Schools and the Equal
Opportunity Problem

CESifo Seminar Series

edited by Hans-Werner Sinn

See http://mitpress.mit.edu for a complete list of titles in this series.

Schools and the Equal Opportunity Problem

edited by Ludger Woessmann
and Paul E. Peterson

CESifo Seminar Series

The MIT Press
Cambridge, Massachusetts
London, England

MIT Press books may be purchased at special quantity discounts for business or sales promotional use. For information, please email special_sales@mitpress.mit.edu or write to Special Sales Department, The MIT Press, 55 Hayward Street, Cambridge, MA 02142.

This book was set in Palatino on 3B2 by Asco Typesetters, Hong Kong. Printed and bound in the United States of America.

Library of Congress Cataloging-in-Publication Data

Schools and the equal opportunity problem / Ludger Woessmann and Paul E. Peterson, editors.
  p.   cm. — (CESifo seminar series)
Includes bibliographical references and index.
ISBN 978-0-262-23257-9 (alk. paper)
1. Educational equalization—Europe—Congresses. 2. Educational equalization—United States—Congresses. 3. Educational change—Europe—Congresses. 4. Educational change—United States—Congresses. 5. Equality—Europe—Congresses. 6. Equality—United States—Congresses. I. Woessmann, Ludger. II. Peterson, Paul E.

LC213.3.E85S36   2007
379.2'6—dc22

2006046908

10 9 8 7 6 5 4 3 2 1

Contents

Series Foreword

This book is part of the CESifo Seminar Series. The series aims to cover topical policy issues in economics from a largely European perspective. The books in this series are the products of the papers and intensive debates that took place during the seminars hosted by CESifo, an international research network of renowned economists organized jointly by the Center for Economic Studies at Ludwig-Maximilians-Universität, Munich, and the Ifo Institute for Economic Research. All publications in this series have been carefully selected and refereed by members of the CESifo research network.

Acknowledgments

The papers collected in this volume were initially presented at the conference on Schooling and Human-Capital Formation in the Global Economy: Revisiting the Equity-Efficiency Quandary, which took place at the CESifo Conference Center in Munich in September 2004. The conference was jointly organized by CESifo Munich and the Program on Education Policy and Governance (PEPG) located within the Taubman Center for State and Local Government at the John F. Kennedy School of Government, Harvard University. The Program was supported in part by a grant from the John M. Olin Foundation. The included papers are a peer-reviewed selection from the 17 papers that were presented at the conference. We hope that the volume documents a fruitful example of building bridges, bringing together leading scholarly perspectives from both sides of the Atlantic.

Our thanks go to all contributors for sharing their research results with an international audience. We would like to particularly thank the conference discussants, whose expertise helped substantially in improving initial drafts: Christopher Berry, Lex Borghans, Torberg Falch, Randall Filer, William Fischel, Roland Fryer, Robert Gary-Bobo, William Howell, Ferran Mane, Pedro Martins, George Psacharopoulos, Margaret Raymond, Richard Romano, Vincent Vandenberghe, Martin West, and Rudolf Winter-Ebmer. The work by numerous anonymous referees, who lent additional support to the selection and improvement of the papers in this volume, is also gratefully acknowledged. Finally, we would like to thank the CESifo support staff, most notably Roisin Hearn, Deirdre Hall, and Deborah Murgia, who ensured that the conference was a wonderful event, as well as Antonio Wendland and Mark Linnen, who coordinated the work from the PEPG side.

I

The Problem

1

Introduction: Schools and the Equal Opportunity Problem

Paul E. Peterson and Ludger Woessmann

As an educational objective, equal opportunity is a Johnny come lately. Starting with Prussia in 1763, basically all Western European countries and the United States introduced compulsory mass state-sponsored primary education by the end of the nineteenth century.[1] But until recent decades, the main purposes of mass education, as expressed by those who campaigned on its behalf, were neither to enhance social mobility nor flatten the income distribution but rather to save souls, create loyal citizens, and enhance economic productivity (Peterson 1985; Gradstein, Justman, and Meier 2005). Any egalitarian consequences were serendipitous.

But after World War II, when socialist parties came to power in Europe, the demand for equal educational opportunity intensified, and most countries opened their school doors to almost all young people at least through the age of 16. Secondary education had come even earlier in the United States, though without the same equal-opportunity justification. That changed with the rise of the civil rights movement, whose leaders insisted that schooling be both desegregated and egalitarian. In the wake of these events, research agendas changed, especially after the pioneering work of University of Chicago sociologist James Coleman (cf., e.g., Coleman et al. 1966), whose work foreshadowed much of the subsequent scholarly research agenda—not excluding the essays published in this volume.

Much educational research today remains focused on those reforms that are expected to address the equal opportunity problem. In this regard, the expectations of advocates run high. Lengthening the years of schooling—through adolescence and into young adulthood—is expected to place the next generation on a more even footing. Extending schooling downward to an ever younger age is expected to compensate for lack of adequate stimulation at home. Similar results are expected from concentrating fiscal resources on the education of the needy. Mixing students of contrasting abilities and backgrounds is often done in the hope that the less advantaged will learn from the others. Accountability systems have been put into place to ensure that instruction is directed at all students, even those with fewer initial skills. And school choice is often said to be a means of giving to the families of the poor access to opportunities otherwise reserved for the well-to-do.

The essays in this volume, initially presented at an international conference held in Munich Germany in September 2004, explore the consequences of these and other school reforms for equal educational opportunity in advanced industrial societies, focusing mainly on countries in Europe and North America. The conference was jointly sponsored by CESifo and the Program on Education Policy and Governance at Harvard University.

1.1 Why Schools Do Not Build a New Social Order: Two Meanings of Equal Opportunity

Despite the intense interest in the topic, there is little agreement on the meaning of equal educational opportunity. For some, equal opportunity means only that everyone is treated the same way within the school house and each is given instruction appropriate to his or her ability, so that all are given the same chance to build on the capabilities they bring to the school door. For others, equal opportunity asks schools to remedy the deficiencies that some children bring with them to school so that only random chance determines which members of the next generation rise to the highest positions of society.

For those who hold the second perspective, the essays included in this volume will prove disappointing. On the whole, they show, quite convincingly, that many of the proposed school reforms can hardly be expected to alter substantially the opportunity structure of a society. The inevitable conclusions one reaches after reading this collection are in fact little different from those reached by George Counts, the radical pessimist, who, in the midst of the Great Depression, answered in the negative the question posed by his book title: *Dare the School Build a New Social Order?* (1932). Not much seems to have changed since Counts wrote that book.

But whether that should give rise to extreme pessimism depends on what one means by equal educational opportunity. Most school officials—indeed, most citizens—even in the wake of the socialist movements of Europe and the civil rights movement in the United States, do not expect schools to alter profoundly the structure of society. Very few agree with the normative claim that "schools are supposed to equalize opportunities across generations," despite the fact that "people naturally wish to give their own children an advantage" (Hochschild and Scovronick 2003, 2). Instead, they expect schools simply to take students as they are, not transform the character that family influences imprinted on them.

Indeed, most people expect the family's warm embrace, not the indifferent educational arm of the state, to bear the principal responsibility for securing the long-term welfare of the next generation. Most parents devote enormous amounts of time, energy, and financial resources to the enhancement of their children's well-being. It is better for a child to have two parents within the home than just one—in part, perhaps, because the child learns more if the family has greater financial resources that can be put to educational use. While finances may be quite important and fathers do play a significant role, the time and talent of the mother, best measured by her endowments and education, usually prove to be of greatest significance (White 1982; Meyer 1996; Jencks and Phillips 1998; Rothstein 2004). In most homes, her care, conversation, and instruction make much of the difference.

Necessarily, this gives rise to inequality. Families vary in quality, perhaps today more than ever before—at least in the United States. Some parents have great personal and professional resources to devote to their children's well-being. Others are barely able to take care of themselves, much less their children. Two changes in modern society may be accentuating the differences among families. On the one side, marriage partners are increasingly chosen from among those with similar endowments, especially since women became breadwinners (Oppenheimer 1988; Mare 1991). On the other side, ever higher percentages of children are being raised in single-parent families. These trends may well be intensifying educational disparities. Two-income families, as compared with single-parent households, typically devote to their children's education much more time, talent, and financial capital (Jencks 1979; McLanahan and Sandefur 1994; Neal 2006).[2]

With the family crucial to a child's educational potential, the contribution that schools can make will be necessarily limited. While school time differs somewhat across countries, children are in school around six hours a day, five days a week, for three-fourths of the year. During that time, they are under the care of teachers who usually are responsible not for just one to three children but somewhere between 10 and 30. And even dedicated professionals do not have quite the same vested interest in the well-being of a child as do his or her mother and father, who are both genetically programmed to care deeply about their children's welfare. As even the best teachers often explain, they have little capacity to alter a child's trajectory from the direction provided by the home.

That the family is the most powerful of all socializing institutions was well known to the ancients. The Greek philosopher Plato (1992), tacitly acknowledging the power of familial influence, proposed that future guardians of the state, at an early age, be taken out of the home and raised in a highly structured educational environment to ensure that mix of qualities the philosopher-king required. Such modern Platonists as Hochschild and Skovronek (2003, as quoted above), to achieve their egalitarian dream, would have to construct a comprehensive compulsory system of mass residential education that removes not just guardians but all children, at as early an age as possible, from the highly variable influences of the home.

So if equal opportunity means equal performance at the time compulsory education comes to an end, then one can be quite sure that the egalitarian ideal will never be realized. When faced with its practical meaning, most people would reject such an ideal, in any case. Imagine telling committed parents, who devoted themselves assiduously to the education of their child, that, as a consequence, their child would be placed in an adverse school setting. Only then could other children, who had less supportive parents, catch up. It is difficult to imagine any society organizing itself along such lines.

Equal educational opportunity might be conceptualized more narrowly, however. Opportunities at school might be said to be equal, if all who enter the schoolhouse were given the same opportunities to enhance the endowments brought to the school threshold. Given this interpretation of equal opportunity, one would not anticipate anything like an equality of outcomes but would settle for no additional inequality over and above what would have existed had the school intervention not taken place. Publicly provided opportunities would be egalitarian in that the school's added value would be similar for all. In such a world, social inequalities would persist, but the public school system would not be responsible for their exaggeration or perpetuation.

1.2 The Educational Impact of Families in Different Countries

It is this second, more limited understanding of equal opportunity that seems operative in much of modern-day education. In most advanced industrial societies, schools do not appear to do much to alter the opportunity structure in one direction or another (Anderson 1961). The impact of family background remains powerful in societies that have greatly expanded their educational systems. For example, recent evidence taken from international test performance data collected by the Third International Mathematics and Science Study (TIMSS) revealed that effects of family background on students' academic performance are very large in all participating countries and that the average European effect was remarkably similar in size to the effect in the United States (Woessmann 2004).

In table 1.1, we report similar new evidence that comes from a more recent international test, the Program for International Student Assessment (PISA), conducted in 2000 on representative national samples of 15-year-old students by the Organization for Economic Cooperation and Development (OECD).[3] On average, those in tenth grade perform 30 test points higher on this test than do ninth graders. The results also show that both in the three largest European countries—France, Germany, and Great Britain—and in the United States, students' educational performance is strongly linked to such family-background features as parental occupation, work status, country of origin, family status, and the number of books at home.

For several reasons, the number of books at home can be understood as a powerful encompassing proxy for the educational, social, and economic background of the students' families, proposed and frequently used in sociological research (e.g., De Graaf 1988; Esping-Andersen 2004). In general, a large number of books indicates a family environment that highly esteems education and promotes children's academic effort (cf. Mullis et al. 2004), proxies for the social background of the parents, and also captures economic aspects because books have to be paid for. The number of books at home has repeatedly proved to be the single most important predictor of student performance on international achievement tests. In addition, Schütz, Ursprung, and Woessmann (2005) show on a different dataset that (at least for the limited number of countries for which the data are available) the association between household income (not available in PISA) and books at home does not vary significantly between countries. With household income

Table 1.1
Impact of family background on student academic performance

	France	Germany	Great Britain	United States
Books at home (residual category: less than 11 books):				
11–50 books	38.00***	33.65***	31.49***	32.75***
	(6.02)	(8.26)	(6.59)	(7.78)
51–100 books	53.22***	50.49***	37.18***	53.14***
	(5.95)	(8.57)	(7.42)	(8.37)
101–250 books	61.89***	66.47***	53.84***	67.49***
	(6.03)	(9.00)	(7.69)	(8.29)
251–500 books	75.77***	89.26***	67.05***	90.39***
	(6.66)	(9.33)	(7.82)	(8.76)
More than 500 books	55.99***	94.96***	77.29***	96.48***
	(9.32)	(9.91)	(8.93)	(10.17)
Parents' work status (residual category: none full-time):				
At least one full-time	18.66***	16.27***	20.99***	36.58***
	(6.06)	(6.09)	(5.97)	(9.53)
Both full-time	26.44***	12.53*	17.24***	29.30***
	(6.26)	(6.60)	(5.75)	(10.45)
Parents' job (residual category: in-between):				
Blue collar	−23.80***	−30.88***	−21.59***	−23.32***
	(6.58)	(7.52)	(8.34)	(8.85)
White collar	29.85***	18.03***	34.52***	28.45***
	(3.83)	(4.49)	(4.19)	(4.97)
Born in country:				
Student	26.35**	5.25	−2.14	9.18
	(11.67)	(8.28)	(9.55)	(13.21)
Mother	11.46*	−0.81	0.09	−5.82
	(6.29)	(8.04)	(7.58)	(12.18)
Father	6.08	38.62***	11.33	5.71
	(5.63)	(8.30)	(10.01)	(10.85)
Living with both parents	7.00	4.69	16.78***	26.04***
	(5.13)	(5.29)	(3.97)	(5.22)
Female	−19.43***	−20.10***	−10.70**	−11.39**
	(3.46)	(4.41)	(4.46)	(5.15)
Age (months)	0.88*	0.38	1.53***	−0.22
	(0.50)	(0.55)	(0.52)	(0.65)
Students (unit of observation)	2,590	2,818	5,165	2,115
Schools (unit of clustering)	177	219	362	152
R^2	0.218	0.299	0.210	0.263

Source: Own calculations based on the PISA micro database.
Note: Least-squares regression within each country, weighted by students' sampling probabilities. Dependent variable: PISA math test score. Standard errors robust to clustering at the school level and heteroscedasticity in parentheses. Regressions include imputation controls. Significance levels (based on standard errors robust to clustering at the school level): ***1%, **5%, *10%.

as maybe the "ideal" measure of family background, at least from an economic perspective, this gives substantial weight to the validity of books at home as an encompassing family-background proxy in cross-country comparisons. By contrast, the cross-country comparability of other family-background proxies (such as parental education) may be limited, for example, by substantial cross-country differences in what specific educational programs mean.[4]

With books at home as an internationally comparable proxy for parental education and for other characteristics of families that are conducive to student learning, it is astounding to observe that 15-year-olds with more than 500 books in their family home perform the equivalent of as much as two to three school years better on the PISA test than do those with fewer than 10 books in the home (table 1.1). Not only are these family-background effects large in all four countries, but their size in Germany and the United States is very similar. Impacts in Great Britain are only slightly smaller. If one assumes that the carryover from high school academic performance into future economic success is high, as many studies suggest (e.g., Bishop 1992; Murnane, Willett, and Levy 1995; Neal and Johnson 1996; Currie and Thomas 2001), then the school system does not seem to have led to particularly high social mobility rates in any of the three countries. Admittedly, the impact of the number of the books in the home on achievement is somewhat less in France, but even in that country nearly the equivalent of two grade levels of learning divides students coming from families with having 500 or more books in the home from those with less than 10.[5]

Though family background has major impacts on student achievement in all four countries, it is possible that certain features of the French educational system moderate that impact. France is well known for its écoles maternelles, which provide a widespread and extensive preschool program for children from all backgrounds. Recent international evidence by Schütz et al. (2005) shows that universality of preschool programs (as well as comprehensive education) is indeed systematically related to higher social mobility across countries—while many other education policies are not. This finding is also consistent with the Dutch evidence provided by Edwin Leuven and Hessel Oosterbeek in this volume (chapter 8), which shows that lowering the compulsory school attendance age and thus universal education before standard ages is the only one of the five educational interventions they considered that lifted the educational achievement of disadvantaged students.

Meanwhile, educational systems in other countries may reinforce family influences. For example, the German emphasis on preparing for a particular vocation early in life may slot students into social roles that resemble their parents. In the United States, the decentralization of school policymaking, coupled with extensive residential segregation by race and income, may reinforce existing social patterns. And Steve Machin, in his essay on the expansion of British higher education (chapter 2), finds that it has reinforced and enhanced, not mitigated, social distinctions. Children of the better off are much more likely to pursue advanced studies than are children from working-class families. With higher education heavily subsidized by the government, the net effect is an organized arrangement that intensifies social differentiation—quite the opposite of what egalitarians expected from educational expansion.

1.3   The Original Purposes of Schooling

That educational expansions sometimes reinforce—not relieve—social inequalities is not necessarily surprising, once it is understood how little a role the egalitarian principle has played in the history of Western mass education. The very word *school* derives from the Greek word meaning "leisure," for in ancient Athens only those who were freed from the obligations of manual labor could afford to educate themselves (Drucker 1961). Nor did matters change during those centuries when learning was mainly confined to the monastery. For the masses, reading was virtually impossible until Gutenberg's invention of the printing press, whose use became widespread by the early part of the sixteenth century, making it possible to put words rapidly into print for the benefit of those outside the palace, castle, and monastery.

Exploiting the possibilities of this new invention, religious reformers, in both their Lutheran and Calvinist guises, urged the faithful to read the "Word" rather than relying on priestly injunctions, ceremonial exercises, and sacerdotal imagery (Pelikan 2005). Inasmuch as each individual was being urged to read the sacred text for himself or herself, literacy spread rapidly, especially throughout northern portions of Europe and, later, the northern portion of the North American continent, where Protestantism took root. Even to this day, these parts of the world remain among the most literate.

If the motivations were originally religious, the consequences were economic, as wealth was enhanced by the spread of literacy. Max

Weber (2001) attributed the more rapid economic growth to higher savings rates in Protestant countries, which he attributed to a belief system that asked adherents to defer gratification. But it is more likely that capitalism prospered in Protestant countries because instruction in reading the Bible generated the human capital crucial to economic growth.[6] A similar argument for the religious origins of human-capital-driven economic success has been made for the selection of urban skilled occupations in crafts and trade by Jews since the eighth century. As Botticini and Eckstein (2005a, 2005b) argue in their human-capital interpretation of Jewish history, the ultimate root of Jewish economic success as merchants lay in a centuries-old Judaic rule that required male Jews to be able to read the Torah in the synagogue and to teach the reading of the Torah to their sons.

In Europe, as religiosity receded, political considerations came to the fore. Once it became clear that a mass system of education, no less than a citizen-army, strengthened the nation state, political leaders took notice. Although public schools originated in the Netherlands, it was Bismarck who best understood the connection between public education and nation-building, giving rise to the old shibboleth that "the Prussian schoolmaster defeated France in the War of 1870 that created imperial Germany" (Drucker 1961, 21). While German railways probably had more to do with the outcome of the war than did their schools, the saying nonetheless captures a reality. Faced with the task of unifying disparate political jurisdictions that had a common tongue but numerous dialects, Bismarck used the schools to foster a common language and sense of nationhood (Lamberti 1989; Gradstein, Justman, and Meier 2005, ch. 2). His success inspired European neighbors to follow suit.

Across the Atlantic, political objectives were no less important. In the United States, the need was not to amalgamate previously independent political jurisdictions but to incorporate waves of immigrants, who spoke different languages and worshipped in their own way. To Horace Mann and others who built the common school, immigrants from southern and eastern Europe, with different cultural heritages, seemed "in need of moral improvement" as well as in instruction in the English language, both of which they thought could be best accomplished by state-run, Protestant-controlled public schools (Kaestle 1983; Glenn 1987).

The notion that schools could become the engine of economic growth had yet to take hold, however. For many in the business and industrial communities, schools were simply a costly public expense that diverted resources from more productive uses. If there were to be public schools that provided more than the basics, they should concentrate on training students for specific trades and occupations that were the mainstay of the industrial economy. A telling anecdote was recorded by Peter Drucker (1961, 15):

A man who is now chief executive of one of America's largest businesses did not dare admit when applying for his first job, in 1916, that he had an advanced degree in economics. "I told the man who hired me that I had been a railroad clerk since I was 14," he says, "otherwise I would have been turned down as too educated for a job in business." Even in the late twenties, when I myself started [Drucker continued], commercial firms in England or on the Continent still hesitated before hiring anyone as a junior clerk who had finished secondary school.

For the House of Labor, schools were often seen as a way of lifting the price of adult manual labor while at the same time protecting children from the abuses of the workplace (Peterson 1985, ch. 3). Campaigns to enact compulsory education and child labor laws went hand in hand. More thoughtful labor leaders and many of the more ambitious within the working community realized that schooling was a way to escape the drudgery of farm and factory. But even then, schools were seen as escape hatches for the few, not a means of changing social mobility patterns more generally. Even as radical and brilliant a black leader as W. E. B. DuBois called for not equal education for all but for a "Talented Tenth" that would lead its people to the promised land (DuBois 1953, 52, 54; Cremin 1988, 121–122).

By contrast, ordinary citizens saw secondary schooling and beyond as a chance to get ahead. Their demand for secondary schooling found expression first within the United States, probably because decisions could be made locally, in particular school districts, without a need for reaching a national consensus on the matter (Peterson 1985, ch. 3; Goldin 2001). As one community built a high school, its neighbor took notice. While the practice spread swiftly, even as late as the 1920s, secondary schooling, though increasingly widespread, was hardly universal. In fact, the greatest decade of growth in secondary education within the United States came during the Great Depression—not because Franklin Roosevelt or any local school board had an equal opportunity vision but because work opportunities were so limited that young people had nothing else to do. School boards were overwhelmed: classrooms became overcrowded, and teachers were badly paid—sometimes, as in Chicago, in "scrip" rather than dollar bills

(Peterson 1985, ch. 9). Still, the system had no easy way of shutting off a bottom-up demand.

So the spread of secondary schooling in the United States was accidental, driven by individual decision making and external economic forces rather than any broad policy decision. Yet that did not prevent the American model from becoming idealized at the end of World War II. To the victor went if not the spoils then at least the imputed wisdom. The revived socialist parties of Europe, with little resistance from conservatives, convincingly called for "Secondary Education for All." Without anyone quite realizing it, a new consensus had been forged. State-run schools for all were soon to become compulsory from somewhere around age five or six (maybe seven) to somewhere around age 15 or 16, with further opportunities for those who wanted to continue. Debates revolved around not whether the job needed to be done but what institution—church or state—should be doing it. The latter question was answered differently from one country to the next, depending on the play of political and social forces in each.

A group of economists at the University of Chicago—Theodore Schultz (1961) and Gary Becker (1964) being the most prominent—helped to consolidate the consensus by articulating a human-capital theory of economic growth. Increasing wealth depended not just on a country's industrial plant or its savings rate, long thought to be key, but also on the quality of its labor force. Once the point was made theoretically, empiricists followed up by showing that the more years a person spent in school, the more he or she earns later in life (e.g., Becker 1964; Mincer 1974; Card 1999)—even throughout the adult years, as Sofia Sandgren's study of a cohort of Swedish males (chapter 3) convincingly shows. In other words, investments in education, like investments in the workplace, generate a rate of return. Remarkably, that rate typically outpaces more traditional capital investments.

When human-capital theory was first enunciated, little attention was given to the potential trade-off between equity and efficiency. More schooling for all was expected to generate new opportunities for the many, while at the same time enhancing the quality of the labor force. Both labor and business as well as parties of all political stripes embraced schools as solutions. Though educators always wanted more resources than taxpayers were willing to concede, publicly financed education was a dynamic growth sector throughout much of the postwar period. Schools grew in number, size, enrollment, age range of students served, financial underpinning, and professional credentials

earned by teachers and administrators. Not only was secondary education for all taken for granted, but the tertiary system (universities,
advanced institutes, and further education) burgeoned at a near exponential rate.

In more recent decades, scholars have begun to realize that all is not
so simple (for an early warning, see Anderson 1961). True, the rate of
return to individual investment in human capital remains strongly
positive, perhaps today more than ever. True, steady improvements in
labor-force quality are essential if societies are to become increasingly
productive. But educational expansion, by itself, is not necessarily the
most efficient way of enhancing human capital. Nor does expansion
ensure social mobility. If everyone finishes secondary education, everyone is still at the same place that their own endowments and family
support left them—unless something unusual happens in school.
In short, one can achieve large increments in human capital without
achieving a detectable shift in the opportunity structure.

1.4   School Expenditure and Class-Size Reduction

More than any other single political development in the United States,
the civil rights movement spawned by the 1954 U.S. Supreme Court
decision in *Brown v. Board of Education* focused attention on the equal-
opportunity problem. By overturning an 1896 court decision that had
found racially separate schools to be acceptable under the equal protec-
tion clause of the U.S. Constitution as long as those separate schools
had equal facilities, *Brown* declared segregated schools to be inherently
unequal, regardless of their facilities. Building on the momentum initiated by the *Brown* decision, the civil rights movement reached its high-
water mark with the passage of the Civil Rights Act of 1964, a law that
accelerated the desegregation of southern schools and outlawed racial
discrimination in all sectors of public life.

The impact of these events on scholarly conversations was no less
dramatic. Most notably, the Civil Rights Act required the U.S. Institute
of Education to conduct a national survey of American schools that
would document any disparity in educational resources available
to black and white Americans. Asked to lead the study, James Coleman collected a vast amount of information about the characteristics
of schools and students. Most significantly, he commissioned the first
large-scale national survey of student achievement. Issued in 1966,

the study's statistical analyses are primitive by today's standards (Coleman et al. 1966; to facilitate readability, the text refers only to Coleman). Yet many of the findings from the study have proven extraordinarily robust to more sophisticated investigations that have since been conducted in both Europe and the United States.

One result had been widely anticipated. The test-score performances of black students trailed, on average, those of their white peers by a wide margin. Nor was anyone surprised to learn that learning was also strongly influenced by other demographic characteristics, including mother's education, father's education, family income, and many other demographic characteristics (cf. Coleman et al. 1966 for details of the mentioned results). Yet the report's findings defined precisely the magnitude of the equal-opportunity problem, though it also instigated a largely fruitless debate over the extent to which heredity or environment was the determining factor (Herrnstein and Murray 1994; Goldberger and Manski 1995; Heckman 1995; Rothstein 2004; for a thoughtful synthesis and interpretation, see Jencks and Phillips 1998).

Significantly, Coleman also found that schools were doing little to ameliorate that problem, either within or across racial groups. Coleman, in fact, showed that, once adjusted for regional and urban-rural differences, blacks and whites, on average, went to schools that had similar levels of per-pupil expenditure and similar teacher-pupil ratios, staff credentials, and most other indicators of material quality. Even more astonishing, once demographic characteristics were taken into account, school characteristics had little effect on student performance, a totally unexpected finding that continues to reverberate. Higher expenditure did not generate higher student test-score performance. Nor did the other material characteristics of the school have more than a trivial effect on student performance. Children, on average, do not seem to learn more if their teachers have more credentials or are paid more; if they are taught in smaller classes or in more well-equipped, modern buildings with more extensive library collections; or if they are better off in many other material ways. So disturbing were these findings that the School of Education at Harvard University held a multiyear seminar devoted to a careful review of the work, under the direction of the noted statistician Frederick Mosteller and future New York senator Daniel P. Moynihan. After reanalyzing the data, the participants in the seminar concluded that Coleman and his team got the story right the first time (Mosteller and Moynihan 1972).

Most studies since then, whether conducted in the United States or Europe, using the simple techniques of Coleman's day or the more advanced now available, have continued to affirm the original findings (Hanushek 2002; Neal 2006; Woessmann 2005a and the references therein). Three chapters in this volume extend that literature to current equal opportunity problems by examining the extent to which the refocusing of additional material resources on the disadvantaged can alter the distribution of educational outcomes. Julian R. Betts and Paul E. Roemer (chapter 9) show that schools would need to spend eight to 10 times as much money on the education of blacks as whites if one were to rely only on additional expenditures as the sole intervention strategy for achieving equity across racial groups. Similarly, Eric A. Hanushek (chapter 7) shows that equalizing standard teacher inputs or reducing class sizes for the disadvantaged does not help to reduce the existing inequality between racial groups in Texas. For Europe, Leuven and Oosterbeek (chapter 8) similarly show that several Dutch policies that refocused resources toward disadvantaged students (class-size reductions, extra resources for personnel, extra resources for computers, and extended compulsory school-leaving age) did not reduce the equal opportunity problem.

Of all the Coleman findings with respect to material resources, the one that remains the most controversial has to do with class size—the ratio of pupils to teachers at a school. Coleman and many others have found little effect, one way or another (Hanushek 1996; Hoxby 2000)—a finding that many ordinary teachers, parents, and students find hard to believe. Supporting this common-sense view, a major experimental study found positive effects on student learning from a reduction in class size in Tennessee (Mosteller 1995; Krueger 1999). More recently, an international study of class size found few effects of class size except in two countries where teachers were poorly paid and teacher quality appeared to be particularly low, suggesting that reductions in class size could be a useful way of enhancing student performance if teacher quality is low (Woessmann and West 2005). Those results would be consistent with the quasi-experimental study of class size carried out in the Netherlands and reported in this volume by Leuven and Oosterbeek (chapter 8). They find little effect of class-size reduction, a finding that might be expected in a country with a relatively well paid teaching force. The topic is sure to remain an area of intense research for years to come.

1.5   Peer Groups and School Tracking

In a second provocative finding, Coleman identified the quality of one's peer group at school as one of the most important school-related factor affecting learning. Blacks learned more if they went to school with whites. More generally, socially less advantaged students did better if they were in schools with more advantaged ones. The reverse was not true. White performances were not adversely affected by the presence of blacks.

These findings were extremely encouraging for those leading the drive to desegregate schools. In addition, the findings contradicted a long-standing practice of separating students according to ability—on the assumption that students learned the most when working with those whose accomplishments were similar. In many European countries, students in early adolescence were and are still sent to different secondary schools. The more able are assigned to a more academically focused program of studies, and the less able to a school with a more general or vocational curriculum. In most parts of the United States, students attended and still attend the same comprehensive high school but are nonetheless assigned to different course tracks—academic, general, or vocational "tracks." Many European countries that have by now adopted the comprehensive school model usually employ similar tracking procedures.

Citing the Coleman findings, many school reformers began to eliminate both dual school systems and tracking within schools. If the less able can be helped without cost to the more accomplished, the policy can enhance both equal opportunity and overall human capital. That remains an open question to which various answers are given in this volume. Using advanced econometric techniques and extensive panel data from North Carolina to distinguish correlation from causation, Jacob Vigdor and Thomas Nechyba show in chapter 4 that the peer effects estimated by standard techniques such as in Coleman's study and elsewhere do not reflect true causal relationships. They point out that ability cannot be easily measured by conventional techniques, that individuals whose own higher ability is not precisely measured sort into observably more able peer groups, and that such sorting can give rise to the false appearance of peer effects unless the analysis can capture the sorting process. Similarly, Hanushek (chapter 7) uses panel data from Texas to show that there are hardly any effects of peers' ability or socioeconomic status on student performance. As a result of these investigations, the question of peer effects, once thought to be settled, is returning to the top of the research agenda.

In chapter 5, this research is carried further. To identify the effect of mixing students, Fernando Galindo-Rueda and Anna Vignoles use data from the United Kingdom at a time (the mid-1970s) when both selective and comprehensive school systems existed next to each other in different local units. Their results suggest that about the only effect that the move to mixing students had was to reduce the performance of the highest-ability students. Thus, while inequality in outcomes was reduced, forcing the best to a lower level is hardly the way that one would hope to address the equal-opportunity problem. Note that this would suggest that there are nonlinear peer effects in that the best lose from mixing but nobody gains. However, the extent to which their results can be generalized to other contexts remains unclear. The immediate effects of social and academic mixing may be quite different from their long-run effects. The shocks of school restructuring, with its attendant movement of students from one school to another, can depress performance, as Hanushek shows in chapter 7.

The distinction between short-term and long-term consequences may help to reconcile the Galindo-Rueda and Vignoles findings in chapter 5 with the cross-country evidence of Hanushek and Woessmann (2006) suggesting that, over the long run, mixing can reduce inequality in performance without hurting either average performance or that of the very best students. With the ambiguity that remains from these various studies, it is all the more welcome to have the theoretical model developed by Giorgio Brunello, Massimo Giannini, and Kenn Ariga (chapter 6), which considers some of the key economic factors that may well determine the optimal age at which students should be placed into selective school settings.

1.6   Output Orientation and Performance Standards

Perhaps Coleman's greatest contributions are not so much his specific findings as the lines of thinking that he opened up. For one thing, he focused public attention on the outcomes of education (how much students were learning) rather than just on inputs (years of education, expenditures, class size, teacher salaries, and teacher credentials) that had previously been taken as the primary indicators of school quality.

In 1969, shortly after the Coleman report was issued, the U.S. Education Commission of the States launched the National Assessment of Educational Progress (NAEP), a national examination given to a nationwide sample of students that was designed to provide information on the performances of 9-, 13-, and 17-year-olds. By undertaking the survey periodically, NAEP was expected to document progress over time. At roughly the same time, an international group of scholars formed the International Association for the Evaluation of Educational Achievement, which subsequently launched the first systematic collection of comparable data on the achievement of high school students in mathematics and science across many advanced industrial societies. International surveys were fielded periodically over the next several decades, eventually evolving into the regular Trends in International Mathematics and Science Study (TIMSS) with its most recent administration in 2003. Beginning in 2000, TIMSS has been supplemented by the PISA survey discussed previously.[7]

The results from the NAEP, TIMSS, PISA, and other similar surveys have proven to be no less eye opening than many of the Coleman findings. For one thing, the NAEP, which was expected to steady national "progress," revealed stagnation instead, with high school graduates performing no better in 2005 than they were in 1970 (U.S. Department of Education 2005; Peterson 2006). Meanwhile, the TIMSS and PISA surveys showed Japanese and other Asian students, not those in Europe or North America, to be achieving at the highest levels in math and science (e.g., Mullis et al. 2004 and many previous studies). Just exactly how newcomers to the industrial world could have advanced so quickly to the educational pinnacle remains a mystery that analysts are still attempting to decipher. Several analyses of the international tests have underlined the importance of comprehensive exit exams popular in Asia (cf. Bishop 2006 and Woessmann 2005b, among others). Those exams, administered during the last year of secondary schooling, are substantive in content, can be passed at various levels of accomplishment, and carry great weight with universities and employers. By defining clear objectives and providing tiers of accomplishment, such exams appear to motivate students, staff, and families to higher levels of performance. The chapter in this volume by John H. Bishop and Ferran Mane (chapter 10) contributes to this discussion with U.S. evidence showing positive effects of exit exams and higher graduation requirements.

1.7 School Choice

Finally, Coleman, always open to new ideas and never satisfied with what he found, no matter how startling, broke new ground again with a second study, *Public and Private Schools: An Analysis of High School and Beyond*, once again commissioned by the U.S. Department of Education (Coleman, Hoffer, and Kilgore 1981, 1982; Coleman and Hoffer 1987). In this study, data were gathered on student performances and background characteristics as well as a variety of school characteristics of both public and private high schools. When the results were reported, the public was surprised to learn that students were learning more in Catholic schools, previously regarded as low-cost, inferior alternatives to which families sent their children for religious, not educational, reasons. Yet once again, its findings have proven robust to alternative estimations conducted with more sophisticated techniques on alternative datasets (e.g., Neal 1997; for recent reviews of the literature, see Neal 2002; Wolf 2006). However, subsequent research has brought out a previously unappreciated point contained within Coleman—namely, that the benefits of a Catholic education are much greater for minority students, especially African Americans, than they are for white students.

The Coleman study has spurred numerous policy interventions designed to enhance school choice, both among public schools and between the public and private sectors. Researchers are only beginning to tease out the impact of the many choice interventions being attempted in both Europe and the United States (cf. Howell and Peterson 2002 and Hoxby 2003 for the United States; Bradley and Taylor 2002, Levačić 2004, and Sandström and Bergström 2005 for examples from Europe). This volume contains two valuable contributions to the discussion. In chapter 11, Simon Burgess, Bredon McConnell, Carol Propper, and Deborah Wilson use extensive administrative data of English students to show that given residential choices, the size of the choice set of nearby schools is positively related to postresidential stratification of students across schools by ability and socioeconomic status. The second chapter on school choice in this volume, by Daniele Checchi and Tullio Jappelli (chapter 12), presents Italian evidence that parents who enroll their children in private schools give a lower ranking of the quality of their local public schools than parents who enroll their children in public schools, suggesting that parents faced with low-quality public schools may find an escape in the private sector.

1.8   Conclusions: Is Educational Efficiency the Best Route to Equity?

Many topics on the effects of schools on the equal opportunity problem are initiated in Coleman's work. But perhaps his most profound
legacy (whether intended or not) was the induced change in the perceived meaning of equality of educational opportunity (cf. Coleman
1968). Before Coleman's research, equal educational opportunity was
interpreted largely in conventional terms: schools should provide
equal services to all students. But when Coleman showed that equal
resources—equal expenditures, equal facilities, equally credentialed
teachers—did not yield equal results, the definition of equal opportunity was transformed to require even more than equalizing resources:
compensatory education concentrated extra resources on the disadvantaged. Confirming and extending Coleman's initial findings, research
in this volume from both the United States and Europe suggests that
even sizeable differential spending on the disadvantaged will not yield
an equality of results.

Given how little of the equal opportunity problem can be attributed
to differences in measurable, material school characteristics, schools
have been asked to address the problem in other ways. Schools have
explored many alternatives—detracking, more flexible curricula,
greater attention to the child's sense of self than their educational
attainments, testing to make sure that no child is left behind, and
choice for low-income families. The effects of detracking and many
other options depend crucially on the exact nature of peer effects,
which is still not very well understood. While advancing our understanding, the U.S. and European evidence presented in this volume
also does not provide unambiguous answers on peer effects, although
cautioning that any causal peer effect may well be very small at best.
Some presented results suggest that high performance standards—
if rightly implemented—lend some hope for alleviating inequalities.
Targeted-choice programs may also help disadvantaged students
who are trapped in low-quality schools, but much depends on their
design, and their long-term efficacy remains quite unknown. Thus,
while showing some routes for possible advancement, the evidence
collected in this volume also raises considerable doubts about the effectiveness of many school policies to alter dramatically the opportunity
structure.

On the basis of what is known, one should not expect miracles in the
near term. When equal opportunity is defined as equality of outcome,

schools will inevitably fall short, though one can hardly fault them for doing as much as can reasonably be done to help the least advantaged. Too much is learned elsewhere, families are too diverse, and children themselves are too heterogeneous to expect that much from schools. But if an older, more widely accepted definition of equal opportunity is accepted, then the problem becomes a good deal more tractable. Schools can and should be expected to challenge all students to their highest potential. That is best done through an efficient system of education that uses available resources to challenge each child so as to realize their potential. In that sense, an efficient educational system can be egalitarian. As Theodore Schultz (1981, 88) observed a quarter century ago, "The complementarity between efficiency and equity in schooling is being overlooked in the quest for equity. An optimum level of efficiency in our big school systems would in all probability contribute more to the cause of equity than any of the many reforms now being imposed."[8]

Notes

1. Ramirez and Boli (1987, 3) state that virtually every Western European country adopted mass state-sponsored primary education "in the 'long' nineteenth century, from Prussia (1763) to Belgium (1914)"; cf. also Flora (1983). On the United States, see Tyack (1974), Cremin (1988), and Goldin (1999, 8), who observes that "during the middle of the nineteenth century … fully free, publicly funded common schools diffused throughout the nation." For a history of postprimary education in the industrial world, see Goldin (2001).

2. For additional studies and discussions of the literature, see Meyer (1996), Mulligan (1997), Phillips, Brooks-Gunn, Duncan, Klebanov, and Crane (1998), Blau (1999), and Fryer and Levitt (2004).

3. For details of the database, see Fuchs and Woessmann (2004) and the references therein. Additional technical details of the specification and results of table 1.1 are available from the authors on request.

4. Given that we see books at home and parental education as alternative proxies for the same issue and given the discussed superiority of the books proxy, parental education was not included in the specifications. However, using parental education instead of books at home led to a quite similar overall assessment of family-background effects in the four countries, only now even stronger in Germany than in the United States.

5. We prefer these estimates of social mobility based on the size of the coefficient on crucial family-background measures to looking at the R^2 of the whole regression because the latter depends on the extent of inequality that is already given in the parental generation. When interested in the relative extent to which school systems alter social mobility, the assessment should be influenced not by how unequal the society is in the older generation but only by how much any existing inequality is carried over to the next generation, which is captured by the size of the family-background coefficient (cf. Goldberger and

Manski 1995, 769, for a related argument). For reasons discussed above, we view books at home as a very encompassing measure of family background. Given that the results reported in table 1.1 control for some other features of family background, it should be noted that the qualitative results on the books-at-home variable across the four countries do not change in a specification that does not include some or all of these other controls.

6. We thank C. Arnold Andersen and Mary Jean Bowman for bringing this point to our attention. However, careful research documenting the connection remains to be done.

7. Reading achievement in primary schools is now regularly administered by the Progress in International Reading Literacy Study (PIRLS).

8. Similarly, Arrow, Bowles, and Durlauf (2000) postulate that in many cases there may well be an equity-efficiency complementarity rather than a tradeoff.

References

Anderson, C. A. (1961). "A Skeptical Note on Education and Mobility." *American Journal of Sociology* 66(1), as reprinted in A. H. Halsey, Jean Floud, and C. Arnold Anderson (eds.), *Education, Economy and Society*. New York: Free Press.

Arrow, K., S. Bowles, S. Durlauf (eds.). (2000). *Meritocracy and Economic Inequality*. Princeton, NJ: Princeton University Press.

Becker, G. S. (1964/1993). *Human Capital: A Theoretical and Empirical Analysis, with Special Reference to Education* (3rd ed.). Chicago: University of Chicago Press.

Bishop, J. H. (1992). "The Impact of Academic Competencies on Wages, Unemployment, and Job Performance." *Carnegie-Rochester Conference Series on Public Policy* 37: 127–194.

Bishop, J. H. (2006). "Drinking from the Fountain of Knowledge: Student Incentive to Study and Learn." In E. A. Hanushek and F. Welch (eds.), *Handbook of the Economics of Education*. Amsterdam: North-Holland.

Blau, D. (1999). "The Effect of Income on Child Development." *Review of Economics and Statistics* 81(2): 261–276.

Botticini, M., and Z. Eckstein. (2005a). "From Farmers to Merchants, Voluntary Conversions and Diaspora: A Human Capital Interpretation of Jewish History." Discussion Paper, Tel Aviv University.

Botticini, M., and Z. Eckstein. (2005b). "Jewish Occupational Selection: Education, Restrictions, or Minorities?" *Journal of Economic History* 65(4): 922–948.

Bradley, S., and J. Taylor. (2002). "The Effect of the Quasi-Market on the Efficiency-Equity Trade-off in the Secondary School Sector." *Bulletin of Economic Research* 54(3): 295–314.

Card, D. (1999). "The Causal Effect of Education on Earnings." In O. Ashenfelter and D. Card (eds.), *Handbook of Labor Economics* (vol. 3A). Amsterdam: North-Holland.

Coleman, J. S. (1968). "The Concept of Equality of Educational Opportunity." *Harvard Educational Review* 38(1): 7–22.

Coleman, J. S., E. Q. Campbell, C. J. Hobson, J. McPartland, A. M. Mood, F. D. Weinfeld, and R. L. York. (1966). *Equality of Educational Opportunity: Summary Report*. Washington, DC: U.S. Government Printing Office.

Coleman, J. S., and T. Hoffer. (1987). *Public and Private High Schools: The Impact of Communities.* New York: Basic Books.

Coleman, J. S., T. Hoffer, and S. B. Kilgore. (1981). *Public and Private Schools: An Analysis of High School and Beyond.* Washington, DC: National Center for Education Statistics, U.S. Government Printing Office.

Coleman, J. S., T. Hoffer, and S. B. Kilgore. (1982). *High School Achievement: Public, Catholic and Private Schools Compared.* New York: Basic Books.

Counts, G. S. (1932). *Dare the School Build a New Social Order?* New York: Day.

Cremin, L. A. (1988). *American Education: The Metropolitan Experience, 1876–1980.* New York: Harper & Row.

Currie, J., and D. Thomas. (2001). "Early Test Scores, School Quality and SES: Long-run Effects on Wage and Employment Outcomes." *Research in Labor Economics* 20: 103–132.

De Graaf, P. M. (1988). "Parents' Financial and Cultural Resources, Grades, and Transition to Secondary School in the Federal Republic of Germany." *European Sociological Review* 4(3): 209–221.

Drucker, P. F. (1961). "The Education Revolution." In A. H. Halsey, J. Floud, and C. A. Anderson (eds.), *Education, Economy and Society.* New York: Free Press. As reprinted from P. F. Drucker, *Landmarks of Tomorrow* (New York: Harper and Row, 1959), 114–125.

DuBois, W. E. Burghardt. (1953). *The Souls of Black Fold: Essays and Sketches.* New York: Blue Heron Press. Reprinted from the original (1903).

Esping-Andersen, G. (2004). "Untying the Gordian Knot of Social Inheritance." *Research in Social Stratification and Mobility* 21: 115–138.

Flora, P. (1983). *State, Economy, and Society in Western Europe 1815–1975: A Data Handbook in Two Volumes.* Vol. 1, *The Growth of Mass Democracies and Welfare States.* Frankfurt: Campus.

Fryer, R., and S. Levitt. (2004). "Understanding the Black-White Test Score Gap in the First Two Years of School." *Review of Economics and Statistics* 86(2): 447–464.

Fuchs, T., and L. Woessmann. (2004). "What Accounts for International Differences in Student Performance? A Re-examination using PISA Data." Working Paper 1235, CESifo, Munich.

Glenn, C. L., Jr. (1987). *The Myth of the Common School.* Amherst: University of Massachusetts Press.

Goldberger, A. S., and C. F. Manski. (1995). Review Article: *The Bell Curve* by Herrnstein and Murray. *Journal of Economic Literature* 33(2): 762–776.

Goldin, C. (1999). "A Brief History of Education in the United States." Historical Paper No. 119, NBER Working Paper Series on Historical Factors in Long-Run Growth, National Bureau of Economic Research.

Goldin, C. (2001). "The Human-Capital Century and American Leadership: Virtues of the Past." *Journal of Economic History* 61(2): 263–292.

Gradstein, M., M. Justman, and V. Meier. (2005). *The Political Economy of Education: Implications for Growth and Inequality.* Cambridge, MA: MIT Press.

Hanushek, E. A. (1996). "Student Resources and Student Performance." In G. Burtless (ed.), *Does Money Matter?* Washington, DC: Brookings Institution.

Hanushek, E. A. (2002). "Publicly Provided Education." In A. J. Auerbach and M. Feldstein (eds.), *Handbook of Public Economics* (vol. 4). Amsterdam: North Holland.

Hanushek, E., and L. Woessmann. (2006). "Does Early Tracking Affect Educational Inequality and Performance? Differences-in-Differences Evidence across Countries." *Economic Journal* 116(510): C63–C76.

Heckman, J. J. (1995). "Lessons from *The Bell Curve*." *Journal of Political Economy* 103(5): 1091–1120.

Herrnstein, R. J., and C. Murray. (1994). *The Bell Curve: Intelligence and Class Structure in American Life*. New York: Free Press.

Hochschild, J., and N. Scovronick. (2003). *The American Dream and the Public Schools*. Oxford: Oxford University Press.

Howell, W. G., and P. E. Peterson. (2002). *The Education Gap: Vouchers and Urban Schools*. Washington, DC: Brookings Institution.

Hoxby, C. M. (2000). "The Effects of School Size on Achievement: New Evidence from Population Variation." *Quarterly Journal of Economics* 115(4): 1239–1285.

Hoxby, C. M. (ed.). (2003). *The Economics of School Choice*. Chicago: University of Chicago Press.

Jencks, C. (1979). *Who Gets Ahead*. New York: Free Press.

Jencks, C., and M. Phillips (eds.). (1998). *The Black-White Test Score Gap*. Washington, DC: Brookings Institution.

Kaestle, C. F. (1983). *Pillars of the Republic: Common Schools and American Society, 1780–1860*. New York: Hill and Wang.

Krueger, A. B. (1999). "Experimental Estimates of Education Production Functions." *Quarterly Journal of Economics* 114(2): 497–532.

Lamberti, M. (1989). *State, Society and the Elementary School in Imperial Germany*. New York: Oxford University Press.

Levačić, R. (2004). "Competition and the Performance of English Secondary Schools: Further Evidence." *Education Economics* 12(2): 177–193.

Mare, R. D. (1991). "Five Decades of Educational Assortative Mating." *American Sociological Review* 56(1): 15–32.

McLanahan, S., and G. Sandefur. (1994). *Growing Up with a Single Parent, What Hurts, What Helps*. Cambridge, MA: Harvard University Press.

Meyer, S. E. (1996). *What Money Can't Buy: Family Income and Children's Life Chances*. Cambridge, MA: Harvard University Press.

Mincer, J. (1974). *Schooling, Experience, and Earnings*. New York: National Bureau of Economic Research.

Mosteller, F. (1995). "The Tennessee Study of Class Size in the Early School Grades." *The Future of Children* 5(2): 113–127.

Mosteller, F., and D. P. Moynihan. (1972). *On Equality of Educational Opportunity*. New York: Random House.

Mulligan, C. B. (1997). *Parental Priorities and Economic Inequality*. Chicago: University of Chicago Press.

Mullis, I. V. S., M. O. Martin, E. J. Gonzalez, and S. J. Chrostowski. (2004). "TIMSS 2003 International Mathematics Report: Findings from IEA's Trends in International Mathematics and Science Study at the Fourth and Eighth Grade." Chestnut Hill, MA: TIMSS and PIRLS International Study Center, Boston College.

Murnane, R. J., J. B. Willett, and F. Levy. (1995). "The Growing Importance of Cognitive Skills in Wage Determination." *Review of Economics and Statistics* 77(2): 251–266.

Neal, D. (1997). "The Effects of Catholic Secondary Schooling on Secondary Achievement." *Journal of Labor Economics* 15(1): 98–123.

Neal, D. (2002). "How Vouchers Could Change the Market for Education." *Journal of Economic Perspectives* 26(4): 25–44.

Neal, D. (2006). "How Families and Schools Shape the Achievement Gap." In P. E. Peterson (ed.), *Generational Change: Closing the Test-Score Gap*. Lanham, MD: Rowman and Littlefield.

Neal, D. A., and W. R. Johnson. (1996). "The Role of Premarket Forces in Black-White Wage Differences." *Journal of Political Economy* 104(5): 869–895.

Oppenheimer, V. K. (1988). "A Theory of Marriage Timing." *American Journal of Sociology* 94(3): 563–591.

Pelikan, J. (2005). *Whose Bible Is It? A History of the Scriptures throughout the Ages*. New York: Viking.

Peterson, P. E. (1985). *The Politics of School Reform, 1870–1940*. Chicago: University of Chicago Press.

Peterson, P. E. (2006). "Toward the Elimination of Race Differences in Educational Achievement." In P. E. Peterson (ed.), *Generational Change: Closing the Test-Score Gap*. Lanham, MD: Rowman and Littlefield.

Phillips, M., J. Brooks-Gunn, G. J. Duncan, P. Klebanov, and J. Crane. (1998). "Family Background, Parenting Practices, and the Black-White Test Score Gap." In C. Jencks and M. Phillips (eds.), *The Black-White Test Score Gap*. Washington, DC: Brookings Institution.

Plato. (1992). *Republic*. Translated by G. M. A. Grube and C. D. C. Reeve (2nd ed.). Indianapolis, IN: Hackett.

Ramirez, F. O., and J. Boli. (1987). "The Political Construction of Mass Schooling: European Origins and Worldwide Institutionalization." *Sociology of Education* 60(1): 2–17.

Rothstein, R. (2004). *Class and Schools: Using Social, Economic, and Educational Reform to Close the Black-White Achievement Gap*. Washington, DC: Economic Policy Institute.

Sandström, F. M., and F. Bergström. (2005). "School Vouchers in Practice: Competition Will Not Hurt You." *Journal of Public Economics* 89(2–3): 351–380.

Schultz, T. W. (1961). "Investment in Human Capital." *American Economic Review* 51(1): 1–17.

Schultz, T. W. (1981). *Investing in People: The Economics of Population Quality*. Berkeley: University of California Press.

Schütz, G., H. W. Ursprung, and L. Woessmann. (2005). "Education Policy and Equality of Opportunity." Working Paper 1518, CESifo, Munich.

Tyack, D. B. (1974). *The One Best System: A History of American Urban Education*. Cambridge, MA: Harvard University Press.

U.S. Department of Education, Institute of Education Statistics. (2005). *NAEP 2004: Trends in Academic Progress, Three Decades of Student Performance in Reading and Mathematics*. National Center for Education Statistics 2005-464.

Weber, M. (2001). *The Protestant Ethic and the Spirit of Capitalism* (2nd ed.). New York: Routledge.

White, Karl R. (1982). "The Relation between Socioeconomic Status and Academic Achievement." *Psychological Bulletin* 91: 461–481.

Wolf, P. (2006). "School Choice by Mortgage or Design." In P. E. Peterson (ed.), *Generational Change: Closing the Test-Score Gap*. Lanham, MD: Rowman and Littlefield.

Woessmann, L. (2004). "How Equal Are Educational Opportunities? Family Background and Student Achievement in Europe and the United States." Working Paper 1162, CESifo, Munich.

Woessmann, L. (2005a). "Educational Production in Europe." *Economic Policy* 20(43): 445–504.

Woessmann, L. (2005b). "The Effect Heterogeneity of Central Exams: Evidence from TIMSS, TIMSS-Repeat and PISA." *Education Economics* 13(2): 143–169.

Woessmann, L., and M. R. West. (2006). "Class-Size Effects in School Systems around the World: Evidence from Between-Grade Variation in TIMSS." *European Economic Review* 50(3): 695–736.

2

Education Expansion and Intergenerational Mobility in Britain

Stephen Machin

2.1 Introduction

Education matters for economic and social outcomes and for the distribution of welfare in society. Possessing more higher-quality education has sizable impacts on wages and education impacts on other non-pecuniary outcomes.[1] Moreover, education has the potential to affect an individual's life course and is often championed as a means by which people from less advantaged backgrounds can advance themselves up the social ladder, thereby fostering increased intergenerational mobility.

The relationship between education and the extent of intergenerational mobility in economic status forms the subject matter of this chapter. To study the possible links between the two, I consider how intergenerational mobility has altered over time in a period when post-compulsory education expanded rapidly as the organization of the education system was restructured. Making a link between education expansion and changes over time in mobility thus permits a consideration of the idea that education can act as a "great leveler" that promotes intergenerational mobility.

The chapter looks at these issues using rich cohort data from Britain. The starting point is to study changes in intergenerational mobility through time. The analysis then links the findings to changing patterns of educational attainment, particularly in the context of expansion of the higher-education system (see figure 2.1, which illustrates the scale of expansion in Britain, to be discussed more fully below).[2] Particularly important to the study of the latter issue is the way in which relationships between education and family income have altered through time and link directly to the observed changes in intergenerational mobility.

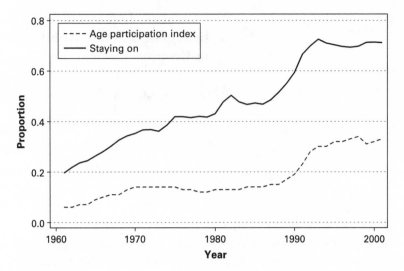

Figure 2.1
Changes in education participation, United Kingdom. *Source:* Department for Education and Skills. *Notes:* "Staying on" denotes staying on in education after the compulsory school leaving age. The higher-education "Age participation index" is the number of young (underage 21) home initial entrants expressed as a proportion of the averaged 18- to 19-year-old population.

The results paint something of a depressing picture for those who believe education can promote increased intergenerational mobility. There is actually strong evidence that the extent of intergenerational mobility has fallen across the birth cohorts I follow over time in Britain. This increase in immobility has occurred alongside a rapid expansion of postcompulsory education. This is because children from richer families benefited disproportionately from this change in the education system, and rather than alleviating inequality across generations, the expansion reinforced and exacerbated already existent intergenerational inequalities.

These results must be placed in context. First of all, they refer to cross-cohort comparisons for the intergenerational work based mostly on two time periods and for the education and income work on three points in time. Second, the results do not say whether education can in general act as a "great equalizer." It clearly plays this role in some circumstances where education policies are pursued in specific ways (for example, when education expansions are appropriately financed). However, in the case of this episode of recent history, results show that education expansion did not have the equalizing role that many people desire.

The chapter is structured as follows. In section 2.2, I present the core findings on changes over time in the extent of intergenerational mobility. In section 2.3, I consider the role played by education in accounting for the intertemporal shifts in intergenerational mobility. Section 2.4 considers changing relationships between education and family income in more detail. Section 2.5 concludes.

2.2 Changes in the Extent of Intergenerational Mobility

2.2.1 Approach

The extent of intergenerational mobility in economic or social status at a point in time is often evaluated using a simple log-linear regression of children's outcomes on parent's outcomes for family i as follows:[3]

$$ln\ Y_i^{CHILD} = \alpha + \beta\ ln\ Y_i^{PARENTS} + \varepsilon_i,$$

where Y is the measure of economic or social status of interest and ε is an error term. The coefficient β measures the extent of intergenerational mobility, reflecting how strongly children's status is associated with parental economic status. The literature usually proceeds to say that a value of zero for β (where child Y and parental Y are uncorrelated) corresponds to complete intergenerational mobility and a value of unity for β (child Y is fully determined by parental Y) corresponds to complete immobility.

A lot of work has produced estimates of β for different measures of Y. While sociologists have studied social-class mobility in detail,[4] economists tend to focus more on labor-market earnings or family income, and I also do this.[5] However, unlike most of the work that simply estimates β at a point in time from data on children and parents, I am interested in the way it has altered through time and look at cross-cohort changes, estimated from British birth-cohort data.

Much of the debate in the intergenerational-mobility literature is concerned with whether a given estimate of β is small (suggesting a lot of mobility) or big (suggesting a lot of immobility). Yet there is clearly little or no agreement on what constitutes big or small. For example, the .4 "consensus" estimate in Solon (1999) that emerges from regressions of son's earnings on father's earnings seems to be interpreted differently by different people, and value judgments may well shape people's views. Looking at changes over time is useful in this regard

since one can benchmark against an initial level and say something
about whether mobility is getting better or worse.[6]

2.2.2 Cohort Data

The data requirements for studying intertemporal changes in intergenerational mobility are demanding. However, some rich British
data sources permit such an analysis to be undertaken, albeit only for
changes at particular points in time rather than for trends based on
more frequently observed data. In particular, two birth cohorts cover
everyone born in Britain in a week of March 1958 and everyone born
in a week of April 1970. They follow individuals from birth to adulthood and obtain a large amount of information along the way. The
first of these is the National Child Development Study (NCDS), which
consists of the birth population of a week in March 1958 with follow-
up samples at cohort member ages 7, 11, 16, 23, 33, and 42. The second,
the British Cohort Study (BCS), is similar in style. It covers a full birth
population in a week of April 1970 with data subsequently collected at
ages 5, 10, 16, 26, and 30. Both of these surveys have information about
parental income at age 16, detailed measures of educational attainment
and measures of earnings at an almost comparable point in time (age
33 in 1991 the NCDS and age 30 in 2000 in the BCS).

Ideally, measures of the same permanent economic status (whether
wages or income) would be available for both generations from both
cohort studies. This would permit changes in β to be estimated using
the regression framework above. Unfortunately, owing to different survey designs, this is not possible since the NCDS parental-income data
comes from separate measures of father's earnings, mother's earnings,
and other income (all defined after taxes), and the BCS has data on
only parents' combined income. Estimates therefore must be based on
the relationship between the cohort member's earnings or income and
combined parental income. While this method will produce different
estimates than the usual regression of child earnings or income on
one parent's earnings or income will produce, it remains the case that
changes in the intergenerational parameter over time are measured on
a consistent basis, thus allowing a discussion of changes over time in
the extent of intergenerational mobility.

2.2.3 Estimates

Table 2.1 shows the results from intergenerational-mobility regressions
for the NCDS and BCS70 birth cohorts. The table presents estimates

Table 2.1
Changes in intergenerational mobility in Britain

	Intergenerational elasticities (standard errors)						
	Regression coefficients birth cohort		Inequality-adjusted regression coefficient birth cohort		Cross-cohort change	Sample sizes birth cohort	
	1958	1970	1958	1970		1958	1970
Panel A. Basic model:							
Sons	0.175	0.250	0.166	0.260	0.095	2,246	2,053
	(0.021)	(0.021)	(0.020)	(0.024)	(0.031)		
Daughters	0.310	0.317	0.168	0.227	0.059	1,908	2,017
	(0.041)	(0.030)	(0.022)	(0.022)	(0.031)		
Panel B. Augmented model:							
Sons	0.109	0.186	0.103	0.194	0.091	2,246	2,053
	(0.023)	(0.026)	(0.022)	(0.027)	(0.035)		
Daughters	0.183	0.215	0.099	0.154	0.054	1,908	2,017
	(0.047)	(0.037)	(0.026)	(0.026)	(0.037)		
Panel C. Family-income model:							
Sons	0.159	0.300	0.123	0.261	0.139	2,110	2,015
	(0.028)	(0.026)	(0.022)	(0.022)	(0.031)		
Daughters	0.219	0.307	0.137	0.221	0.085	2,156	2,285
	(0.033)	(0.029)	(0.021)	(0.021)	(0.029)		

Source: Estimates from Blanden et al. (2004). 1958 birth cohort data are from the National Child Development Study, 1970 birth cohort data are from the British Cohort Study.

Notes: Earnings are measured at age 33 in 1991 for the 1958 cohort and at age 30 in 2000 for the 1970 cohort, while parental income is at cohort member age 16 in both (1974 in the 1958 cohort and 1986 for the 1970 cohort). Standard errors in parentheses. All regressions control for parents' age and age-squared. Augmented regressions include controls for ethnicity, parental education, family structure, whether father was unemployed during childhood, and maths and reading test score quintiles at age 10/11. In the family income regressions, the dependent variable is the sum of cohort member's earnings plus those of any partner.

from regressions of cohort members' log(earnings) on log(family income) for sons and daughters separately, reporting three different specifications for each. It is important to be clear on comparability across cohorts, and there is a close (though not perfect) correspondence in the data used. Earnings are measured at age 33 in 1991 for the 1958 cohort and at age 30 in 2000 for the 1970 cohort, while parental income is at cohort member age 16 in both (1974 in the 1958 cohort and 1986 for the 1970 cohort).

The first specification, given in panel A, relates cohort members' log(earnings) to log(family income).[7] It is thus the equation

$$\ln E_i^{CHILD} = \alpha' + \beta' \ln Y_i^{PARENTS} + \varepsilon_i',$$

where E is labor-market earnings and Y is now parents' combined income.

One feature of the time period being studied is that income inequality rose in Britain. Thus, it is important to adjust for changes in inequality when looking at patterns over time. This adjustment can be made by scaling the regression coefficient on log(family income) by the ratio of the standard deviation of parental income to the standard deviation of child earnings (see Grawe 2000). The adjusted estimates given in the table are those standardizing for inequality change (these become the conditional correlation coefficients since the regressions also control for age).

The results from the basic specification produce a clear pattern. The estimated intergenerational parameter is significantly higher for the younger BCS cohort than for the NCDS cohort. For example, for sons the inequality-adjusted intergenerational parameter is .166 in the NCDS and rises to .260 in the BCS, with the .095 change being statistically significant. The same increasing pattern is seen for daughters, with a rise from .168 to .227, with the change being slightly smaller at .059. Hence, the rise in the estimated parameter reveals significant falls in the extent of intergenerational mobility.[8]

One might worry that the observed changes reflect compositional changes in the characteristics of families, in differing childhood experiences of cohort members, or perhaps in different ability levels across the cohorts. Panel B thus presents estimates when a set of extra factors, Z, are added to the basic specification. In the standard omitted-variable bias formula, one will worry that β' could be biased if an important factor in Z is omitted and, in the cross-section, the bias (for the bivariate regression above) is given by

$\delta.[Cov(ln\ Y_i^{PARENTS}, Z_i)/Var(ln\ Y_i^{PARENTS})]$,

where δ is the coefficient on Z when it is also included in the estimating equation and where

$$[Cov(ln\ Y_i^{PARENTS}, Z_i)/Var(ln\ Y_i^{PARENTS})]$$

is the coefficient from a regression of Z_i on $ln\ Y_i^{PARENTS}$, where $Cov(.)$ denotes a covariance and $Var(.)$ a variance. One can use this bias formula to assess the importance of particular Z factors in accounting for the rise in β over time. It is evident that stronger correlations between Z and child E or parent Y in a particular cohort will have implications for the change in the intergenerational parameter over time.

Take the case of ability. If ability is more strongly correlated with either child E or parent Y (or both) in a given time period, then when one controls for ability, this will shift β' by more in the cohort in which it is more strongly correlated. Thus, the change in β' will be different from that given in panel A, where no other factors are conditioned upon.

Panel B presents estimates where the following Z variables are added to the panel A specifications: ethnicity, parental education, single-parent family structure, whether father was unemployed during childhood, and math and reading test-score quintiles at age 10/11. It is clear that, at a point in time, the estimate of the intergenerational elasticity falls, suggesting that these factors do account for an important part of the intergenerational correlation. But it is striking that they fall by very similar amounts across cohorts and that the change over time is barely affected by their inclusion. As such, it seems that the change in intergenerational mobility is not due to these prelabor-market factors associated with the cohort members' childhood and family situations.

Panel C uses a different dependent variable and relates the total family income of cohort members (now including spouse's income if a spouse is present) and relating this to total parental income in the basic model. Again, there is strong evidence of a rise in the intergenerational-mobility parameter over time.

2.2.4 Transitions

The advantage of the regression approach is that it summarizes the extent of mobility in a single number through an average coefficient. However, this is less forthcoming in that it is unclear about the way in which the nature of the mobility process is altering. One can explore this in more detail by looking at transition matrices, which show where

Table 2.2
Quartile transition matrices for sons and daughters

	Earnings quartile			
Parental income quartile	Bottom	Second	Third	Top
National Child Development Study: Sons				
Bottom	.31	.29	.23	.17
Second	.30	.24	.23	.23
Third	.23	.26	.26	.26
Top	.17	.20	.29	.34
British Cohort Study: Sons				
Bottom	.39	.25	.22	.14
Second	.28	.29	.24	.19
Third	.20	.28	.27	.25
Top	.13	.17	.28	.42
National Child Development Study: Daughters				
Bottom	.27	.31	.25	.17
Second	.30	.24	.22	.24
Third	.25	.24	.26	.24
Top	.19	.20	.27	.34
Boston Cohort Study: Daughters				
Bottom	.33	.31	.23	.13
Second	.28	.28	.25	.19
Third	.24	.22	.28	.26
Top	.16	.19	.26	.39

Notes: Immobility Index for sons: NCDS 2.78, BCS 2.95. Immobility Index for daughters: NCDS 2.69, BCS 2.86.

child-parent pairs are moving across the distribution of economic status.

Table 2.2 thus reports quartile transition matrices for NCDS and BCS sons and daughters. They show the proportion in each parental-income quartile that moves into each quartile of the sons' or daughters' earnings distribution. The extent of immobility can be summarized by an immobility index that computes the sum of the leading diagonal and its adjacent cells. These are reported at the top of the tables. These numbers can be interpreted relative to the immobility index in the case of perfect mobility. If all individuals had an equal chance of experiencing an adult income in each quartile, all cells would contain 0.25, and the immobility index would be 2.5. As we might expect, given what we learned from the regression analysis, all the immobility indices we observe in the table are above this number.

It is clear that the transition analysis of table 2.2 confirms the regression finding that mobility has fallen between the cohorts. In almost every case, a higher proportion remain in the same quartile as their parents in the later cohort, and there are less extreme movements between generations. For example, in the NCDS, 17 percent of sons and daughters with parents in the bottom quartile rise to the top; in the BCS, this falls to 14 percent for sons and 13 percent for daughters. Moving in the other direction, the growth in immobility is similar, with almost one-fifth (17 percent for sons and 19 percent for daughters) of those who start in the top quartile falling to the bottom in the NCDS, while in the BCS the corresponding percentages are 13 for sons and 16 for daughters. The overall pattern of reduced mobility is very much confirmed by the pattern of results in the transition matrices.

This section has considered how the extent of intergenerational mobility has changed across two British birth cohorts, the first born in March 1958 and the second in April 1970. One sees sharp falls in cross-generation mobility of economic status between the cohorts, reflecting that the economic status of the 1970 cohort is more strongly connected to parental economic status than the 1958 cohort. In the next two sections of the chapter, I consider how education is connected to these findings.

2.3   Educational Attainment and Changes in Intergenerational Mobility

The previous section makes it clear that intergenerational mobility has fallen across the 1958 and 1970 cohorts but also that a number of prelabor-market factors do not seem to account for the observed changes. In this section, I consider whether educational attainment is able to account for any of the change.

2.3.1   Rising Educational Attainment

As with many other countries, educational attainment in terms of qualifications has been rising sharply in Britain. Table 2.3 shows that there has been rapid upgrading of the educational status of the workforce between 1975 and 1998. The table uses General Household Survey data to report the percentage of workers in five bands according to their highest qualification: degree or higher, having a higher vocational qualification,[9] teaching/nursing, an intermediate group (comprising those with A levels, just GCSEs, or lower vocational qualifications), and no educational qualifications.

Table 2.3
Employment shares by education, 1975 to 1998 (percentages)

	1975	1980	1985	1990	1995	1998
Men:						
Degree or higher	5.8	8.2	12.1	12.5	15.5	16.3
Higher vocational	4.7	6.8	10.5	11.4	11.7	12.1
Teaching and nursing	1.2	1.3	1.4	1.2	1.3	2.0
Intermediate	38.3	41.2	40.7	47.9	50.7	50.7
No qualifications	50.2	42.6	35.4	27.1	20.7	18.9
Women:						
Degree or higher	2.2	3.6	6.2	7.5	10.8	12.5
Higher vocational	.7	1.3	2.0	2.9	3.8	2.7
Teaching and nursing	5.8	6.8	8.4	7.9	7.4	7.7
Intermediate	33.1	39.6	46.5	52.1	54.3	53.7
No qualifications	58.3	48.8	36.8	29.6	23.6	23.3

Source: Calculated from General Household Surveys. For 1975 through 1995, statistics are based on three pooled years with the central year reported in the table.

The upper panel of table 2.3 shows that the incidence of men with a degree rose from 5.8 percent in 1975 to 16.3 percent by 1998. Similarly, the share of men with a higher vocational qualification went up rapidly from 4.7 to 12.1 percent. But most striking is the falling proportion of men with no qualifications, which goes down from just over half (at 50.2 percent) in 1975 to less than 20 percent (18.9) by 1998. The patterns for women, in the bottom panel of the table, are even more marked. The proportion of women in employment with a degree rises over fivefold from a very low initial level of 2.2 percent in 1975 up to 12.5 percent by 1998. There has been much less of a shift into higher vocational qualifications compared to men, as only 2.7 percent of working women possessed such qualifications in 1998. However, mirroring the experience of males, there has been a sharp fall in the size of the group with no qualifications, which plummets from 58.3 percent in 1975 to 23.3 percent by 1998.

2.3.2 Educational Attainment and Changes in Intergenerational Mobility

This makes it clear that changing education composition may be important. Table 2.4 reports what happens when the educational attainment of cohort members, measured by their highest educational qualifications, are controlled for in the intergenerational-mobility equa-

Table 2.4
Changes in intergenerational mobility and educational upgrading

| | Intergenerational elasticities (standard errors) | | | | | |
| | Regression coefficients cohort | | Inequality adjusted regression coefficient cohort | | Cross-cohort change | Sample sizes |
	1958	1970	1958	1970		
Panel A. Sons:						
Table 2.1 upper panel	0.175	0.250	0.166	0.260	0.095	NCDS: 2,246
	(0.021)	(0.021)	(0.020)	(0.024)	(0.031)	BCS: 2,053
Plus son's education	0.105	0.170	0.099	0.177	0.078	NCDS: 2,246
	(0.020)	(0.023)	(0.019)	(0.024)	(0.031)	BCS: 2,053
Panel B. Daughters:						
Table 2.1 upper panel	0.310	0.317	0.168	0.227	0.059	NCDS: 1,908
	(0.041)	(0.030)	(.022)	(0.022)	(0.031)	BCS: 2,017
Plus daughter's education	0.154	.0167	0.084	0.119	0.036	NCDS: 1,908
	(0.037)	(0.030)	(0.020)	(0.021)	(0.029)	BCS: 2,017

Source: From Blanden et al. (2004).
Notes: Standard errors in parentheses. All regressions control for parents' age and age-squared. Educational attainment is modeled via educational qualification dummies (less than O level, O level or equivalent, greater than O level but less than degree, degree or higher).

tions. There is, indeed, evidence that highest qualification matters. For the point-in-time (within-cohort) comparisons, they account for around 30 percent of the intergenerational transmission of income for sons and 40 to 50 percent of the transmission for daughters. Moreover, they explain some of the rise in the intergenerational elasticities. For sons, the estimate of the cross-cohort rise falls by around 20 percent on inclusion of the education variables. For daughters, it accounts for 40 percent of the cross-cohort rise. As such, the educational variables seem to explain both point-in-time intergenerational mobility and its evolution over time.

Considering the transition matrices is suggestive of even more of an education effect. Table 2.5 shows transition matrices that control for education. For both sons and daughters, an important portion of the observed fall in mobility is accounted for by the education variables. For sons, the immobility index rises by .10 conditional on education compared with .17 in the unconditional matrices in table 2.2. For

Table 2.5
Quartile transition matrices for sons and daughters conditional on education

Parental income quartile	Earnings quartile			
	Bottom	Second	Third	Top
National Child Development Study: Sons				
Bottom	.30	.26	.25	.19
Second	.28	.25	.24	.23
Third	.22	.27	.25	.26
Top	.20	.25	.24	.31
British Cohort Study: Sons				
Bottom	.33	.26	.22	.19
Second	.27	.27	.25	.21
Third	.23	.24	.27	.26
Top	.17	.22	.26	.35
National Child Development Study: Daughters				
Bottom	.27	.29	.23	.21
Second	.27	.24	.25	.23
Third	.25	.23	.25	.27
Top	.21	.24	.26	.29
British Cohort Study: Daughters				
Bottom	.30	.26	.24	.19
Second	.27	.24	.25	.24
Third	.23	.25	.24	.28
Top	.20	.24	.26	.30

Notes: Immobility Index for sons: NCDS 2.66, BCS 2.76. Immobility Index for daughters: NCDS 2.62, BCS 2.65.

daughters, the conditional rise is .03 compared with an unconditional rise of .17. Thus, the nonlinearities allowed for in the transition-matrix approach do seem to imply a bigger education effect for both sons and daughters as compared to the average regression approach considered earlier (the immobility index is reduced by 41 percent for sons and by 80 percent for daughters). As such, the increased educational attainment of the younger birth cohort seems to matter in interpreting the fall in intergenerational mobility observed across cohorts.

2.3.3 Why Could Education Matter for Changes in Intergenerational Mobility?

It is worth considering how changing education might be a transmission mechanism underpinning the change in intergenerational mobility. Solon (2004) has formalized ideas about how education acts as a transmission mechanism underpinning the extent of intergenerational mobility. In a simple version of his model, in generation t labor-market earnings E are a function of human capital H so that $E_t = \phi_t H_t + u_t$, where u_t is a random-error term. If children's human-capital accumulation then relates to parental income, we can write $H_t = \psi_t Y_{t-1} + v_t$ (v_t being an error term). One can combine these equations to generate an intergenerational mobility function like the ones from which parameter estimates are reported in table 2.1: $E_t = \phi_t \psi_t Y_{t-1} + \omega_t$, where $\omega_t = \phi_t v_t + u_t$.

Here the intergenerational mobility parameter is $\phi_t \psi_t$, so that intergenerational mobility will be higher in a given generation t if (a) there are lower returns to human capital for children (ϕ_t is lower) or (b) if children's human capital is less sensitive to parental earnings (ψ_t is lower).

A critical factor is thus how sensitive education is to parental income (ψ_t). This relates back to the discussion in the introduction to this chapter about how well education does enable people to escape poor childhoods, increase their earning potential, and thus enhance the extent of intergenerational mobility. In the next section of the chapter, I consider changing education-income relations to see if they are consistent with the scope for changing educational attainment across the income spectrum as being a factor underpinning falling intergenerational mobility.

2.4   The Expansion of Postcompulsory Schooling and Changes in Intergenerational Mobility

Over the period where intergenerational mobility fell, there was a sizable expansion in the British education system. Postcompulsory participation rates, especially in higher education, rose sharply indeed. To be a possible candidate explanation for the mobility falls, one needs to investigate the extent to which this expansion was equally or unequally distributed across the parental-income distribution, and this is what is done in this section of the chapter.

2.4.1   Expansion of the Higher-Education System

Student numbers in higher education have quadrupled in the United Kingdom since the 1960s. Figure 2.1 shows the Department for Education and Skills (DfES) higher-education age-participation index, which measures the proportion of young people in higher education between 1960 and 2001. It contrasts the pattern of change in this index with the growth in staying on beyond the compulsory school-leaving age. The figure shows sharp increases in both from 1960 onward. The staying-on series appears to have been on a fairly steadily increasing path (although it is subject to cyclical variations) from the start of the series through to the mid-1980s. From the late 1980s, there appears to be a step change as staying on rates rise much faster, from 51 percent in 1988 to a new plateau of around 70 percent in the late 1990s and early 2000s.[10] The increase in university participation is also very rapid. There was a sharp expansion in the 1960s, where the age-participation index doubled from 6 to 14 percent. It then rose marginally from this level until the late 1980s, after which it grew even more rapidly than the 1960s change. By 2001, it had reached 33 percent, rising up from under 20 percent at the start of the 1990s.[11]

2.4.2 Higher-Education Expansion and Family Income

To study links with shifts in intergenerational mobility, it is critical to assess how the expansion of the education system links to family background and whether differential shifts in participation rates and qualification attainment can be seen across different family-income groups. The principal data issue that emerges is the requirement to match up data on children's education with the income of their parents. I am again able to use the NCDS and BCS cohort studies, but these are a little out of date for an education analysis since they contain information on young people in higher education (such as attending university) in the early 1980s and early 1990s. But data from the British Household Panel Survey (BHPS), a longitudinal survey that began in 1991, can be used to form a third, more up-to-date cohort to facilitate an examination of changing relations between education and family income for cohorts of children who could have entered higher education from the late 1970s and early 1980s through to the late 1990s.

Table 2.6 presents some descriptive analysis showing the proportion of young people who acquire a degree by age 23 broken down by parental-income groups (the top quintile, the middle 60 percent, and the bottom quintile) from the three cohorts, in 1981, 1993, and 1999, respectively. The numbers in the table clearly demonstrate wide gaps in degree acquisition by income group. In 1981, for example, 20 percent of children from the top income quintile had a degree by age 23, whereas the comparable number was only 6 percent in the bottom

Table 2.6
Degree acquisition by age 23 and parental income

	Degree acquisition by age 23			
	Lowest 20 percent	Middle 60 percent	Highest 20 percent	Educational inequality
NCDS 1981	.06	.08	.20	.14 (.01)
BCS 1993	.07	.15	.37	.30 (.02)
BHPS 1999	.09	.23	.46	.37 (.05)
Change 1981–1993	.01	.07	.17	.15 (.02)
Change 1993–1999	.02	.08	.09	.07 (.06)
Change 1981–1999	.03	.15	.26	.23 (.06)

Notes: Sample sizes are NCDS: 5,706, BCS: 4,706, BHPS: 580. The year we establish degree attainment is 1999 on average for the BHPS. For the NCDS and BCS, all individuals need to have graduated by 1981 and 1993, respectively. Standard errors in parentheses. Rows and columns may not add up precisely due to rounding.

quintile. One natural metric of gauging the extent of educational inequality is the gap between the top and bottom quintiles. In 1981, this was 14 percentage points, which (as the standard errors in parentheses show) was strongly significant in statistical terms.

Looking at changes through time shows a sharp increase in higher-education inequality between 1981 and 1999. In table 2.6, the top-bottom quintile measure of inequality rises considerably through time, from 14 percent in 1981, through to 30 percent by 1993, and up to a huge 37 percentage points by 1999. The magnitude of these changes is large and demonstrates a considerable widening of the gap between the university attainment of the richest and poorest in the two decades the data spans. The standard errors for these changes show that the rise in educational inequality was strongly significant between 1981 and 1993, a little less precisely determined between 1993 and 1999 (largely owing to relatively small sample sizes in the BHPS), and strongly significant over the full 18 years between 1981 to 1999. The descriptive analysis therefore uncovers a big, statistically significant change in the association between income and degree attainment between the early 1980s and late 1990s. Thus, in the era of higher-education expansion, children from richer families raised their higher-education participation by more than those from poorer families. This is completely in line with the notion that the increased sensitivity of higher education (here, degree acquisition) to parental income is a key factor underpinning falling intergenerational mobility over time.

The purpose of this chapter is to document these changes, to show the magnitude of the changes, and to make clear how they link to shifts in intergenerational mobility. Nonetheless, it is worth remarking that education policy is likely to have played a role. Over the time of expansion, student finance became less redistributive (Goodman and Kaplan 2003), making it relatively harder for children from poorer families to obtain funding to participate in higher education.[12] This may well have acted as a deterrent effect to further reinforce the widening educational inequality, especially if low-income students are more averse to taking on debt (see Callender 2003 for evidence on this).

2.4.3 Statistical Models

As with the analysis of changes in intergenerational mobility, one might also be concerned that other changes may have occurred at the same time as the strengthening of the education-income relationship. One can therefore consider statistical models that relate degree acquisition to parental income. The starting point is a probit model relating the probability of having a degree by age 23, the 0-1 variable D for person i in cohort c to their parent's log income Y and a set of control variables Z:

$$D_{ic} = \kappa_c + \theta_c f(Y_{ic}) + \lambda_c Z_{ic} + \xi_{ic},$$

where $f(.)$ denotes the functional form for parental income, which is the independent variable of interest, and ξ is an error term. If we continue to use quintiles[13] as in the descriptive analysis of table 2.6, the equation becomes

$$D_{ic} = \kappa_{1c} + \sum_{j=2}^{5} \theta_{1jc} Q_{jic} + \lambda_{1c} Z_{ic} + \xi_{1ic},$$

where the Q_j variables are dummy variables for quantiles of the log income distribution—in this case, quintile dummies (leaving out the lowest quintile, $j = 1$, as the reference group).

Owing to the discrete nature of the dependent variable, the marginal impact of Q_5, the top quintile dummy, from a probit model is

$$\Upsilon_c = Pr[D_{ic} = 1 \mid Q_{5ic} = 1, Q_{4ic} = 0, Q_{3ic} = 0, Q_{2ic} = 0]$$

$$- Pr[D_{ic} = 1 \mid Q_{5ic} = 0, Q_{4ic} = 0, Q_{3ic} = 0, Q_{2ic} = 0]$$

$$= \Phi(\kappa_{1c} + \theta_{15c} + \lambda_{1c} Z_{ic}) - \Phi(\kappa_{1c} + \lambda_{1c} Z_{ic}),$$

Table 2.7
Changes in higher education-income associations, specifications with quintile dummies

	Degree acquisition by age 23			Changes over time		
	(1) NCDS 1981	(2) BCS70 1993	(3) BHPS 1999	(4) $(2)-(1)$	(5) $(3)-(2)$	(6) $(3)-(1)$
A. No controls						
Top quintile	.144	.299	.371	.155	.072	.226
	(.013)	(.018)	(.054)	(.022)	(.057)	(.056)
B. Basic controls						
Top quintile	.143	.295	.365	.152	.070	.221
	(.013)	(.0180)	(.057)	(.022)	(.060)	(.059)
C. Basic controls, plus test scores						
Top quintile	.061	.183		.122		
	(.012)	(.018)		(.022)		

Notes: Sample sizes as for table 2.6. Marginal effects are derived from probit models of staying on beyond age 16 on dummy variables for quintiles of family income as described in the text of the main body of the chapter. Bootstrapped standard errors in parentheses. Basic controls are sex, parental age bands, number of siblings, and no father figure at age 16. Test scores are the quintiles obtained in math and reading scores at ages 10 and 11. Rows and columns may not add up precisely due to rounding.

where $\Phi(.)$ is the standard normal cumulative distribution function. For a model with no Z controls, this will simply be the measure of educational inequality defined as the gap between the top and bottom income quintiles that we considered in table 2.6. In terms of changes over time (say, across cohorts c and c'), then a measure of changing educational inequality over time is $\Delta Y_{c'c} = Y_{c'} - Y_c$ (for which one can also calculate appropriately bootstrapped standard errors).

Table 2.7 reports estimates of educational inequality and its changes over time from statistical probit models where the functional form for $f(.)$ is taken to be the set of quintile dummy variables. Panel A of the table includes no control variables and therefore reproduces the descriptive numbers from table 2.6, with $\Delta Y_{c'c}$ rising by a strongly significant .23 between 1981 and 1999. Panel B then includes a basic set of family characteristics (sex of child, family composition, and parental age). These additions change the magnitude of the estimates very little and serve to slightly enhance, though very moderately, the patterns found in the unconditional models.

The specification in panel C of the table adds test-score quintiles for reading and math at age 11 (NCDS) and age 10 (BCS). Unfortunately, these data on test scores are available only for the first two cohorts but are one of the big advantages of these data sources. This is because the transmission of ability across generations is seen by many as an obvious route leading to higher attainment among children of better-off parents. According to this line of thinking, the addition of controls for ability should substantially reduce the remaining educational inequality. This is certainly the case, with the estimate of ψ_c falling from .14 to .06 in the NCDS and from .30 to .18 in the BCS. But it is striking that the fall is of similar magnitude across cohorts. Thus, the pattern of rising degree-income relations is not damaged by the inclusion of test scores, as the rise in educational inequality $\Delta\psi_{c'c}$ is estimated as a strongly significant .12, or 12 percentage points. Conditional on family characteristics and test scores, the probability of getting a degree at age 23 was 12 percentage points higher for young people in 1993 as compared to 1981.

2.5 Conclusions

Empirical study of cross-cohort data on children and their parents shows that in Britain the extent of intergenerational mobility has been falling. That is, for a more recent birth cohort, an individual's position in his or her own generation's income distribution is more strongly affected by where the individual's parents were in their own generation's income distribution. Education acts as a transmission mechanism affecting mobility, but over the period studied, where there was an important expansion of access to postcompulsory education, it acts not to foster increased mobility but rather to reinforce inequalities across generations.

The findings reported here come from looking at largely descriptive cross-cohort comparisons. Nonetheless, these comparisons reveal that the kinds of education expansions studied here can be shown to matter for patterns of social mobility. This is revealed in the British case, where an increased sensitivity of educational attainment to parental income emerging from the observed education expansion lies behind the observed pattern of falling intergenerational mobility in economic status. This is a feature of the particular expansion studied, where rather than giving opportunities that enabled children from poorer backgrounds to participate in postcompulsory education, the expansion benefited children from parents further up the income distribution.

There are other potentially important factors to look at in trying to understand why economic mobility across generations fell in the time periods studied in this chapter. The analysis reported here focuses on an individual's economic success as a function of parental income, but it is also evident that the changing nature of families and changes in the distribution of work across families (for example, with the rise of dual-earner households over time) may well be important. Similarly, scope for changes in the extent of assortative matching in family formation may play a role (see Blanden 2004a for a first look at this). Also, placing the British experience of falling mobility into an appropriate international context seems important given the suggestion, albeit still a very preliminary one, of less or smaller change occurring in other countries (Blanden 2004b; Mayer and Lopoo 2004; Levine and Mazumdar 2002).

From a policy perspective, it seems key to understand how expansions of the education system can end up disproportionately benefiting children from richer backgrounds. In the British context, this happened in earlier time periods: in the 1950s, when richer children stayed on at school; in the 1970s and 1980s, when they did better in terms of leaving school with qualifications; and in the 1990s, in terms of getting into higher education. However, as the children from poorer families start to catch up, then it seems that the children from families with more resources have already moved on and "colonized" the next stage. The equilibrium implied by this process of colonization seems to shift over time, typically before education policy has scope or time to exert a redistributive effect. If people want education to act as a leveler or equalizer in society, as it clearly can under appropriate policy design and implementation, a dynamic, forward-looking approach to education policy is required. Central to this is acquiring a better understanding of what causes intergenerational inequalities and how trends in educational inequality arise and persist.

Acknowledgments

This work draws on and further develops some of my joint work with Jo Blanden, Alissa Goodman, Paul Gregg, and Anna Vignoles. The views and interpretations expressed are mine alone. I am grateful to my discussant Roland Fryer, to other participants in the CESifo/PEPG conference, and to two referees and the editors for a number of helpful comments.

Notes

1. See Card (1999) for an extensive and comprehensive discussion of the impact of education on wages. A recent review of the impact of education on noneconomic outcomes (like health and well-being) is Heshmati (2004).

2. See also the in-depth discussion in Machin and Vignoles (2005).

3. See Solon's (1999) review for a more in-depth discussion.

4. See, among many others, Erikson and Goldthorpe (1992).

5. It may be interesting to do some work on intergenerational correlations of occupational status and link them to economic-status measures with the hope of building a bridge between the economic and sociological approaches. This, however, is beyond the scope of the current study.

6. There is hardly any work on changes over time in intergenerational mobility. Mayer and Lopoo (2004) consider very small samples from the U.S. Panel Survey of Income Dynamics (PSID), finding little change in the extent of intergenerational mobility in the United States. The results I report on here come from Blanden et al. (2004) and use much larger samples from British cohort data.

7. It also conditions on parental age to net out the fact that the parental earnings may be measured at different points in the life cycle.

8. An important consideration is whether these results could be contaminated by measurement error in income as there is only a single measure of this for each cohort in the table 2.1 results. Indeed, point-in-time estimates will be biased downward if parental income is measured with error (Solon 1989, 1999). This has been explored in other work (Blanden et al. 2004), where two sets of robustness checks suggest that this is unlikely to affect the result of falling mobility over time. First, simulations show that, under certain assumptions about measurement error in the BCS (ranging from zero to sizable amounts), the amount of measurement error needed in the NCDS income data to offset the rise in the intergenerational mobility parameter would be implausibly large. Second, in the BCS cohort, income data are available for cohort members ages 10 and 16, and so one can time average the two income measures in the hope of smoothing out some of the measurement error. When this is done, the BCS intergenerational mobility parameter does rise but only moderately. Thus, the rise in the intergenerational correlation does not seem attributable to differential bias owing to measurement error in income across the two cohorts considered.

9. The most important higher vocational qualifications include Higher National Certificates (HNC), Higher National Diplomas (HND), and full City and Guilds awards.

10. It appears likely that this rise was a consequence of the introduction of a new examination system for 15- and 16-year-olds, the General Certificate of Secondary Education (GCSE) in 1988, and the consequent improvement in exam results (see Blanden and Machin 2004).

11. A discussion of the factors that lie behind the growth of higher-education participation is given in Kogan and Hanney (2000). In part, the rise in participation was demand-led as students responded to the changes in the economy and the shift toward service-industry jobs. Widening wage differentials between graduates and nongraduates, especially in the 1980s (Machin 1996, 1999, 2003) likely played a role here, and it seems

likely that higher-education participation may have been linked to perceived changes in economic incentives, at least among some groups.

12. The political economy and redistributive implications of universal subsidies to higher education are considered in more detail in Fernandez and Rogerson (1995).

13. The functional form assumptions for $f(.)$ are studied in more detail in Blanden and Machin (2004). They show similar patterns of temporal change with income marginal effects rising over time (with differing magnitudes) for different $f(.)$ functions, including specifying $f(.)$ as log(income), decile dummies, or a discrete above/below median-income formulation.

References

Blanden, J. (2004a). "Intergenerational Mobility and Assortative Mating in the UK." Centre for Economic Performance photocopy.

Blanden, J. (2004b). "International Comparisons of Intergenerational Mobility." Centre for Economic Performance photocopy.

Blanden, J., A. Goodman, P. Gregg, and S. Machin. (2004). "Changes in Intergenerational Mobility in Britain." In M. Corak (ed.), *Generational Income Mobility in North America and Europe*. Cambridge: Cambridge University Press.

Blanden, J., and S. Machin. (2004). "Educational Inequality and the Expansion of UK Higher Education." *Scottish Journal of Political Economy* 51: 230–249 (special issue on the economics of education).

Callender, C. (2003). "Attitudes to Debt: School Leavers and Further Education Students' Attitudes to Debt and Their Impact on Participation in Higher Education." Report commissioned by Universities UK and the Higher Education Funding Council.

Card, D. (1999). "The Causal Effect of Education on Earnings." In O. Ashenfelter and D. Card (eds.), *Handbook of Labor Economics* (vol. 3). Amsterdam: Elsevier-North Holland.

Erikson, R., and J. Goldthorpe. (1992). *The Constant Flux: A Study of Class Mobility in Industrial Societies*. Oxford: Oxford University Press.

Fernandez, R., and R. Rogerson. (1995). "On the Political Economy of Education Subsidies." *Review of Economic Studies* 62: 249–262.

Goodman, A., and G. Kaplan. (2003). "'Study Now, Pay Later' or 'HE for Free'? An Assessment of Alternative Proposals for Higher Education Finance." Commentary No. 94, Institute for Fiscal Studies.

Grawe, N. (2000). "Lifecycle Bias in the Estimation of Intergenerational Income Persistence." Research Paper, Statistics Canada Analytical Studies Branch.

Heshmati, A. (2004). "Inequalities and Their Measurement." Discussion Paper 1219, IZA. Available at ⟨ftp://ftp.iza.org/dps/dp1219.pdf⟩.

Kogan, M., and S. Hanney. (2000). *Reforming Higher Education*. London: Jessica Kingsley.

Levine, D., and B. Mazumder. (2002). "Choosing the Right Parents: Changes in the Intergenerational Transmission of Inequality between 1980 and the Early 1990s." Working Paper 2002-08, Federal Reserve Bank of Chicago.

Machin, S. (1996). "Wage Inequality in the UK." *Oxford Review of Economic Policy* 12(1): 47–64.

Machin, S. (1999). "Wage Inequality in the 1970s, 1980s and 1990s." In R. Dickens, P. Gregg, and J. Wadsworth (eds.), *The State of Working Britain*. Manchester: Manchester University Press.

Machin, S. (2003). "Wage Inequality since 1975." In R. Dickens, P. Gregg, and J. Wadsworth (eds.), *The Labour Market under New Labour*. London: Palgrave MacMillan.

Machin, S., and A. Vignoles (eds.). (2005). *What's the Good of Education? The Economics of Education in the United Kingdom*. Princeton: Princeton University Press.

Mayer, S., and L. Lopoo. (2004). "Changes in the Intergenerational Mobility of Sons and Daughters." In M. Corak (ed.), *Generational Income Mobility in North America and Europe*. Cambridge: Cambridge University Press.

Solon, G. (1989). "Biases in the Estimation of Intergenerational Earnings Correlations." *Review of Economics and Statistics* 71: 172–174.

Solon, G. (1999). "Intergenerational Mobility in the Labor Market." In Orley Ashenfelter and David Card (eds.), *Handbook of Labor Economics* (vol. 3A). Amsterdam: Elsevier Science.

Solon, G. (2004). "A Model of Intergenerational Mobility Variation over Time and Place." In M. Corak (ed.), *Generational Income Mobility in North America and Europe*. Cambridge: Cambridge University Press.

3 Education and Earnings over the Life Cycle: Longitudinal Age-Earnings Profiles from Sweden

Sofia Sandgren

3.1 Introduction

Studies on earnings differences over the working lives of people with different levels of education have generally been limited to cross-sectional census data. The respondents have then been divided into age groups, and the earnings converted into time-series profiles by adjusting for secular growth in incomes. Hence, such figures do not show how individuals' incomes differ as they grow older but rather show how incomes differ between age groups on a given occasion or how they would develop over the lifetime in a stationary economy (Becker 1993; Mincer 1974; Willis 1986). Furthermore, when estimating wage premiums on cross-sectional data, an average premium is often estimated for all age groups, which disguises the fact that premiums may well fluctuate with age and experience. More recently, longitudinal cohort analyses have revealed that cross-sectional studies give a biased picture of how wage premiums develop (Creedy 1991; Heckman, Lochner, and Todd 2003).

The Malmö Longitudinal Study consists of data on the cohort of men and women born in 1928 in Malmö, Sweden. It includes data on earnings over their working lives, from age 20 to 65 years, which is the mandatory retirement age in Sweden. Hence, this material makes it feasible to construct an actual picture of life-cycle earnings and to show how wage premiums on education vary with age. Furthermore, there are exceptionally good ability measures in the dataset, which enable a study of how a potential ability bias in the return to education may vary over time and with the educational level.

In this chapter, I investigate how earnings and wage premiums have developed over the lives of the male respondents in the Malmö study. To the best of my knowledge, this is the first study where actual earnings over whole working lives have been used when studying earnings profiles, wage premiums, and ability biases.

One of the main findings in the present chapter is that real earnings for those with higher levels of education decline considerably after a peak between 40 and 45 years of age, while the earnings for the less educated are even during their whole working lives. In addition, the ability bias is found to be largest for the less educated groups, which also have the largest variation in innate ability. The level of education for this cohort of men turns out to be highly correlated with their parents' social class, with few men from the lower social classes achieving a higher level of education. Furthermore, the estimated actual longitudinal age-earnings profiles turn out to be fairly comparable with standard cross-sectional profiles.

The chapter is organized as follows. The next section gives a brief background to the study. Thereafter, the data (the Malmö study) and the empirical model are discussed in sections 3.3 and 3.4. Section 3.5 presents the results on how earnings differ over time and age for the Malmö cohort, and in section 3.6 wage and ability premiums are estimated. Finally, in the last sections, I discuss the results and conclude.

3.2 Background

It is widely accepted that earnings increase with formal schooling. Several explanations have been offered to explain this, with the traditional human-capital and signaling theories being dominant (Arrow 1973; Becker 1993; Mincer 1974; Spence 1974; Willis 1986). Furthermore, a number of studies (Blackburn and Neumark 1993; Griliches 1977; Lam and Schoeni 1993; Mellander 1998) have shown that when background factors that are positively correlated with the educational level are not included in the wage regression, the wage premium for schooling tends to be positively biased—which is referred to as the *omitted-variable bias*.[1]

Much has been written on the subjects mentioned above, but there has been less examination of how earnings and premiums develop with time and age. Mincer (1974) and Becker (1993) have been the pioneers in life-cycle analyses using cross-sectional data (U.S. Census, 1940 and 1960). Their estimated profiles are fairly similar: the higher educational levels have a steeper curve and a later peak than the lower educational groups. The peaks occur between 50 and 60 years of age, although Mincer's curves dip toward the end of the working life while

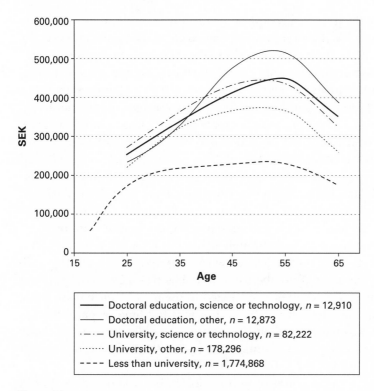

Figure 3.1
Cross-sectional age-earnings profiles, Swedish men 1999, $n = 2,074,533$. *Source:* Johnny Ullström, VINNOVA/SCB, 2004.

Becker's do not. An example of age-earnings profiles estimated on Swedish cross-sectional data are shown in figure 3.1. The figure is based on all gainfully employed men in Sweden in 1999 and is relatively comparable to Mincer's figure.

In Sweden, several articles have been written on how the premiums for schooling have fluctuated over a shorter period of time, between 1968 and 1991 (Björklund 1999; Björklund and Kjellström 2002; Edin and Holmlund 1993). A common finding in these studies is that the premiums fell sharply from the late 1960s to the mid-1970s. In the 1990s, a tendency toward increasing premiums has been discernible.

3.3   The Data

This chapter uses the Malmö Longitudinal Study, which is one of the longest individual longitudinal databases existing. It covers many aspects of the lives of a cohort of men and women, from the ages of 10 to 65 years. A doctoral student named Siver Hallgren initiated the study in 1938. The aim was to study the relation between social background and cognitive ability, and the chosen sample consisted of all third-graders in the province of Malmö in 1938. Malmö is the third largest city in Sweden, located in the southern part of the country. A vast amount of background information was collected, and an ability test was distributed and converted into intelligence quotients. In 1964, data on each student's acquired level of education were collected through a questionnaire, which was supplemented with register information. Four questionnaires were distributed—in 1964, 1971, 1984, and 1994. They provide data on, among other things, profession, work experience, unemployment, and retirement. Furthermore, data on earnings have been collected through registers on 14 separate occasions from 1948 to 1993, thus covering the whole working lives of these individuals. The original number of individuals was 1,542 (834 men and 708 women). This chapter is restricted to the men because there is not reliable information on whether work was full-time or part-time. As the latter was more common for women, it is difficult to use women's earnings information in a comparison with men's. Of the 834 men, 657 were still alive in 1993.

There is a vast amount of information in the Malmö study, but in this chapter, only the following variables are used: educational level, occupational category, gender, earnings, ability, and social class. Educational level was reported in six different categories: discontinued primary school, primary school, vocational school, lower secondary school, upper secondary school, and university. During this period, primary school (*folkskola*) in the province of Malmö consisted of seven years of schooling. Vocational school involved one or two years after primary or secondary school. Lower secondary school (*realskola*) was normally begun after fourth grade in primary school and lasted for four or five years. Compared with vocational school, lower secondary school was a more theoretical continuation of primary school. Upper secondary school involved further theoretical studies for three or four more years.

There is tax register data on earnings for the years 1948, 1953, 1958, 1963, 1968, 1971, 1974, 1978, 1982, 1986, 1990, and 1993. Earnings are yearly and hence do not include information on whether the individual was working full- or part-time or maybe only part of the year. To come to terms with this problem, I have checked wage statistics for the relevant years and regarded as part-time workers those persons who presumably earned too little to have worked full-time.[2]

The data do not indicate if the earnings were acquired through gainful work or if pensions or other kinds of transfers were received. However, it is possible to ascertain this for most of the individuals from the occupational data given in the surveys. From the surveys, there is information on each individual's occupation from 1942 until 1993, and this information is translated into work experience where the individual is assigned one year of experience for each year he has reported an occupational category. For individuals who have not answered the surveys, dummies have been constructed to take this into consideration.

The social class of the family in 1938 was assigned to one of four categories on the basis of four items of information: father's occupation, family income in 1937, number of children at home, and whether the family was on social welfare. A dummy for the highest social class is used in the regressions.

For 79 individuals, information is missing on the acquired-schooling level. These individuals are excluded from the empirical analysis, together with three outliers with earnings more than three times as high as the average. This leaves a sample of 752 men. The differences between the original sample and the slightly reduced sample are small; see table 3.1 for descriptive statistics. I allow the program to use all individuals with earnings reported for each year tried.[3]

The correlation coefficient between the social class of the parents and own achieved education for these men is 0.50. Among the men born into the lowest social class, 90 percent achieved only primary or vocational education. In contrast, 60 percent of those from the highest social class achieved a higher education. Of the university-educated men, 71 percent came from the highest social class.

There is always a question of representativeness for data from a geographically limited area. First, one advantage of the present sample is that because it includes the population of third graders in Malmö in one particular year, there is no problem with representativeness within this area. Second, Malmö is not considered to be different from other Swedish cities in any significant aspects. Thus, there seems to be no reason to believe that the working career for people born in Malmö should differ from that of other individuals of the same age in Sweden. Unfortunately, analyzing representativeness in more detail has not been feasible because comparable datasets are not available. This lack

Table 3.1
Descriptive statistics (standard deviation in parentheses)

	Original sample $n = 834$	Subsample $n = 752$
Primary school		0.47
		(0.50)
Vocational school		0.26
		(0.44)
Lower secondary school		0.12
		(0.33)
Upper secondary school		0.09
		(0.28)
Academic education		0.06
		(0.24)
Social class, high	0.12	0.10
	(0.32)	(0.30)
IQ	97.73	97.16
	(16.02)	(15.87)
Earnings 1958	13,214	13,109
	(6,893)	(6,850)
Earnings 1963	19,683	19,416
	(13,039)	(12,769)
Earnings 1968	35,010	33,863
	(26,679)	(20,530)
Earnings 1971	40,713	40,189
	(28,280)	(25,004)
Earnings 1974	52,551	52,068
	(32,687)	(28,435)
Earnings 1978	77,440	76,264
	(44,728)	(41,709)
Earnings 1982	107,377	103,450
	(79,311)	(58,652)
Earnings 1986	137,404	132,650
	(120,443)	(73,602)
Earnings 1990	188,683	183,918
	(137,324)	(119,455)
Earnings 1993	202,734	196,349
	(138,614)	(106,972)

of randomness of the sample in geographical terms is an important caveat in interpreting the results below, but it seems likely that there is interesting knowledge to be drawn from studying a restricted sample over such a long time.

3.4   The Empirical Model

In the empirical model, I use the standard Mincer (1974) semilogarithmic equation, with a dummy for each educational level:

$$\ln Y_{it} = \alpha_t + \beta_{lt}S_{li} + \lambda_t X_{it} + \delta_t X_{it}^2 + \varphi_t S_{li} R_{it} + \vartheta_{lt} S_{li} PT_{it}$$

$$+ \rho_t Q_{it} + \zeta_t Z_i + e_{it}. \tag{3.1}$$

On the left-hand side, $\ln Y_{it}$ gives the logarithm of the yearly earnings for individual i at year t. The schooling level S_{li} is represented by four dummy variables: vocational studies, lower secondary school, upper secondary school, and university education. Primary school or less is the reference group. Given the four dummies, the wage premium is not assumed to be the same for all schooling levels but might differ with each level. The individual's total years of work experience by the year in question t is given by X_{it}, included in quadratic form. R is a dummy for those individuals on retirement pensions that year.[4] The dummy PT controls for those who are considered part-timers, and both R and PT are used in interaction with the schooling dummies. Q is the dummy for those without any information on work experience in year t, and Z is a dummy for those belonging to the highest social class during childhood.[5]

In this model, β_{lt} gives the premium for the lth level of education in year t, compared to those who have only primary education, conditional on experience and social class. However, if schooling and innate ability are positively correlated and ability is not included in the equation, β_{lt} might be positively biased because part of the effect of ability will be captured by the schooling level achieved. When ability is included in the model, we have

$$\ln Y_{it} = \alpha_t + \beta'_{lt}S_{li} + \gamma'_t A_i + \lambda_t X_{it} + \delta_t X_{it}^2 + \varphi_t S_{li} R_{it} + \vartheta_{lt} S_{li} PT_{it}$$

$$+ \rho_t Q_{it} + \zeta_t Z_i + e_{it}, \tag{3.1'}$$

where A is a parameter for the ability of individual i. With a positive ability bias in (3.1), this model will result in lower estimates of β_{lt}, and

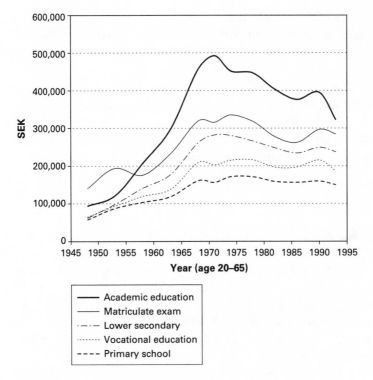

Figure 3.2
Longitudinal age-earnings profiles, Malmö cohort men, in 1993 values

the difference between β_{lt} and β'_{lt} gives the ability bias of the schooling coefficient when ability is omitted.

3.5   Earnings over Time

Actual age-earnings profiles for the men in the Malmö study are presented in figure 3.2. Earnings are depicted in 1993 SEK, deflated with the consumer price index. In figure 3.2, average earnings for different years are given. Notice that, with only a few exceptions, all individuals were born in 1928, and hence they were 20 years of age at the first reported survey year, 1948, and 65 years of age at the last reported year, 1993. The formal retirement age in Sweden is 65 years.

The profiles are fairly comparable with those estimated on cross-sectional data given in section 3.2, although the peak was reached earlier among the men from Malmö—at approximately 43 or 46 years of age, compared to 55 years of age in the Swedish cross-sectional figure

(figure 3.1). For all educational groups, the earnings profiles dip toward the late 1970s and early 1980s, but it is above all the university educated who experienced a significant decrease in their real earnings.[6] For the most educated men, average real earnings dropped by almost 20 percent between 1971 and 1990. For the other groups, the drop was significantly less. For the men with primary or vocational school education, earnings leveled off at just over 40 years of age and were fairly stable from then onward. The steep decrease between 62 and 65 years of age for the highest educated may seem rather surprising. However, many of the men had already retired at this age.

3.6 Premiums over Time

Table 3.2 presents the wage premiums estimated by models (3.1) and (3.1′), as well as the estimates for ability, and the relative ability bias. Starting with equation (3.1), the wage premium reached its peak in 1971 for all groups except the one with vocational school education, which had its highest premiums in 1968. However, those with only vocational education had premiums with a rather low spread over their whole lives. Between 1953 and 1993, they fluctuated between 0.07 and 0.16 in model (3.1). If we disregard the premiums for 1948 and 1953 (20 and 25 years of age) for the university educated, the premiums for this group differ between 0.46 and 0.92 log points and are highly significant each year. In a few cases, the estimates are within each other's confidence intervals (95 percent)—mainly for the years before 1968.

After the peak in the early 1970s, premiums dropped markedly for all educational groups, except for those with vocational education. The same pattern was shown in the previous section on real earnings. For Sweden, a number of studies have shown this large drop in educational premiums in the 1970s but also a recovery in the late 1980s (Edin and Holmlund 1995; Hibbs 1990; Zetterberg 1994). The recovery is harder to discern in the Malmö material; the wage premium between 1990 and 1993 tends to develop differently depending on the educational level. It is likely that this discrepancy compared to the earlier studies is due to the fact that the Malmö study consists of a cohort whose members reached retirement age in the early 1990s. This probably had a great influence on the estimated premiums in table 3.2, whereas the other studies were done on cross-sectional material consisting of Swedish citizens between 16 and 64 years of age.

Table 3.2
Wage premiums with and without ability included (equations 3.1 and 3.1′)

	1948	1953	1958	1963	1968	1971
Education level:						
Vocational school						
Eq. (3.1)	0.066	0.074	0.102	0.094	0.163	0.148
	(.054)	(.030)	(.030)	(.029)	(.035)	(.032)
Eq. (3.1′)	0.052	0.069	0.091	0.063	0.131	0.113
	(.084)	(.032)	(.029)	(.030)	(.037)	(.034)
Bias %	*21*	*8*	*11*	*33*	*20*	*24*
Lower secondary school						
Eq. (3.1)	0.070	0.141	0.219	0.236	0.385	0.416
	(.085)	(.063)	(.056)	(.051)	(.049)	(.055)
Eq. (3.1′)	0.037	0.128	0.198	0.182	0.325	0.356
	(.086)	(.071)	(.059)	(.052)	(.053)	(.058)
Bias %	*47*	*9*	*10*	*23*	*16*	*14*
Upper secondary school						
Eq. (3.1)	0.718	0.293	0.359	0.393	0.563	0.621
	(.511)	(.134)	(.081)	(.064)	(.059)	(.055)
Eq. (3.1′)	0.687	0.279	0.336	0.327	0.493	0.548
	(.505)	(.137)	(.082)	(.065)	(.064)	(.061)
Bias %	*4*	*5*	*6*	*17*	*12*	*12*
Academic education						
Eq. (3.1)	0.168	0.285	0.461	0.559	0.894	0.924
	(.295)	(.215)	(.155)	(.114)	(.087)	(.111)
Eq. (3.1′)	0.120	0.271	0.432	0.479	0.810	0.843
	(.294)	(.217)	(.158)	(.116)	(.092)	(.117)
Bias %	*29*	*5*	*6*	*14*	*9*	*9*
IQ, Eq. (3.1′)	0.0022	0.0007	0.0013	0.0034	0.0036	0.0035
	(.002)	(.001)	(.001)	(.001)	(.001)	(.001)
n	286	361	479	653	627	689
R^2						
Eq. (3.1)	0.575	0.546	0.613	0.595	0.665	0.623
Eq. (3.1′)	0.578	0.546	0.614	0.604	0.670	0.630

Notes: Dependent variable = log earnings. Heteroscedastic robust standard errors in parentheses.

	1974	1978	1982	1986	1990	1993
Education level:						
Vocational school						
Eq. (3.1)	0.120	0.138	0.130	0.109	0.132	0.056
	(.032)	(.036)	(.031)	(.033)	(.048)	(.065)
Eq. (3.1')	0.077	0.106	0.101	0.100	0.106	0.023
	(.034)	(.036)	(.033)	(.036)	(.049)	(.066)
Bias %	*36*	*23*	*22*	*8*	*20*	*59*
Lower secondary school						
Eq. (3.1)	0.349	0.334	0.305	0.301	0.243	0.407
	(.053)	(.057)	(.055)	(.051)	(.061)	(.111)
Eq. (3.1')	0.273	0.279	0.257	0.283	0.221	0.321
	(.055)	(.057)	(.060)	(.056)	(.064)	(.111)
Bias %	*22*	*16*	*16*	*6*	*21*	*17*
Upper secondary school						
Eq. (3.1)	0.550	0.525	0.486	0.393	0.431	0.611
	(.049)	(.062)	(.057)	(.061)	(.076)	(.143)
Eq. (3.1')	0.456	0.456	0.423	0.370	0.364	0.530
	(.053)	(.064)	(.061)	(.068)	(.079)	(.145)
Bias %	*17*	*13*	*13*	*7*	*15*	*13*
Academic education						
Eq. (3.1)	0.769	0.813	0.775	0.766	0.799	0.787
	(.084)	(.088)	(.089)	(.086)	(.086)	(.138)
Eq. (3.1')	0.664	0.734	0.704	0.739	0.721	0.696
	(.089)	(.090)	(.093)	(.095)	(.092)	(.140)
Bias %	*14*	*10*	*9*	*4*	*10*	*12*
IQ, Eq. (3.1')	0.0046	0.0035	0.0031	0.0011	0.0033	0.0033
	(.001)	(.001)	(.000)	(.001)	(.001)	(.001)
n	*693*	*695*	*674*	*650*	*618*	*586*
R^2						
Eq. (3.1)	0.534	0.555	0.630	0.622	0.518	0.481
Eq. (3.1')	0.549	0.561	0.634	0.623	0.524	0.489

The estimates of the other variables in the model are not reported. However, the estimates for experience are small and insignificant, with very few exceptions. This is most likely because the individuals are all of the same age and therefore have approximately the same level of work experience. In most cases, the coefficients for the interactions between part-time work and the various levels of schooling are jointly significant, if not separately significant.[7] The same is the case with the interactions between retirement and schooling. To the extent that they are significant, they indicate a negative impact. The interactions strongly increase the fit of the model. The rather large fluctuation of R^2 is seen in other Swedish studies covering the same time period, with the highest values for the years around 1970 and decreasing thereafter.

When ability (intelligence quotients from 1938) is included in the model, the expected result is obtained: the estimates for schooling are reduced. The coefficient for ability is not significant until 1963, perhaps caused by the fact that it takes a while for the employees to show their true ability and establish themselves in the labor market. From 1963 onward, the estimates for ability are highly significant, with a coefficient between 0.003 and 0.005. The ability bias is discernible from 1953. The schooling coefficients have the same development over time as in the original model but on a slightly lower level. However, the ability bias is consistently proportionally higher for the lower educational categories than for the higher, even if the absolute bias is higher for the latter. The estimates are within each other's confidence intervals.

That proportional biases are consistently larger for the lower levels of education may seem a surprising result. In other words, the premium for vocational school compared with primary school was more biased than the premium for a university education compared with primary school. However, it must be remembered that the individuals who went all the way through a university education were a chosen few. Many adolescents with the potential to complete both upper secondary school and a university education did not go further than vocational, lower secondary, or even primary school. As mentioned earlier, it was very much a matter of social class if you were given the chance to achieve a higher education. Hence, the variation in ability among the less educated should be greater than among the highly educated. This appears to be the case. In table 3.3, the standard deviations and

Table 3.3
Variation of IQ among education levels ($n = 752$)

Education level	Standard deviation	Coefficient of variation
Primary school	14.82	16.57
Vocational school	14.65	14.76
Lower secondary school	12.08	11.26
Upper secondary school	11.27	10.15
Academic education	11.62	10.29

the coefficients of variation for IQ among the different educational levels are shown.

The expected pattern is found. The spread of ability is highest among the least educated and lowest among those in the two highest educated groups. Hence, it seems that because the variation of ability is higher in the larger group of less educated men, it has a greater significance for the wage premiums of this group if ability is omitted from the model, compared to the two educational groups where the individuals are more of the same ability. With the exception of two years, the estimates for ability (and the ability bias) are surprisingly stable over the years.

3.7 Discussion

To my knowledge, this is the first study where actual earnings over the whole working life have been depicted. Earlier studies on the same theme are normally done from cross-sectional data and are based on average estimates of premiums over the age groups. When we compare the figures created in this chapter with those estimated on cross-sectional data, it must be remembered that the actual development has been affected by institutional, structural, and personal changes over these persons' life cycles. For example, the compression of wages shown during the 1970s and 1980s could have been caused by high unemployment among the highly educated men, which would have reduced their real earnings. Nevertheless, only two men reported themselves unemployed during the 1970s, and none of them belonged to the two highest educational groups. General unemployment was extremely low in Sweden during this period (Ohlsson and Olofsson 1998). Inflation, on the other hand, was high, which may have affected the real value of earnings. However, as the real wage for the less educated men does not decrease much at all, this seems unlikely to be a significant explanation. Another explanation could be an increased supply of university-educated individuals during this time period (Edin and Holmlund 1995). However, according to Arai and Kjellström (1999), this change in the supply of highly educated labor does not really correspond to the drop in earnings (premiums).

It is most likely that the actual decrease in real earnings, which was most pronounced among the highest-educated men, was caused by the solidarity wage policy. The goal of this policy was that the same work should receive the same pay, but it also aimed at a general reduction of wage differences. Even though it was formulated and initiated earlier, the solidarity wage policy was most active and influential during the 1970s. The negotiations and agreements between employer and employee organizations were made centrally, and thus there is no reason to believe that this development was peculiar only to Malmö.

Furthermore, the policy was more prevalent within the public sector, and according to the 1984 questionnaire, a majority of the highest-educated men worked within the public sector. In another study (Zetterberg 1994), it is shown that the public sector had lower wage growth during this period than did the private sector. However, as information on which sector the men worked in is available only from 1984 and only for approximately 75 percent of the men, it is hard to know with certainty which sector they worked in when the decrease in real earnings occurred.[8] Nevertheless, there are reasons to believe that the sectoral composition of the individuals in the sample is representative for all workers of a similar age in Sweden.

It is interesting to note that while the solidarity wage policy is often expected to have decreased the wage dispersion by increasing wages for low-income earners, the results in this chapter indicate another picture. The decrease in earnings dispersion seems to have come around from above, by a reduction in the earnings of the high-income earners. This lack of development for the individuals with lower levels of education is noteworthy and is an important difference from both Mincer's and Becker's figures, which were based on cross-sectional data. Among the Malmö men with less than lower secondary school education, the increase in earnings is modest from the earliest years, and from 40 years of age, the earnings remain almost the same until retirement age.

When trying to find an explanation for the sharp decrease in earnings for some of the men in the 1970s, it is important to remember that such a decrease is seen in most figures based on cross-sectional data.

The difference is that the decrease in this case occurs approximately 10 to 15 years earlier, but then again, we must take into account the institutional and structural changes during the time period.

The very steep decrease in earnings for the university educated between 1990 and 1993 is most likely an illustration of the retirement scheme. The pension starts as a percentage of the individual's earlier earnings. However, there is a maximum amount that the individual can receive as a pension. Therefore, men with higher incomes naturally received a lesser percentage of their earlier earnings than those with lower earnings.

I estimated the wage premium on 12 occasions during these men's lives. The wage premium followed a development similar to that of real wages but with a somewhat larger spread between the educational levels. Thus, the premiums decreased during the late 1970s and early 1980s even for the two highest-educated groups of men. This is consistent with other Swedish studies using cross-sectional data (Björklund 1999; Björklund and Kjellström 2002; Edin and Holmlund 1995; Zetterberg 1994).

The large and significant difference between the premiums for those with vocational school and lower secondary school education is an interesting result. These educational levels consisted of more or less the same number of years in the educational system, though the education was of a different kind, lower secondary school being more theoretical in character. The number of years of formal schooling is often used in the analysis of wage premiums instead of levels of schooling. These results are an illustration of how misleading such a measure of education can be, at least in the Swedish context. The large difference in the coefficients is probably caused by differences in the kind of jobs these men had. Those who went through vocational school may have ended up in fairly low-paid blue-collar jobs, while those who went through lower secondary school instead became employed in better-paid white-collar work. The difference could also be a case of general versus specialized education; the men with a lower secondary education, which can be considered more general than a vocational education, were better equipped to meet with changes in the working life. Part of the explanation could also be the selection effect. However, even when I control for both social class and ability, this large difference between the premiums for the levels is evident.

Finally, an ability measure was included in the model. An interesting finding when comparing the ability bias between the different educational levels was that the relative bias was much larger for the lower levels of education. A positive ability bias was found for all levels, for almost every year tried, but the relative biases were constantly highest for the lowest-educated men. As mentioned above, studies of wage premiums often use a linear model with years of schooling,[9] where such an effect will not be detected. As the variation of ability was found to be much larger within the lowest-educated groups, it obviously has a larger effect on the earnings for the less educated if they have a higher ability than others with similar education, compared to higher-educated men.

In his article in 1976, Griliches estimated ability bias for young men in America. He obtained lower estimates for ability, approximately 0.002. In addition, Griliches found a lower proportional bias—around 10 percent, which is comparable to what I found for the university-educated men from Malmö.

As the men who were born into the lower social classes generally achieved a lower education than those from the higher social classes, they were deemed to receive lower wages. However, it seems as if the solidarity wage policy actually reduced the earnings differences related to social class. The correlation between social class and earnings is highest for the years 1963 and 1971 (the correlation coefficients in these years are 0.41 and 0.40, respectively) and decreases thereafter until 1990 (0.29).

3.8 Conclusion

I have used the longitudinal data of the Malmö Longitudinal Study to analyze different aspects of earnings, education, and ability. One of the main conclusions of the findings is that there was a steep decrease in real earnings for many of the highest-educated men in the 1970s, when the men were in their forties. The most likely cause of this decrease is the active solidarity wage policy that prevailed during the period and that aimed to reduce wage differences. The decrease in real earnings for the higher-educated men resulted in a lower correlation between earnings and parental social class for this cohort.

Another finding is that real earnings for the least educated changed rather marginally during their whole working lives. Furthermore, the relative ability bias is found to be largest for the less educated groups, among whom the variation of ability is also much larger. Thus, in this group, there were probably many men who were well suited to go through both upper secondary school and a university education but who, because of their social background, were never given the chance to do so.

Acknowledgments

I wish to thank participants at the CESifo/PEPG conference in Munich on Schooling and Human-Capital Formation in the Global Economy: Revisiting the Equity-Efficiency Quandary for valuable comments on the chapter. In addition, I wish to thank Gunnar Eliasson, Erik Mellander, Gunnar Isacsson, Torberg Falch, and Johnny Zetterberg. Financial support from VINNOVA (the Swedish Agency for Innovation Systems) is gratefully acknowledged. The usual disclaimer applies.

Notes

1. On the other hand, if the schooling variable is not correctly defined and collected, the wage premium tends to be negatively biased instead—the *measurement-error bias*. Hence, it is difficult to know whether the schooling coefficient is ultimately positively or negatively biased.

2. Those who earned less than the following amounts are regarded as part-time workers: 1948, 4,000 SEK; 1953, 5,000 SEK; 1958, 7,000 SEK; 1963, 8,000 SEK; 1968, 10,000 SEK; 1971, 12,000 SEK; 1974, 15,000 SEK; 1978, 22,000 SEK; 1982, 30,000 SEK; 1986, 43,000 SEK; 1990, 55,000 SEK; 1993, 65,000 SEK.

3. The model was also tried on a smaller sample that consists of exactly the same men each year; that is, it includes only those with earnings reported each year in question from 1958 onward. I did not exclude those without reported earnings for 1948 or 1953, nor did I try this smaller sample for these years, as many of the university educated had not yet entered the labor market at this time. The difference between the premiums for the two samples was small; in fact, except for the estimates for the university educated, the differences were negligible. However, because the number of persons with university education in the smaller sample is very small (10 individuals), I chose not to investigate this further.

4. Used only for the years 1982, 1986, 1990, and 1993, as no men retired earlier than 1982.

5. As experience is a variable constructed from data in the surveys, which are from four different occasions, up to four dummies have to be used for the later years in the sample to handle the fact that X measures accumulated work experience.

6. This result does not seem to be driven by outliers. About half of the individuals in this group had a decline in real earnings.

7. When those considered as part-timers are excluded from the sample, the estimates for schooling variables are almost unchanged. When they are included in the sample without specific dummy variables, the estimates of both schooling and R^2 are reduced.

8. The regressions are also done with a dummy for work in the public sector, and the results indicate a better development of wages for those employed in the private sector than for those in the public sector. However, remember that the information on work in the public or private sector is reliable only for the year 1984 and only for those who answered the questionnaire for this year.

9. I have also tried a linear model, which results in a positive ability bias for each year except the first two and 1986, as is also the case in the nonlinear model. The ability bias is then between 10 percent and 15 percent.

References

Arai, M., and C. Kjellström. (1999). "Returns to Human Capital in Sweden." In R. Asplund (ed.), *Human Capital in Europe*. Helsingfors: ETLA.

Arrow, K. (1973). "Higher Education as a Filter." *Journal of Public Economics* 2(3): 193–216.

Becker, G. S. (1993). *Human Capital*. Chicago: University of Chicago Press.

Björklund, A. (1999). "Utbildningspolitik och utbildningens lönsamhet." In L. Calmfors and M. Persson (eds.), *Tillväxt och ekonomisk politik*. Lund: Studentlitteratur.

Björklund, A., and C. Kjellström. (2002). "Estimating the Return to Investments in Education: How Useful Is the Standard Mincer Equation?" *Economics of Education Review* 21: 195–210.

Blackburn, M. L., and D. Neumark. (1993). "Omitted Ability Bias and the Increase in the Return to Schooling." *Journal of Labor Economics* 11(3): 521–544.

Creedy, J. (1991). "Lifetime Earnings and Inequality." *Economic Record* (March): 46–58.

Edin, P.-A., and B. Holmlund. (1995). "The Swedish Wage Structure: The Rise and Fall of Solidarity Wage Policy." In R. Freeman and L. Katz (eds.), *Differences and Changes in Wage Structures*. Chicago: University of Chicago Press.

Griliches, Z. (1976). "Wages of Very Young Men." *Journal of Political Economy* 84(4): S69–S86.

Griliches, Z. (1977). "Estimating the Returns to Schooling: Some Econometric Problems." *Econometrica* 45(1): 1127–1160.

Heckman, J., L. J. Lochner, and P. E. Todd. (2003). "Fifty Years of Mincer Earnings Regressions." Working Paper No. 9732, National Bureau for Economic Research.

Hibbs, D. A. (1990). "Wage Dispersion and Trade Union Action in Sweden." In Inga Persson (ed.), *Generating Equality in the Welfare State*. Oslo: Norwegian University Press.

Lam, D., and R. F. Schoeni. (1993). "Effects of Family Background on Earnings and Returns to Schooling." *Journal of Political Economy* 101(4): 710–740.

Mellander, E. (1998). "On Omitted Variable Bias and Measurement Error in Returns to Schooling Estimates." Working Paper No. 494, Research Institute of Industrial Economics, Stockholm.

Mincer, J. (1974). *Schooling, Experience, and Earnings*. New York: Columbia University Press.

Ohlsson, R., and J. Olofsson. (1998). *Arbetslöshetens dilemma*. Stockholm: SNS Förlag.

Spence, M. A. (1974). *Market Signaling: Informational Transfer in Hiring and Related Screening Processes*. Cambridge: Harvard University Press.

Willis, R. J. (1986). "Wage Determinants: A Survey and Reinterpretation of Human Capital Earnings Functions." In O. Ashenfelter and R. Layard (eds.), *Handbook of Labor Economics*. Amsterdam: North-Holland.

Zetterberg, J. (1994). "Avkastning på utbildning i privat och offentlig sektor." Arbetsrapport nr. 125, Fackföreningsrörelsens institut för ekonomisk forskning, Stockholm.

II Solutions A: Change the Peer Group?

4

Peer Effects in North Carolina Public Schools

Jacob Vigdor and Thomas Nechyba

4.1 Introduction

The economics of education literature has long struggled to identify the inputs that matter most in the production of school quality. Such inputs may include per-pupil spending in schools, measurable qualifications of teachers and administrators, background and involvement of parents, or governance structure of the school. Increasingly, however, peer effects have emerged as a potential input that may play an important independent role in determining student outcomes. Peer effects are now widely discussed in policy circles and are routinely included as crucial components in theoretical and computational models of school choice (as, for example, in Epple and Romano 1998; Nechyba 2000; Ferreyra 2006). At the same time, they remain rather poorly understood, with empirical investigations often limited by both methodological constraints as well as severe data limitations. Perhaps the most important limitation is the relative absence of controlled trials that randomly assign individuals to peer groups. The use of observational, rather than experimental, data will introduce a positive selection bias into peer-effect estimates to the extent that unobservably more able individuals sort into observably more able peer groups.

In this chapter, we utilize a comprehensive administrative dataset tracking North Carolina public school students to explore the relationship between peer characteristics and student achievement in elementary school. Several features of the North Carolina dataset enable us to pay careful attention to empirical issues that have plagued existing literature. We are, for instance, able to match students with their classmates. This provides us with an opportunity to use very basic econometric tools of school and teacher fixed effects to address the endogenous selection of individuals into peer groups. Our ability to track students longitudinally also permits us to examine whether the appearance of peer effects predates the actual exposure to a group of peers—a telltale sign that the effects actually reflect selection into peer groups. Finally, we present analysis of a subsample of students who witnessed substantial turnover in their elementary schools between the fourth and fifth grades. Although these students did not switch schools themselves, changes in school-attendance zones resulting from policy shifts or the opening of new schools imply that their peer groups were subject to potentially large changes.

In our most basic regression specifications, we estimate significant relationships between peer characteristics and student achievement. These relationships are robust to the addition of school fixed effects, suggesting that the sorting of families across schools and districts, the predominant form of sorting on observables in North Carolina elementary schools (Clotfelter, Ladd, and Vigdor 2006), does not significantly bias the coefficients. The relationships also appear quite persistent, with the impact of fifth-grade peers still apparent in eighth grade.

Three further empirical tests, however, lead us to the conclusion that the peer effects we observe do not truly reflect a causal relationship. First, the inclusion of teacher fixed effects reverses the sign of the co-efficients on our peer-ability measures. Second, the relationship between fifth-grade peer ability and individual outcomes is still evident even when we analyze fourth-grade test scores, controlling separately for schoolmate characteristics in fourth grade. Third, significant peer effects are not in evidence within a set of schools that undergo a plausibly exogenous shock to peer-group composition, attributable to the opening of new schools and other shifts in attendance-zone boundaries. These findings cast doubt not only on the associations we measure but on many of those reported in earlier literature on peer effects in educational settings.

4.2   The Peer-Effect Literature

A growing literature in economics, sociology, and psychology documents strong correlations between peer-group characteristics and individual outcomes. Within this literature, there exists great variation both in terms of the outcomes considered and the definition of an individual's peer group. Studies including Arcidiacono and Nicholson (2005), Bryk and Driscoll (1988), Caldas and Bankston (1997), Gaviria and Raphael (2001), Jencks and Mayer (1990), Link and Mulligan

(1991), Mayer (1991), Robertson and Symons (1996), and Zimmer and Toma (1999) investigate peer effects in educational settings, defining peer-group characteristics as characteristics of a school's student body. Some additional studies, summarized by Slavin (1987, 1990), have examined within-classroom peer effects, with a special emphasis on the effect of ability grouping within schools, and Betts and Zau (2002) estimate significant peer effects at both the grade and classroom levels.[1] Only recently, however, have researchers begun to grapple seriously with the econometric difficulties of truly identifying peer effects, with earlier studies (reviewed in Nechyba et al. 1999) primarily documenting suggestive correlations. In all, the existing literature has been inconclusive on the existence, nature, and magnitude of peer effects in schools (and in neighborhoods).

The failure of previous studies to arrive at a consensus reflects two essential challenges in estimating the importance of peer or neighborhood characteristics on student achievement. The first of these challenges arises from the difficulty in econometrically separating a group's influence on an individual's outcome from the individual's influence on the group (Manski 1993; Moffitt 1998; Nechyba et al. 1999). Many studies avoid this challenge by examining the relationship between exogenous characteristics of a peer group (such as race or gender) and the endogenous outcomes of an individual, rather than focus on the relation of endogenous outcomes between individual and peers. Other studies, such as Hanushek et al. (2001) and ours, use lagged peer-outcome measures to circumvent these issues. Use of either strategy entails some limitation in the interpretation of results, as the failure to distinguish exogenous from endogenous social effects leaves unanswered the question of whether intervening to change one student's outcome will generate social multiplier effects (Manski 1993).

The second challenge stems from the endogenous choice of peer groups and neighbors in most situations. Individuals who choose to associate with a "good" peer group, for example, may be "good" persons themselves in ways that are difficult to quantify or observe. In our context, households may select into schools based on their characteristics, and within schools they may choose classrooms (and teachers) or be assigned to classrooms based on these characteristics. Estimates of the relationship between peer characteristics and individual outcomes will therefore generally display a positive omitted-variable bias unless an exogenous source of variation in peer achievement can be identified. Policy experiments where individuals are randomly assigned to peer groups (or where plausibly exogenous changes in peer groups occur) offer one such potential source of exogenous variation.[2] Alternatively, school and classroom fixed-effect strategies can be employed to purge estimates of bias associated with nonrandom sorting into schools and within schools.[3] We employ fixed-effect strategies and, toward the end of the chapter, use a variant on the policy-experiment strategy.[4]

While we follow the existing literature by presenting estimates that admittedly confound exogenous and endogenous social effects, the dataset we employ has significant advantages over data used in previous studies—advantages that are particularly useful in uncovering evidence of the degree to which selection is responsible for the appearance of peer effects. We identify the same types of relationships between achievement and peer characteristics that others have identified using different datasets, but our investigation of endogenous selection of peer groups casts doubt on whether these relationships are causal. Through the use of school fixed effects, we can rule out selection into schools as a major confounding source, but three other independent tests for selection suggest strongly that the peer effects we initially estimate are due to selection and do not represent true peer effects.

We are able to perform these tests in large part because of the unusual quality of the data we have available. The link of students to teachers within schools allows us to employ within-school teacher fixed effects; the longitudinal nature of the data allows us to test for the impact of fifth-grade peers on fourth-grade achievement; and the large changes in attendance zones provide us with an arguably exogenous source of variation in peer quality.[5] The fact that we find peer effects similar to what others have found in our baseline model but then find strong evidence that these effects are not causal when we take advantage of unique features of our data may then cause us to view peer-effect estimates that have not been subjected to such robustness checks with some skepticism.

Most studies on peer effects have not (as suggested in Nechyba et al. 1999) been able to address effectively the endogeneity issues central to the estimation of peer effects. We cannot claim at this point to have done so fully either, but it is nevertheless striking to us that three separate checks for selection all suggest that peer effects that are robust to (school) fixed effects and appear persistent across years are due to sorting, not a causal relationship between peer characteristics and individual achievement. While it therefore would be premature to attempt to fully reconcile the various different estimates of peer effects in light of the evidence presented in this chapter, our evidence is suggestive of a general upward bias of these estimates in the literature. This does not imply that peer effects are less important than what many suspect, but it may cause us to reevaluate such issues as peer-group definitions.

4.3 Data

Our estimation employs a dataset recording information on every public-school student in the state of North Carolina between the 1994–1995 and 2000–2001 school years. Standardized end-of-grade tests are administered annually to students in North Carolina beginning in third grade and continuing until eighth grade. Each student test-score record contains information on the school attended and the identity of the teacher administering the test. This teacher information permits us to match students who share a classroom within a school. This method of sorting students into classrooms is effective only in elementary school, where students spend nearly all their time with the same group of peers and receive most of their instruction from a single teacher. In secondary school, where one math or English teacher serves multiple classes' worth of students, this method is ineffective.[6] For this reason, we focus our peer-group analysis on the characteristics of a student's classmates and schoolmates in the fifth grade. Virtually all North Carolina school districts assign fifth-grade students to elementary schools.

As table 4.1 indicates, the North Carolina administrative data provide us with more than 900,000 student-year observations, corresponding to some 230,000 fifth-grade students spread across four individual cohorts. For ease of interpretation, we normalize student test scores to have mean zero and variance 1.[7] In addition to standardized test-score information, we observe basic demographic information on each student, including race, sex, and participation in the federal free- or reduced-price-lunch program. Beyond these widely available measures, we have teacher-reported information on parental education for each student.[8]

We form a set of basic peer-characteristic variables for each student in the dataset, including racial composition and measures of peer ability. Our peer-ability variables use data on third-grade standardized-test performance for those classmates who can be tracked two years.

Table 4.1
Summary statistics ($n = 939,453$ student/year observations)

	Mean	Standard deviation	Minimum	Maximum
Math score	0.039	0.987	−3.605	3.652
Reading score	0.035	0.982	−4.021	2.968
Parent completed high school	0.443	0.497	0.000	1.000
Parent completed trade/business school	0.044	0.205	0.000	1.000
Parent completed community or technical college	0.138	0.345	0.000	1.000
Parent completed four-year college	0.229	0.420	0.000	1.000
Parent completed graduate school	0.057	0.233	0.000	1.000
Classroom peer groups:				
Average math score of peers (twice lagged)	0.052	0.432	−3.522	2.344
Average reading score of peers (twice lagged)	0.048	0.413	−7.328	2.012
Std. dev. in math score of peers (twice lagged)	0.856	0.247	0.000	8.406
Std. dev. in reading score of peers (twice lagged)	0.864	0.265	0.000	7.797
% males in class	0.505	0.093	0.000	1.000
% blacks in class	0.286	0.245	0.000	1.000
% Hispanics in class	0.027	0.048	0.000	1.000
Number of students in class	22.913	4.009	1.000	43.000
Grade peer groups:				
Average math score of peers (twice lagged)	0.045	0.335	−3.079	1.701
Average reading score of peers (twice lagged)	0.042	0.312	−2.152	1.828
Std. dev. in math score of peers (twice lagged)	0.902	0.178	0.000	3.302
Std. dev. in reading score of peers (twice lagged)	0.908	0.195	0.000	3.680
% males in grade	0.509	0.058	0.000	1.000
% blacks in grade	0.290	0.235	0.000	1.000
% Hispanics in grade	0.027	0.038	0.000	0.486

Across the entire sample, we are able to link about 80 percent of fifth-grade students to their third-grade test scores. As in existing literature, we use the mean of this lagged achievement variable as a basic ability measure.[9] In addition, we control for the standard deviation of peer lagged test scores.[10] Controlling for both the mean and the standard deviation of our ability measure allows us to test for the presence of nonlinearities in the relationship between peer ability and student achievement. This parameterization provides a clear picture of the aggregate implications of choosing to stratify classrooms by ability or to mix students of varying ability levels evenly across classrooms. If mean-preserving spreads in the test-score distribution increase achievement and the effects of mean peer achievement are negligible, then mixing students of various ability levels in the same classroom will not only maximize aggregate achievement but also present a "win-win" situation, providing students at all points in the test-score distribution with net benefits. If individual achievement increases significantly with both mean peer ability and mean-preserving spreads in peer ability, then mixing ability levels continues to maximize aggregate achievement, but benefits to students at the low end of the ability distribution will be partially offset by costs to students at the high end.[11]

Table 4.1 shows that the mean peer-achievement level within classrooms is slightly higher than the population mean, indicating that lower-performing students tend to be assigned to smaller classrooms, consistent with Lazear's (2001) model of administrative efforts to maximize school output. Mean peer achievement within schools also exceeds the population average, indicating that high-ability students attend larger schools on average. Widespread rural poverty in North Carolina most likely explains this pattern. The distribution of mean peer ability is considerably more dispersed than one would expect if schools and classrooms represented random samples of the overall student population.[12] This is evidence of the stratification of students by ability across classrooms and schools.

The peer standard-deviation measures, at both the school and classroom levels, are slightly lower than the population standard deviation, providing additional evidence that students in North Carolina public-school classrooms are stratified by ability. The classroom-level standard-deviation measure is lower than the grade-level measure, indicating that a portion of the observed ability stratification occurs within schools rather than between them. The peer standard-deviation

measure varies considerably; some schools and classrooms are almost
entirely homogeneous, while others are considerably more heterogeneous than the state itself.

Table 4.1 also reports summary statistics regarding the racial and
gender composition of North Carolina schools and classrooms. North
Carolina is a diverse state that also displays a heterogeneous amount
of diversity in its classrooms and schools. The mean classroom has
roughly 23 students, just over half of whom are male, and nearly one-
third are either black or Hispanic.

4.4   Basic Results

Table 4.2 presents coefficients from basic regression specifications
examining the relationship between peer characteristics and student
math and reading test scores. The first two columns examine the
correlates of math scores, using basic least-squares regression with
grade- and classroom-level definitions of peer groups, respectively.
At the grade level, there is a significant partial correlation between
peer lagged test scores and individual achievement. A one standard-
deviation increase in peer achievement (0.30) predicts an increase in individual test scores equivalent to 2 percent of a standard deviation.
The table also reveals a significant partial correlation between black
share within the grade and the achievement of black students. A similar pattern appears for Hispanic students. For both groups of minority
students, the results suggest that racial or ethnic achievement gaps are
most pronounced in schools serving small minority populations. The
estimated partial correlation between variation in peer ability and individual achievement is very small and not statistically distinguishable
from zero, as is the estimated relationship between grade gender composition and achievement.

For reasons discussed below, we are not eager to attach a causal
interpretation to these results. Nonetheless, it is instructive to note
the magnitude and significance of certain other coefficients in this introductory regression. A student's fourth-grade test score is, not surprisingly, a strong predictor of fifth-grade performance. The lagged
test-score coefficients in this and each other specification in the table
are significantly less than one, suggesting that there is at least some
mean reversion in test scores. Male students score slightly, though
significantly, lower than their female counterparts. Finally, categorical
controls for parental education reveal a strong relationship between

that characteristic and student achievement. The predicted impact of having a college-educated parent, rather than a high school dropout parent, is equivalent to the predicted impact of raising peers' mean achievement from two standard deviations below the statewide mean to two standard deviations above.

Switching the definition of peer group from the grade to classroom level changes the magnitude of many estimated coefficients. The estimated effect of peer test scores on math achievement increases, and the standard deviation of peer test scores has a significant positive effect.[13] Students in classrooms with a higher density of male students tend to perform worse on the math exam.[14] The relationship between classroom racial composition on the test scores of white and Asian students continues to be negligible, though the interacted effects noted in the grade-level specification persist here.

Students are not allocated randomly to classrooms in North Carolina. It can be argued however, that most of this nonrandom allocation occurs at the school level (Clotfelter, Ladd, and Vigdor 2006). While parents assuredly sort into school districts and elementary school-attendance zones on the basis of a school's reputation, available evidence suggests that the amount of sorting on observable characteristics within elementary schools is relatively modest. Estimates presented in the third column of table 4.2, which represents regression models that incorporate school fixed effects, are effectively purged of a great deal of any bias associated with nonrandom sorting across schools.

In the fixed-effect specification, mean peer test scores continue to be a significant predictor of individual math achievement. The point estimate is somewhat smaller than in the previous specification but still larger than the estimate derived from grade-level peer groups. A one standard-deviation (0.40) increase in peer ability predicts a test-score increase equivalent to 3 percent of a standard deviation. The impact of dispersion in peer test scores also retains significance, actually increasing in magnitude relative to the specification without school fixed effects. As in the previous specification, math test scores show evidence of being lower in classrooms with a higher density of males. The relationship between classroom racial composition and student achievement changes notably. Students of all races now appear to receive lower test scores when the share of black or Hispanic students in their classroom is high relative to other classrooms in the same school.

The fourth, fifth, and sixth regressions in table 4.2 replicate the first three specifications, replacing both the dependent variable and peer

Table 4.2
Relationship between peer characteristics on test scores

	Dependent variable: Fifth-grade test score		
	Math achievement		
	Grade	Classroom	
Independent variable	OLS	OLS	Fixed effects
Lagged test score	0.7841***	0.7801***	0.7787***
	[0.0073]	[0.0070]	[0.0071]
Average score of peers	0.0542***	0.0839***	0.0721***
(twice lagged)	[0.0129]	[0.0081]	[0.0075]
Std. dev. in scores of peers	−0.0012	0.0215**	0.0335***
(twice lagged)	[0.0186]	[0.0105]	[0.0091]
% males in peer group	−0.055	−0.0740***	−0.0685***
	[0.0554]	[0.0274]	[0.0221]
% blacks in peer group	−0.0028	−0.0167	−0.1371***
	[0.0196]	[0.0172]	[0.0262]
% Hispanics in peer group	−0.0573	−0.0842	−0.1298**
	[0.0887]	[0.0579]	[0.0516]
%Black*black	0.1076***	0.1173***	0.0320*
	[0.0261]	[0.0238]	[0.0168]
%Hispanic*Hispanic	0.4382**	0.2625*	0.1393
	[0.2004]	[0.1491]	[0.1340]
Class size	0.0029***	−0.0014*	−0.001
	[0.0009]	[0.0007]	[0.0006]
Male	−0.0093***	−0.0088***	−0.0083***
	[0.0023]	[0.0025]	[0.0024]
Black	−0.1508***	−0.1487***	−0.1196***
	[0.0109]	[0.0099]	[0.0076]
Hispanic	−0.0339**	−0.0223*	−0.0092
	[0.0137]	[0.0120]	[0.0112]
Parent completed high school	0.0719***	0.0715***	0.0885***
	[0.0055]	[0.0054]	[0.0048]
Parent completed trade or	0.1144***	0.1136***	0.1374***
business school	[0.0080]	[0.0079]	[0.0072]
Parent completed community	0.1414***	0.1392***	0.1631***
or technical college	[0.0072]	[0.0070]	[0.0066]
Parent completed four-year college	0.2293***	0.2228***	0.2552***
	[0.0084]	[0.0080]	[0.0080]
Parent completed graduate school	0.3290***	0.3196***	0.3436***
	[0.0108]	[0.0103]	[0.0103]
R^2	0.7109	0.7111	0.7341
n	233,287	232,749	232,749

Notes: Standard errors reported in parentheses. Peer variables are defined by fifth-grade peer group at either the grade level or classroom level. Fixed effects regression controls for fifth-grade school. Regressions also control for year effects and include intercept.

Independent variable	Dependent variable: Fifth-grade test score		
	Reading achievement		
	Grade	Classroom	
	OLS	OLS	Fixed effects
Lagged test score	0.7677***	0.7654***	0.7627***
	[0.0090]	[0.0091]	[0.0090]
Average score of peers	0.0901***	0.0893***	0.0609***
(twice lagged)	[0.0095]	[0.0066]	[0.0065]
Std. dev. in scores of peers	−0.01	0.0093	0.0109*
(twice lagged)	[0.0105]	[0.0064]	[0.0060]
% males in peer group	0.0311	−0.0229	−0.0522***
	[0.0345]	[0.0189]	[0.0172]
% blacks in peer group	0.0369***	0.0251**	−0.0512**
	[0.0126]	[0.0110]	[0.0200]
% Hispanics in peer group	0.0565	−0.0079	−0.1175***
	[0.0562]	[0.0387]	[0.0388]
%Black*black	0.0331*	0.0266	−0.0023
	[0.0193]	[0.0175]	[0.0153]
%Hispanic*Hispanic	0.5126***	0.3485***	0.3120***
	[0.1483]	[0.1250]	[0.1182]
Class size	0.0019***	0.0004	0.0003
	[0.0006]	[0.0005]	[0.0005]
Male	−0.0300***	−0.0291***	−0.0306***
	[0.0026]	[0.0027]	[0.0026]
Black	−0.1465***	−0.1396***	−0.1302***
	[0.0092]	[0.0085]	[0.0076]
Hispanic	0.0036	0.0142	0.0127
	[0.0127]	[0.0118]	[0.0114]
Parent completed high school	0.1132***	0.1123***	0.1213***
	[0.0053]	[0.0053]	[0.0052]
Parent completed trade or	0.1668***	0.1662***	0.1781***
business school	[0.0077]	[0.0077]	[0.0078]
Parent completed community	0.1918***	0.1892***	0.2024***
or technical college	[0.0076]	[0.0076]	[0.0078]
Parent completed four-year college	0.2684***	0.2640***	0.2824***
	[0.0093]	[0.0092]	[0.0097]
Parent completed graduate school	0.3354***	0.3301***	0.3429***
	[0.0124]	[0.0121]	[0.0127]
R^2	0.7001	0.7004	0.7086
n	232,525	232,008	232,008

Data obtained from the North Carolina Education Research Data Center's End-of-Grade Tests dataset. *** denotes a coefficient significant at the 1% level, ** the 5% level, * the 10% level.

Table 4.3
Fifth-grade peers and longer-term outcomes

| Independent variable | Dependent variable: End-of-grade math score | | | |
	Fifth grade	Sixth grade	Seventh grade	Eighth grade
Lagged math score	0.7786***	0.8035***	0.8149***	0.8290***
	[0.0071]	[0.0019]	[0.0021]	[0.0022]
Average score	0.0717***	0.0345***	0.0323***	0.0339***
of classmates	[0.0074]	[0.0057]	[0.0051]	[0.0049]
(twice lagged)				
Std. dev. in scores	0.0334***	0.0072	−0.0047	0.0189***
of classmates	[0.0091]	[0.0062]	[0.0056]	[0.0053]
(twice lagged)				
% males in class	−0.0682***	0.0022	−0.0192	−0.0255*
	[0.0221]	[0.0165]	[0.0145]	[0.0140]
% blacks in class	−0.1355***	−0.0766***	−0.0532***	−0.0191
	[0.0263]	[0.0216]	[0.0187]	[0.0177]
% Hispanics in class	−0.1317**	−0.0538	−0.0919**	0.0385
	[0.0518]	[0.0403]	[0.0359]	[0.0357]
%Black*black	0.0319*	0.0345**	−0.001	0.0048
	[0.0168]	[0.0153]	[0.0150]	[0.0148]
%Hispanic*Hispanic	0.1678	0.1472	0.1527	0.2541**
	[0.1357]	[0.1074]	[0.1031]	[0.1104]
Class or grade size	−0.001	0.0007**	0.0003	−0.0001
	[0.0006]	[0.0003]	[0.0002]	[0.0001]
R^2	0.734	0.7533	0.7651	0.7692
n	232,756	240,268	224,911	211,464

Notes: Standard errors reported in parentheses. Peer variables are defined by fifth-grade classroom peers. Regression specifications also control for individual characteristics listed in table 4.2, year fixed effects, an intercept, and fifth-grade school fixed effects. Data obtained from the North Carolina Education Research Data Center's End-of-Grade Tests dataset. "Class or grade size" variable is class size for fifth-grade and grade size for all other specifications. *** denotes a coefficient significant at the 1% level, ** the 5% level, * the 10% level.

test-score variables with reading rather than math test scores. In general, the results in these specifications bear significant resemblance to the math results, though there are several noteworthy contrasts. The mean peer-achievement coefficients derived from grade- and classroom-level peer groups are nearly identical in specifications without fixed effects. In the preferred school fixed-effect model, the coefficient on mean peer achievement, though still significantly greater than zero, is roughly one-third lower than either prior estimate. Classroom sex composition continues to be associated with achievement, at least

| Independent variable | Dependent variable: End-of-grade reading score | | | |
	Fifth grade	Sixth grade	Seventh grade	Eighth grade
Lagged math score	0.7640***	0.7778***	0.7765***	0.7568***
	[0.0084]	[0.0018]	[0.0023]	[0.0021]
Average score	0.0601***	0.0438***	0.0484***	0.0542***
of classmates	[0.0065]	[0.0054]	[0.0052]	[0.0050]
(twice lagged)				
Std. dev. in scores	0.0102*	0.0109**	0.0132**	0.0042
of classmates	[0.0061]	[0.0054]	[0.0055]	[0.0055]
(twice lagged)				
% males in class	−0.0496***	−0.0165	−0.0286**	−0.0674***
	[0.0173]	[0.0145]	[0.0140]	[0.0147]
% blacks in class	−0.0508**	−0.0969***	−0.0162	−0.0825***
	[0.0200]	[0.0176]	[0.0179]	[0.0182]
% Hispanics in class	−0.1171***	−0.0621*	−0.0883**	−0.0183
	[0.0385]	[0.0350]	[0.0348]	[0.0350]
%Black*black	−0.0013	−0.0172	−0.0162	−0.0047
	[0.0153]	[0.0149]	[0.0152]	[0.0154]
%Hispanic*Hispanic	0.3275***	0.1711	0.2138*	0.2049
	[0.1181]	[0.1161]	[0.1145]	[0.1256]
Class or grade size	0.0003	0.0008**	0.0005	0
	[0.0005]	[0.0004]	[0.0003]	[0.0001]
R^2	0.7093	0.7255	0.7121	0.7047
n	232,015	239,557	224,516	211,041

in the fixed-effect specification. There is only limited evidence—a marginally significant coefficient in the fixed-effect specification—to suggest that dispersion in peer reading scores is advantageous to individual students. The link between classroom racial composition and individual achievement is also more tenuous here. In the fixed-effect specification, non-Hispanic students in classrooms with a higher share of Hispanics tend to score lower; Hispanic students themselves, if anything, are positively affected by Hispanic share.

For purposes of policy discussions, the existence of contemporaneous peer effects is of limited interest. More important is the question of whether peer-group composition has lasting effects on students' academic trajectories. Table 4.3 examines the persistence of peer characteristic associations by tracing the impact of fifth-grade peer quality through eighth grade.

Each of the specifications in these tables controls for a standard set of student-level covariates as well as fixed effects grouping students into the schools they attended in fifth grade. Peer-characteristic variables are consistently defined on the basis of a student's classmates in fifth grade, including race, sex, and moments in the third-grade test-score distribution.

For both reading and math achievement, the results are consistent with the hypothesis of a significant persistent effect of fifth-grade peer quality on student achievement. In the math-score regressions, the effect of mean fifth-grade peer ability in the sixth, seventh, and eighth grades is consistently estimated at about one-half the magnitude of the effect measured in fifth grade. Persistent effects are larger in both absolute and relative terms in the reading-score regressions: there is little evidence of decay in the impact of fifth-grade peer ability on student achievement. This persistence occurs even though students presumably have limited contact with their fifth-grade classmates once they enter a middle-school environment, partly because schools are larger at higher grade levels and partly because the structure of middle school implies less exposure to any particular set of classmates.

Other peer characteristics show mixed evidence of persistence. The benefits of being in a class with diverse math-ability levels shows no consistent signs of persistence after fifth grade. The benefits of diverse reading-ability levels, though smaller in initial magnitude, show greater persistence, with significant coefficients estimated in the fifth, sixth, and seventh grades. The negative association between the density of males in the fifth-grade classroom and achievement shows signs of decaying over time, but significant negative impacts, particularly in the case of reading scores, are in evidence as late as eighth grade. Classroom racial composition has a significant instantaneous effect on achievement, but in most cases this effect decays rapidly over time, to the extent that it appears irrelevant for most students by the end of their eighth-grade year. The possible exceptions to this generalization are (1) the estimated negative impact of percent black in a student's fifth-grade classroom on sixth- and eighth-grade reading scores and (2) the large, though imprecisely estimated, math and reading gains to attending a class with a large Hispanic share for Hispanic students. The first of these effects appears too large to be credible, while the second is consistent with a view that initial concentration of Hispanic students is beneficial for those students' later performance.

The persistence of relationships between fifth-grade classmate characteristics and achievement is consistent with the hypothesis that there
are important, lasting impacts of peers on educational outcomes. This
pattern is also consistent, however, with the view that observable peer
characteristics are correlated with unobserved individual predictors of
achievement. In the following section, we focus greater attention on
the immensely important question of whether the relationships we
have estimated to this point are truly causal in nature.

4.5   Are the Estimated Effects Causal in Nature?

As our preferred regression estimates to this point incorporate school
fixed effects, the primary remaining concern is that student sorting
across classrooms within schools generates selection bias in the estimation of peer effects. There is substantial evidence that at least some such
sorting occurs in North Carolina elementary schools, driven primarily
by the desire of some parents to match their students with particular
teachers (Clotfelter, Ladd, and Vigdor 2006). The nonrandom sorting
that would arise from such a process introduces two potential forms of
omitted-variable bias. Assignment to a class with higher-ability peers
may be a function of parents' desire to secure such a high-ability peer
group, and this parental desire may correlate with other unmeasured
aspects of parental investment in education. Parents of high-ability
students may also exert more effort to secure an assignment to a classroom teacher of superior quality. Assignment to a high-ability peer
group would then imply assignment to a superior-quality teacher and
a confounding of peer effects and teacher-quality effects.

In this section, we employ three different strategies to circumvent
these forms of omitted-variable bias. The first two strategies are represented in table 4.4. Because our data consist of four cohorts of fifth-
grade students, we can employ teacher fixed effects in addition to
school fixed effects.[15] Teacher fixed effects eliminate any bias associated with time-invariant teacher quality and address parental sorting
concerns as well if sorting patterns are consistent over time. The peer-
effect coefficients are identified using variation in the characteristics of
students that an individual teacher instructs over time.

In these specifications, the estimated effects of increases in mean peer
ability and mean-preserving spreads in ability are negative and statistically significant—exactly the opposite of our findings in earlier

Table 4.4
Investigating whether peer correlations are causal

	Fifth-grade outcomes with teacher fixed effects		Fourth-grade outcomes	
	Math	Reading	Math	Reading
Lagged test score	0.7739***	0.7569***	0.7586***	0.7521***
	[0.0073]	[0.0092]	[0.0032]	[0.0028]
Mean third-grade score	−0.1042***	−0.1168***	0.0495***	0.0726***
of fifth-grade classmates	[0.0105]	[0.0108]	[0.0049]	[0.0048]
Std. dev. of third-grade score	−0.0451***	−0.0568***	0.0842***	0.0638***
of fifth-grade classmates	[0.0110]	[0.0080]	[0.0122]	[0.0090]
% males among fifth-grade	−0.0353	−0.0490**	−0.0751***	−0.0494***
classmates	[0.0260]	[0.0226]	[0.0133]	[0.0120]
% blacks among fifth-grade	−0.1342***	−0.1537***	−0.0418***	−0.0207
classmates	[0.0313]	[0.0299]	[0.0140]	[0.0128]
% Hispanics among fifth-grade	−0.1093*	−0.1426***	−0.0304	−0.0263
classmates	[0.0611]	[0.0535]	[0.0257]	[0.0233]
%Black*black	0.0333**	0.0036	0.0299*	0.0164
	[0.0160]	[0.0161]	[0.0168]	[0.0161]
%Hispanic*hispanic	0.1267	0.3765***	0.0883	0.0484
	[0.1326]	[0.1156]	[0.1037]	[0.1074]
Fourth-grade schoolmate-characteristic controls	No	No	Yes	Yes
R^2	0.7654	0.7264	0.6764	0.6723
n	232,749	232,008	32,977	32,521

Notes: Standard errors reported in parentheses. Regression specifications also control for individual characteristics listed in table 4.2, year fixed effects, an intercept, and fifth-grade school fixed effects. Data obtained from the North Carolina Education Research Data Center's End-of-Grade Tests dataset. *** denotes a coefficient significant at the 1% level, ** the 5% level, * the 10% level.

tables. This evidence is wholly inconsistent with the view that our earlier results represent the causal impact of peer-group composition on achievement. Note that the coefficients on classmate sex and racial composition on achievement bears much greater resemblance to earlier estimates, implying that these peer-group characteristics matter more than ability measures. In these specifications, as in earlier ones, evidence suggests that Hispanic students perform much better on reading exams in the presence of a higher share of Hispanic classmates.

Our second effort to discern the relative role of selection and causality in our previous estimates focuses on the outcomes of fourth-grade students. Since these students have not yet been exposed to their fifth-grade classmates, there is little reason to think that the composition of their fifth-grade class will influence achievement, particularly when we control for fourth-grade peer-group characteristics. Evidence of a relationship between future peer characteristics and present achievement will bolster the argument that our earlier estimates reflect omitted-variable bias arising from the correlation between peer characteristics and unobserved individual-level predictors of achievement. In fact, this is exactly what we observe in table 4.4: the impacts of mean ability and of mean-preserving spreads in ability among one's future peers are positive, significant, and in some cases larger than our earlier estimates of contemporaneous effects. The sex composition of future classmates is also significantly associated with present achievement, suggesting an important role for omitted-variable bias in earlier estimates of the gender effect as well.[16] The coefficients on racial composition are, by and large, small and only rarely significant, lending more weight to the view that altering a classroom's racial composition leads to important impacts on achievement.

The evidence in table 4.4 suggests that omitted-variable bias is an important concern in the estimation of peer effects in schools using observational data. In light of this concern, a more convincing strategy for identifying the true causal impact of peer characteristics on student achievement would exploit some source of variation exogenous to the individual student and uncorrelated with his or her own ability conditional on observables. As a final exercise, we take advantage of two characteristics of North Carolina public schools that create situations where students are exposed to significantly different peer groups from one year to the next. First, certain parts of North Carolina have experienced rapid population growth in recent years. This growth has led to the construction and opening of many new schools. Wake County, the state's second-largest school system, which serves Raleigh, opened 50 new schools over the 15-year span of 1988 to 2003. Second, rulings from federal courts have led some large districts across the state to change their practices regarding student assignment to schools, moving away from busing plans designed to achieve racial balance and toward other schemes.

Students reassigned to a new school may experience a change in outcomes for several reasons. The composition of their peer group changes, but there may be other factors—including the social strain of adjusting to a new environment or changes in the transportation time to the new school—that have the potential to influence achievement. For this reason, our exploitation of changes in school assignment will focus not on the students who switch but rather on students who are consistently assigned to a school that experiences a significant change in enrollment. These "feeder" schools are those who lose at least 10 percent but less than 50 percent of their student body between one year and the next. We chose the lower threshold because small changes in peer-group composition may be imperceptible to students and the upper threshold because a situation where the majority of students in a school are replaced may be as traumatic to remaining students as a transfer to a new school.[17]

Table 4.5 provides some summary statistics for these feeder schools. While feeder schools are quite representative of the state in terms of racial composition, average student test scores are almost one-tenth of a standard deviation higher, and average parental education levels are also disproportionately high. This stems from the tendency for such schools to be located in rapidly growing, more affluent areas of the state. Since it is conceivable that different peer-influence mechanisms operate in schools serving disproportionately advantaged students, the results below should be interpreted with some degree of caution.

Table 4.6 reports regression results where the sample is restricted to students consistently assigned to feeder schools. These specifications use school-level peer-group definitions, since the variation in peer-group composition we seek to exploit is at the school- rather than classroom-level.[18] The first two regressions are comparable to the grade-level OLS specifications reported in table 4.2 and illustrate that few of the patterns found in our entire sample also hold in this restricted subsample. Higher mean peer achievement in third grade continues to predict higher individual reading test scores in fifth grade. As noted in previous specifications, Hispanic students also show a tendency to score better in schools serving a higher share of Hispanic students. In general, though, peer coefficients in the feeder-school sub-sample are either weaker or more negative than in the whole sample. This pattern is consistent with the view that changes in attendance-zone boundaries disrupt sorting processes that took place at some point in the past, attenuating the correlation between peer characteristics and unobserved individual- or family-level determinants of achievement.

Even in the feeder-school sample, cross-sectional variation in peer characteristics is most likely contaminated by endogenous sorting.

Table 4.5
Summary statistics by feeder school

	Feeder = 0		Feeder = 1	
	Mean	Standard deviation	Mean	Standard deviation
Math score	0.036	0.987	0.117	0.983
Reading score	0.032	0.982	0.123	0.965
Parent completed high school	0.445	0.497	0.402	0.490
Parent completed trade/business school	0.044	0.204	0.049	0.217
Parent completed community or technical college	0.138	0.345	0.131	0.337
Parent completed four-year college	0.227	0.419	0.288	0.453
Parent completed graduate school	0.057	0.232	0.066	0.249
Classroom peer groups:				
Average math score of peers (twice lagged)	0.048	0.433	0.141	0.395
Average reading score of peers (twice lagged)	0.044	0.414	0.139	0.395
Std. dev. in math score of peers (twice lagged)	0.857	0.249	0.851	0.188
Std. dev. in reading score of peers (twice lagged)	0.863	0.266	0.871	0.242
% males in class	0.505	0.094	0.501	0.086
% blacks in class	0.287	0.247	0.262	0.192
% Hispanics in class	0.027	0.048	0.030	0.045
Number of students in class	26.58	23.86	27.75	28.99
Grade peer groups:				
Average math score of peers (twice lagged)	0.042	0.336	0.134	0.303
Average reading score of peers (twice lagged)	0.039	0.312	0.135	0.289
Std. dev. in math score of peers (twice lagged)	0.902	0.180	0.884	0.113
Std. dev. in reading score of peers (twice lagged)	0.909	0.197	0.904	0.152
% males in grade	0.509	0.059	0.505	0.051
% blacks in grade	0.291	0.237	0.266	0.180
% Hispanics in grade	0.027	0.038	0.030	0.033
n	906,239		33,214	

Table 4.6
Analysis of peer effects in feeder schools

	Feeder schools		First difference		Whole sample First difference	
	Level					
	Math	Reading	Math	Reading	Math	Reading
Lagged test score	0.8023*** [0.0084]	0.7616*** [0.0116]				
Average score of peers (twice lagged)	0.0292 [0.0302]	0.0739*** [0.0215]	0.0186 [0.0269]	0.0007 [0.0279]	0.0371*** [0.0064]	0.0143** [0.0063]
Std. dev. in scores of peers (twice lagged)	-0.0406 [0.0666]	-0.0146 [0.0284]	-0.0323 [0.0452]	0.0063 [0.0232]	-0.0065 [0.0094]	-0.0036 [0.0058]
% males in peer group	-0.0947 [0.1157]	0.0936 [0.0911]	0.0395 [0.1174]	0.0927 [0.0875]	0.0157 [0.0264]	0.0013 [0.0202]
% blacks in peer group	-0.0723 [0.0619]	-0.0229 [0.0404]	-0.0105 [0.0642]	-0.0285 [0.0504]	-0.0015 [0.0142]	0.0042 [0.0123]
% Hispanics in peer group	0.3008 [0.1965]	0.0148 [0.1390]	0.0073 [0.1910]	-0.1563 [0.1620]	0.0578 [0.0485]	-0.0031 [0.0376]
%Black*black	0.0268 [0.0694]	0.0283 [0.0503]	-0.0008 [0.0742]	0.0361 [0.0598]	0.0242 [0.0168]	0.0172 [0.0157]
%Hispanic*hispanic	0.9553*** [0.3615]	0.5975* [0.3295]	-0.3183 [0.5571]	0.0957 [0.6218]	0.0873 [0.1778]	0.0059 [0.1657]
Class size	-0.0002*** [0.0001]	-0.0001 [0.0001]	-0.0003*** [0.0001]	-0.0001 [0.0001]	-0.0002*** [0.0001]	-0.0001* [0.0001]
Male	-0.0120** [0.0059]	-0.0465*** [0.0060]	-0.0069 [0.0064]	-0.0115* [0.0068]	-0.0074*** [0.0013]	-0.0082*** [0.0013]

Black	−0.1213***	−0.1465***	0.0128	0.0002	0.0022	−0.0117***
	[0.0241]	[0.0185]	[0.0104]	[0.0089]	[0.0028]	[0.0024]
Hispanic	−0.0763**	−0.0398	−0.0014	0.0344	0.0069	0.0167***
	[0.0329]	[0.0284]	[0.0266]	[0.0268]	[0.0058]	[0.0059]
Parent completed high school	0.0575***	0.1080***	−0.0258	0.003	−0.0066**	0.0111***
	[0.0144]	[0.0151]	[0.0159]	[0.0184]	[0.0031]	[0.0031]
Parent completed trade or business school	0.1131***	0.1422***	0.0044	−0.0223	0.0006	0.0176***
	[0.0208]	[0.0185]	[0.0222]	[0.0227]	[0.0045]	[0.0043]
Parent completed community or technical college	0.1344***	0.1880***	−0.011	0.0034	−0.0011	0.0175***
	[0.0168]	[0.0167]	[0.0179]	[0.0191]	[0.0036]	[0.0034]
Parent completed four-year college	0.2003***	0.2516***	0.0005	0.0154	0.0071*	0.0158***
	[0.0173]	[0.0172]	[0.0173]	[0.0182]	[0.0037]	[0.0034]
Parent completed graduate school	0.2501***	0.2909***	0.0059	−0.0031	0.0257***	0.0163***
	[0.0206]	[0.0211]	[0.0201]	[0.0210]	[0.0045]	[0.0041]
R^2	0.7418	0.7014	0.0028	0.0013	0.0008	0.0004
n	31,923	31,853	29,004	28,940	854,183	851,979

Notes: Robust standard errors reported in parentheses. Peer variables are defined by fifth-grade peers (school-level) for students attending feeder schools in fifth-grade. Specifications also control for year effects and an intercept. Data obtained from the North Carolina Education Research Data Center's End-of-Grade Tests. First differences indicate that the independent peer variables are defined by fifth-grade peer-group characteristic minus fourth-grade peer-group characteristic. The dependent variable in this case is the difference between achievement score in fifth-grade minus achievement score in fourth grade. *** denotes a coefficient significant at the 1% level, ** the 5% level, * the 10% level.

Feeder schools, by definition, have maintained a significant portion of their student body intact from year to year. In a feeder school, the student-body composition at any one point in time is likely to reflect endogenous sorting into the school. It is the change in student-body composition that can be considered exogenous from the perspective of a student permanently assigned to the school. To more directly exploit this source of variation, the third and fourth specifications in table 4.6 take first differences of both the dependent variable and the peer-characteristic variables. Effectively, these regressions seek to determine whether changes in a student's performance between fourth and fifth grade can be linked to changes in classroom composition between fourth and fifth grade.

Before reporting the results of these specifications, it is important to note some limitations associated with differenced models. Since test scores are noisy measures of ability, problems associated with measurement error are exacerbated in differenced specifications. Differencing our dependent variable should lead to less efficient coefficient estimates. Coefficients on differenced independent variables will display an exacerbated attenuation bias toward zero. Put together, these problems imply that we are much less likely to identify meaningful statistical relationships correctly in this specification. To address this concern, we report the results of first-differenced specifications using the entire sample in the last columns of table 4.6. As we report below, these specifications indicate that not all of our results in the differenced feeder-school regressions reflect exacerbated measurement-error problems.

In the feeder-school specifications, very few independent variables have any explanatory power. The regressions explain less than 1 percent of all variation in year-over-year changes in student test scores. The peer-characteristic coefficients are generally smaller than in the level specifications and insignificant.

A basic reading of these results thus corroborates the conclusions of table 4.4: the observed correlation in peer and individual achievement can be attributed primarily to sorting and not any causal impact. The final regressions reported in table 4.6 provide some additional information that is valuable in interpreting these final results. These models replicate the first-difference specification using the full sample of North Carolina fifth-grade students. In the whole sample, there is a statistically significant, though empirically small, association between changes in lagged peer test scores and changes in individual test scores. Thus, attenuation bias and efficiency problems cannot explain away the absence of any result in the feeder-school specifications.

4.6 Conclusions and Future Directions

This chapter contributes to a large and growing literature documenting significant correlations between peer characteristics and student achievement. It raises serious doubts regarding whether a causal interpretation can be assigned to such correlations. Three important pieces of evidence argue against a causal interpretation. First, the correlations we estimate are not robust to the inclusion of teacher-fixed effects, consistent with the view that parents, particularly those with more able students, attempt to secure superior teachers for their children. Second, peer characteristics appear to influence achievement even before the peer contact has actually occurred, a pattern conceivable only when peer characteristics correlate with unobserved (and persistent) individual determinants of achievement. Finally, our analysis of students attending "feeder schools" where significant year-to-year variation in peer-group composition arose from changes in school-assignment policy or the opening of new schools found little evidence that changes in peer-group composition lead to changes in achievement levels.

An optimistic view of our findings is that peer effects may indeed exist, but in observational data they are swamped by omitted-variable bias generated by selection into peer groups. This view suggests that more sophisticated efforts to model the sorting process might yet yield important evidence on the existence and magnitude of peer effects. Our future research agenda incorporates several strategies for disentangling the impact of peer characteristics from family background and other variables that presumably contaminate cross-sectional relationships. The feeder-school analysis represents one such strategy. A similar strategy will be to use the sample of North Carolina elementary schools that appear to assign students randomly to classrooms, at least on the basis of observable characteristics (Clotfelter, Ladd, and Vigdor 2006). Coupled with school-by-year fixed effects, this strategy promises to identify variation in peer characteristics that is truly uncorrelated with individual background variables.

A more ambitious strategy will incorporate further information on student background characteristics and family residential choices by linking student test-score records to student-address data, and via address data to family characteristics derived from consumer credit databases. A link to an external source of data will be advantageous from many perspectives: it will allow us at least some ability to track those students who exit North Carolina public schools for either a non-public alternative school or a public school in another state. In the long run, we expect this enhanced dataset to be rich enough to allow us to estimate a general equilibrium location model incorporating education production with peer effects (Bayer 2000; Bayer, McMillan, and Reuben 2004). By modeling the process of family sorting across schools, we hope to be able to impute the values of latent variables indicating a parent's propensity to agitate for within-school sorting as well. Until the data are in place to perform this estimation, we will continue to explore additional avenues in our quest to identify the true magnitude of causal peer effects in public schools.

Acknowledgments

We are grateful to the Spencer Foundation, National Science Foundation, and William T. Grant Foundation for financial support; to Dennis Epple, Torberg Falch, participants at the 2004 ASSA meetings, two anonymous referees, and participants at the CESifo/PEPG conference on Schooling and Human-Capital Formation in the Global Economy: Revisiting the Equity-Efficiency Quandary for valuable comments; and to Dan Hungerman and Jane Cooley for outstanding research assistance.

Notes

1. A second strand of the literature has considered the implications of neighborhood characteristics for individual outcomes, particularly the developmental consequences of growing up in a poor neighborhood (Brooks-Gunn et al. 1993; Case and Katz 1991; Chase-Lansdale et al. 1997; Duncan 1994; Duncan, Connell, and Klebanov 1997; Ensminger, Lamkin, and Jacobson 1996; Halpern-Felsher et al. 1997; Hanratty, McLanahan, and Pettit 1998; Katz, Kling, and Liebman 2001; Leventhal and Brooks-Gunn 2001; Ludwig, Duncan, and Hirschfeld 2001; Ludwig, Duncan, and Pinkston 2000; Ludwig, Ladd, and Duncan 2001; Rosenbaum 1991; Rosenbaum and Harris 2000; Solon, Page, and Duncan 2000; see Jencks and Mayer 1990, Ellen and Turner 1997, and Gephardt 1997 for literature reviews).

2. Several studies have used policy experiments with explicit randomization of peers (Boozer and Cacciola 2001; Sacerdote 2001) or neighborhoods (Hanratty et al. 1998; Katz et al. 2001; Ludwig, Duncan, and Hirschfeld 2001; Ludwig, Duncan, and Pinkston 2000; Ludwig, Ladd, and Duncan 2001; Leventhal and Brooks-Gunn 2001; Rosenbaum 1991), while others have used idiosyncratic variation in the composition of peer groups—such as the differences between successive cohorts within a school or across classrooms in an elementary school (Hoxby 2000; Hanushek et al. 2001).

3. Our data, unlike data used in many other studies, permit both school and teacher fixed effects—allowing us to control for selection into and within schools.

4. A very different strategy not used in this chapter involves explicitly modeling the assignment process—that is, analyzing neighborhood and schooling choices. The most straightforward implementation of this strategy is to conduct an instrumental-variable analysis that models peer-group characteristics as a function of exogenous variables (Evans, Oates, and Schwab 1992). A more complex approach utilizes discrete-choice models and other econometric methods to analyze neighborhood and schooling consumption decisions (Bayer 2000; Bayer, McMillan, and Rueben 2004; Epple and Sieg 1999; McFadden 1978).

5. The most drastic recent change in desegregation plans in North Carolina occurred in the state's largest district, the Charlotte/Mecklenburg County school system. Following a federal court ruling, this district dropped its desegregation plan and adopted a modified neighborhood-school assignment plan in the 2002–2003 school year. Consequently, the average African American elementary student witnessed an increase in black share of classmates from 52 percent to 57 percent: this increase would be equivalent to one extra black classmate in a class of 20. The Charlotte-Mecklenburg system is about 40 percent black overall, implying that this increase in the proportion of black classmates for black students must be matched by a relatively equal decrease in the proportion for students of other races. Since race correlates very highly with socioeconomic status and standardized test performance, this change in the racial makeup of classrooms suggests changes in other peer characteristics measures as well. See section 4.5 for more on recent school-district changes in North Carolina.

6. Moreover, in middle schools there is no guarantee that a teacher listed as an exam proctor on a student's test form will be the actual instructor of that subject to that student. Each student observation lists a single teacher-identification code associated with both math and reading test scores.

7. Mean math and reading test scores in our estimation sample exceed zero, and the standard deviation is less than one, primarily because the estimation sample omits students tested in exceptionally small classroom groups, which are likely to be special education classes.

8. Because parent education is teacher-reported, this variable may reflect nonclassical measurement error, as some teachers may be systematically misguided as to the distribution of educational attainment among their students' parents or in society more broadly. This measurement error may correlate with other teacher characteristics that have an independent effect on student achievement or may correlate with a teacher's own perceptions of a student's ability level. Any interpretation of parental education effects should therefore be conducted with appropriate caution.

9. We omit a student's own lagged test score from the computation of mean classroom or grade-level peer ability.

10. We have estimated models employing a number of alternative measures of dispersion in the peer-ability distribution; some of these are reported in Vigdor and Nechyba (2006). Models using the square of mean peer ability resemble those reported here: there is evidence of a positive relationship between dispersion in the peer-ability distribution and math test scores. For reasons described below, this relationship should not be assigned a causal interpretation.

11. The allocation of students to classrooms may influence the distribution of achievement levels even in situations where mean student achievement is constant. If individual

school-enrollment decisions are sensitive to the level of peer quality offered to a student of any particular type, the enrollment or achievement-maximizing allocation of students to classrooms may well deviate from the allocation identified in our analysis as aggregate achievement maximizing. For a theoretical analysis of the decision to employ tracking in public schools, see Epple, Newlon, and Romano (2002).

12. For example, if classrooms were random draws from the population, with sample sizes between 16 and 25, we would expect the standard deviation of mean peer ability to be between 0.20 and 0.25. School standard deviations would be even smaller.

13. The finding that classroom-level peer achievement is an equal or greater predictor of individual test scores contrasts with Betts and Zau (2002), who find the opposite relationship in their study of data from the San Diego Unified School District. To further examine this pattern, we estimated models that controlled simultaneously for grade- and classroom-level peer characteristics. In these specifications, classroom-level peer characteristics systematically bore larger and more significant coefficients than grade-level peer characteristics.

14. In additional unreported specifications, we controlled separately for the mean and standard deviation in twice-lagged test scores for male and female classmates and interacted these measures with a student's own gender. The results suggest that raising the performance of male classmates has a positive impact on females and little impact on males and that raising the performance of female classmates has a negative impact on females and a positive impact on males. There were no consistent patterns linking dispersion of male and female ability to outcomes. While these results are in some respects puzzling and intriguing, they should not be assigned a causal interpretation, for reasons identified below.

15. Note that in this specification, school fixed effects are identified by teachers who switch schools. As we are not interested in the estimates of these school fixed effects per se, this is not an important concern.

16. Such a result would also be expected in a world where students are consistently exposed to the same group of peers. This scenario does not appear to accurately describe the experiences of North Carolina elementary school students, however. While schoolmate characteristics are highly correlated over time (the correlations in third-grade test scores of fourth- and fifth-grade schoolmates are 0.82 and 0.81 for math and reading tests), correlations in classmate characteristics are substantially lower (0.60 and 0.56 for math and reading). Moreover, the absence of significant racial composition effects in these specifications argues against a continuity-in-peer group explanation.

17. The feeder-school analysis may provide a misleading view of peer influence to the extent that newcomers to a school are not fully integrated into the environment, either formally or informally. For example, introducing a group of low-performing students to a high-performing school might have a minimal impact if the new students are ostracized by their peers or grouped into separate classrooms. The introduction of new students could also have a disproportionately large impact if it leads to widespread conflict and classroom disruption. For this reason, the feeder-school analysis should be viewed as a source of potential corroborating evidence, rather than a convincing quasi-experimental estimate of true peer effects.

18. In an alternative set of specifications, we used classroom-level peer-group characteristics and instrumented for those characteristics using school-level characteristics. The results of this analysis are qualitatively identical to those reported in table 4.6.

References

Arcidiacono, P., and S. Nicholson. (2005). "Peer Effects in Medical School." *Journal of Public Economics* 89: 327–350.

Bayer, P. (2000). "Tiebout Sorting and Discrete Choices: A New Explanation for Socioeconomic Differences in the Consumption of School Quality." Unpublished manuscript.

Bayer, P., R. McMillan, and K. Reuben. (2004). "An Equilibrium Model of Sorting in an Urban Housing Market." Working Paper No. 10865, National Bureau of Economic Research.

Betts, J. R., and A. Zau. (2002). "Peer Groups and Academic Achievement: Panel Evidence from Administrative Data." Unpublished manuscript.

Boozer, M. A., and S. E. Cacciola. (2001). "Inside the 'Black Box' of Project STAR: Estimation of Peer Effects Using Experimental Data." Unpublished manuscript.

Brooks-Gunn, J., G. J. Duncan, P. K. Klebanov, and N. Sealand. (1993). "Do Neighborhoods Influence Child and Adolescent Development?" *American Journal of Sociology* 99: 353–395.

Bryk, A. S., and M. E. Driscoll. (1988). "The High School as Community: Contextual Influences and Consequences for Students and Teachers." National Center on Effective Secondary Schools, University of Wisconsin, Madison.

Caldas, S. J., and C. Bankston. (1997). "Effect of School Population Socioeconomic Status on Individual Academic Achievement." *Journal of Educational Research* 90: 269–277.

Case, A. C., and L. F. Katz. (1991). "The Company You Keep: The Effects of Family and Neighborhood on Disadvantaged Youths." Working Paper No. 3705, National Bureau of Economic Research.

Chase-Lansdale, P. L., R. A. Gordon, J. Brooks-Gunn, and P. K. Klebanov. (1997). "Neighborhood and Family Influences on the Intellectual and Behavioral Competence of Preschool and Early School-Age Children." In J. Brooks-Gunn, G. J. Duncan, and J. L. Aber (eds.), *Neighborhood Poverty* (vol. 1). New York: Russell Sage Foundation.

Clotfelter, C. T., H. F. Ladd, and J. L. Vigdor. (2006). "Teacher Sorting, Teacher Shopping, and the Assessment of Teacher Effectiveness." *Journal of Human Resources* 41: 778–820.

Duncan, G. J. (1994). "Families and Neighbors as Sources of Disadvantage in the Schooling Decisions of White and Black Adolescents." *American Journal of Education* 103: 20–53.

Duncan, G., J. Connell, and P. Klebanov. (1997). "Conceptual and Methodological Issues in Estimating Causal Effects of Neighborhoods and Family Conditions on Individual Development." In J. Brooks-Gunn, G. Duncan, and J. Aber (eds.), *Neighborhood Poverty* (vol. 1). New York: Russell Sage Foundation.

Ellen, I., and M. Turner. (1997). "Does Neighborhood Matter? Assessing Recent Evidence." *Housing Policy Debate* 8: 833–866.

Ensminger, M. E., R. P. Lamkin, and N. Jacobson. (1996). "School Leaving: A Longitudinal Perspective Including Neighborhood Effects." *Child Development* 67: 2400–2416.

Epple, D., E. Newlon, and R. Romano. (2002). "Ability Tracking, School Competition, and the Distribution of Educational Benefits." *Journal of Public Economics* 83: 1–48.

Epple, D., and R. Romano. (1998). "Competition between brivate and Public Schools, Vouchers, and Peer Group Effects." *American Economic Review* 88(1): 33–62.

Epple, D., and H. Sieg. (1999). "Estimating Equilibrium Models of Local Jurisdictions." *Journal of Political Economy* 107: 645–681.

Evans, W., W. Oates, and R. Schwab. (1992). "Measuring Peer Group Effects: A Study of Teenage Behavior." *Journal of Political Economy* 100: 966–991.

Ferreyra, Maria. (2006). "Estimating the Effects of Private School Vouchers in Multi-District Economies." Working Paper, Carnegie Mellon University.

Gaviria, A., and S. Raphael. (2001). "School-Based Peer Effects and Juvenile Behavior." *Review of Economics and Statistics* 83: 257–268.

Gephardt, M. (1997). "Neighborhoods and Communities as Contexts for Development." In J. Brooks-Gunn, G. Duncan, and J. Aber (eds.), *Neighborhood Poverty* (vol. 1). New York: Russell Sage Foundation.

Halpern-Felsher, B. L., J. P. Connell, M. B. Spencer, J. L. Aber, G. J. Duncan, E. Clifford, W. E. Crichlow, P. A. Usinger, S. P. Cole, L. Allen, and E. Seidman. (1997). "Neighborhood and Family Factors Predicting Educational Risk and Attainment in African American and White Children and Adolescents." In J. Brooks-Gunn, G. J. Duncan, and J. L. Aber (eds.), *Neighborhood Poverty* (vol. 1). New York: Russell Sage Foundation.

Hanratty, M., S. McLanahan, and B. Pettit. (1998). "The Impact of the Los Angeles Moving to Opportunity Program on Residential Mobility, Neighborhood Characteristics, and Early Child and Parent Outcomes." Working Paper No. 98-18, Bendheim-Thoman Center for Research on Child Wellbeing.

Hanushek, E., J. Kain, J. Markman, and S. Rivkin. (2001). "Does Peer Ability Affect Student Achievement?" Working Paper No. 8502, National Bureau for Economic Research.

Hoxby, C. (2000). "Peer Effects in the Classroom: Learning from Gender and Race Variation." Working Paper No. 7867, National Bureau for Economic Research.

Katz, L., J. Kling, and J. Liebman. (2001). "Moving to Opportunity in Boston: Early Results of a Randomized Mobility Experiment." *Quarterly Journal of Economics* 116: 607–654.

Jencks, C., and S. Mayer. (1990). "The Social Consequences of Growing Up in a Poor Neighborhood." In L. Lynn and M. McGreary (eds.), *Inner-City Poverty in the United States*. Washington, DC: National Academy Press.

Lazear, E. P. (2001). "Educational Production." *Quarterly Journal of Economics* 116: 777–803.

Leventhal, T., and J. Brooks-Gunn. (2001). "Moving to Opportunity: What about the Kids?" Working paper.

Link, C. R., and J. G. Mulligan. (1991). "Classmates' Effects on Black Student Achievement in Public School Classrooms." *Economics of Education Review* 10: 297–310.

Ludwig, J., G. Duncan, and P. Hirschfield. (2001). "Urban Poverty and Juvenile Crime: Evidence from a Randomized Housing-Mobility Experiment." *Quarterly Journal of Economics* 116: 655–680.

Ludwig, J., G. Duncan, and J. Pinkston. (2000). "Neighborhood Effects on Economic Self-Sufficiency: Evidence from a Randomized Housing-Mobility Experiment." Unpublished working paper.

Ludwig, J., H. Ladd, and G. Duncan. (2001). "The Effects of Urban Poverty on Educational Outcomes: Evidence from a Randomized Experiment." *Brookings-Wharton Papers on Urban Affairs* 2: 147–201.

Manski, C. F. (1993). "Identification of Endogenous Social Effects: The Reflection Problem." *Review of Economic Studies* 60: 531–542.

Mayer, S. E. (1991). "How Much Does a High School's Racial and Socioeconomic Mix Affect Graduation and Teenage Fertility Rates?" In C. Jencks and P. E. Peterson (eds.), *The Urban Underclass*. Washington, DC: Brookings Institution.

McFadden, D. (1978). "Modeling the Choice of Residential Location." In A. Karlquist et al. (eds.), *Spatial Interaction Theory and Planning Models*. New York: Elsevier North-Holland.

Moffitt, R. A. (1998). "Policy Interventions, Low-Level Equilibria and Social Interactions." In S. Durlauf and H. P. Young (eds.), *Social Dynamics*. Cambridge, MA: MIT Press.

Nechyba, T. (2000). "Mobility, Targeting and Private School Vouchers." *American Economic Review* 90: 130–146.

Nechyba, T., D. Older-Aguilar, and P. McEwan. (1999). "The Effect of Family and Community Resources on Education Outcomes." Unpublished manuscript.

Robertson, D., and J. Symons. (1996). "Do Peer Groups Matter? Peer Group versus Schooling Effects on Academic Attainment." Unpublished manuscript, London School of Economics Centre for Economic Performance.

Rosenbaum, J. (1991). "Black Pioneers: Do Their Moves to the Suburbs Increase Economic Opportunity for Mothers and Children?" *Housing Policy Debate* 2: 1179–1213.

Rosenbaum, E., and L. Harris. (2000). "Short-term Impacts of Moving for Children: Evidence from the Chicago MTO Program." Working paper.

Sacerdote, B. (2001). "Peer Effects with Random Assignment: Results for Dartmouth Roommates." *Quarterly Journal of Economics* 116: 681–704.

Slavin, R. E. (1987). "Ability Grouping and Student Achievement in Elementary Schools: A Best-Evidence Synthesis." *Review of Educational Research* 57: 293–336.

Slavin, R. E. (1990). "Achievement Effects of Ability Grouping in Secondary Schools: A Best-Evidence Synthesis." *Review of Educational Research* 60: 471–499.

Solon, G., M. E. Page, and G. J. Duncan. (2000). "Correlations between Neighboring Children in Their Subsequent Educational Attainment." *Review of Economics and Statistics* 82: 383–392.

Vigdor, J. L., and T. J. Nechyba. (2006). "Peer Effects in Elementary School: Learning from 'Apparent' Random Assignment." Unpublished manuscript.

Zimmer, R. W., and E. F. Toma. (1999). "Peer Effects in Public Schools across Countries." *Journal of Policy Analysis and Management* 19: 75–92.

5   The Heterogeneous Effect of Selection in UK Secondary Schools

Fernando Galindo-Rueda and
Anna Vignoles

5.1 Introduction

During the second half of the twentieth century, several European countries abandoned their systems of selective schooling, whereby students of different levels of academic ability attended separate schools with different curricula. This was largely motivated by the belief that such selective or two-tier schooling systems impact negatively on equality of opportunity, particularly for children from less privileged backgrounds.

Relative to a comprehensive system in which children of all abilities are taught in the same school, a two-tier education system is likely to affect the opportunities and performance of different types of student in a number of potentially unequal ways. First, outcomes will depend on the difference in effectiveness of schools from each tier. Such differences can be due simply to peer effects or to differential resourcing of schools across the two tiers. Thus, an individual's experience of the system will depend not only on her abilities and the specific school she attends but more generally on the school *type* she has been assigned to. Second, the set of rules and criteria that determine the allocation of different students to different school tiers will play a more important role in determining the overall performance of a tiered system relative to a system that subjects most students to the same curriculum and generic school type.

It can be argued that selective systems have the potential to provide a more appropriate education for different types of student as they may provide a curriculum that better meets an individual's educational potential and her needs. However, the fact that one tier can be perceived to be superior to another and does in fact deliver different outcomes naturally leads to concerns about inequality. Furthermore, to be implementable, a selective system presupposes that a given set of measured characteristics, such as those captured by test scores, provides sufficient information with which to assign different children to different school types efficiently. Yet such test scores provide only a limited and snapshot assessment of an individual's educational potential, and the scope for misassignment of students can be very significant.

Proponents of both comprehensive and selective school systems can, on slightly different grounds, claim that their preferred system is best placed to meet the goal of equality of opportunity in education. However, independently of a society's preferences about the nature of educational equality, it is important to determine empirically which system produces better aggregate educational results. We need to know, for example, whether gains for high-ability pupils, caused by stretching such students and providing them with good peer groups, are offset by poorer outcomes for lower-ability pupils, caused by low expectations and poor peer groups. Equally, such an empirical analysis may also identify inefficiencies in the system, whereby the performance of one group can be improved without impinging on that of another group. Finally, inequality of outcomes may in itself also matter to society; hence any evidence of heterogeneous impacts for different types of student from a given system should be considered carefully.

Certainly, selection remains a topical issue in many European countries, such as Germany, where features of selective schooling from a relatively early age still remain in place. In other countries, such as the United Kingdom, various policy initiatives have reopened the debate on how places in popular schools, which are in great demand, should be effectively rationed. In some instances, this has led to increased pressures for both implicit and explicit selection mechanisms to be introduced (or reintroduced) to the school system.[1] For example, policies to increase parental choice may put additional pressure on schools to get better academic results and thus increase their implicit selection of pupils accordingly. In the United Kingdom, there have been moves toward reintroducing more explicit forms of selection, such as the formation of specialist schools that can select a proportion of their students on the basis of aptitude in a particular field (such as arts or technology) rather than on the basis of overall academic ability. As yet, little is known about the potential impact of these changes, and thus selection is still very much a live policy issue.

In this work, we attempt to shed some light on these issues by quantifying the relationships between early cognitive ability, family background, and school selection, on the one hand, and educational achievement, on the other. To do this, we look at a cohort of children born in 1958 who went through secondary school in the United Kingdom during the 1970s, a period of uneven transition from a selective to a comprehensive system in the United Kingdom. The details of this change in educational policy are discussed in section 5.2. We then proceed to describe our data in section 5.3. Crucially for our estimation strategy, our data reflect the period's geographical divide between areas with selective schools—grammar and secondary modern schools—and those with mixed-ability comprehensives, enabling us to compare the outcomes from both types of system, as is explained in section 5.4. We present our key results in section 5.5, and section 5.6 concludes.

5.2 Background

5.2.1 The History of Selection in UK Secondary Schooling
During the 1960s and 1970s, the UK secondary education system underwent a period of significant institutional change, particularly in England and Wales.[2] Prior to the early 1960s, the system could perhaps be best characterized as "elitist." At the secondary level, students of differing abilities were sent to different types of school and received very different types of education. Essentially, there was a tripartite system consisting of "grammar," "secondary modern," and a small and rapidly declining number of "technical" schools. Grammar schools were academically oriented secondary schools, which catered for the top of the ability range, and entry into these schools was based on an ability test administered at age 11, although socioeconomic factors were seen to influence attendance at a grammar school (Steedman 1983). Grammar schools provided for the full age range (11 to 18), and these students were most likely to go on to higher education. Secondary modern schools, on the other hand, provided a lower-level academic education for those who could not get into a grammar school. Secondary moderns generally took pupils only up to the compulsory minimum school-leaving age of 15 (in place until 1973 and 16 afterward). A small number of technical schools provided a vocational-oriented education (again, generally up to age 16).

One important aspect of the selective grammar system is that it encouraged students to take very different curricula at an early age. In England and Wales, prior to the dismantling of the grammar-school system in the 1970s, the student body was effectively divided at age 11. The majority of secondary modern students either left the education system at the age of compulsory schooling (16 since 1973) with few or no qualifications (around 45 percent of the cohort) (Central Advisory Council 1959) or acquired a set of certificates of secondary education (CSEs)[3] at age 16. Grammar students generally acquired Ordinary (O) levels, which were more academically demanding than CSEs, at age 16, and many continued on until age 18 to take Advanced (A) levels. Around one-third of the full cohort left the education system at the end of their compulsory schooling with either CSEs or O levels. Of the remaining 20 percent that continued on to A levels, around one-half went on to higher education—one in 10 of the cohort. Some students who attended a secondary modern did manage to switch to the higher academic stream and stay on past age 16, but this was not common.

This highly selective system was still in place during the 1960s and 1970s. However, in response to concerns about the inequity of this system, policies were introduced in the mid-1960s, by the then Labour government, to move toward mixed-ability schooling.[4] In particular, legislation was enacted to enable local education authorities (LEAs)[5] to establish mixed-ability schools called *comprehensives*. The institutional structure of the English and Welsh education systems meant, however, that the pace of change varied between and within LEAs (Kerckhoff et al. 1996). Certainly, central government was not able to dictate that all LEAs switched to nonselective schooling at a particular time. Indeed, selective grammar schools continue to exist today in certain LEAs, such as Kent. Local political resistance to their abolition has been extremely strong. Nonetheless, by 2004 there were only 25 noncomprehensive secondary schools out of a total of 3,409. These accounted for 20,970 out of a total of 3,324,950 students (Department for Education and Skills 2004).

The manner in which mixed-ability schools were introduced varied from LEA to LEA. Very few LEAs switched all their schools into a nonselective system simultaneously, and thus, within LEAs, there was also considerable variability in the pace at which particular areas and schools moved into the nonselective system.

What is also important to remember is that in some LEAs secondary moderns became comprehensives but nearby grammar schools preserved their selective entry policy. This meant that the comprehensives in these areas did not necessarily teach the full ability range; rather, they continued to attract only students from the bottom of the ability distribution (or thereabouts). Furthermore, secondary moderns that changed into comprehensives often could not accommodate students up to age 18. Students wishing to stay on past age 16 would then have had to change schools altogether, compared to grammar students who could continue in their school up to age 18. In other LEAs, change was more radical with the introduction of wholly new schools, designed specifically as comprehensives.

So what determined the pace of change and the nature of the reorganization in secondary schools across different LEAs? Kerckhoff et al. (1996) showed that the political orientation of the LEA was crucially important. Specifically, LEAs that had Conservative political control experienced slower change toward mixed-ability schooling than LEAs under Labour control. Furthermore, LEAs that were under Labour control initially but that then switched to Conservative control appeared to have been able to reverse or slow plans to move toward comprehensive schooling. It was not quite as clear-cut as a simple political dichotomy. Examples of LEAs under Conservative control that moved swiftly toward comprehensivisation can be found, such as Leicestershire (Kerckhoff et al. 1996).

One might have expected that other factors would determine whether an LEA or schools within an LEA shifted quickly to mixed-ability schooling, such as the level of educational funding in that school or LEA or indeed other characteristics of the neighborhood of the school. Kerckhoff et al. (1996) concluded, however, that most community characteristics of the LEA were not major determinants of the extent of comprehensivization within the LEA. There was, however, weak evidence that better-resourced LEAs made the shift toward mixed-ability schooling more rapidly. The determinants of whether a child was educated in a selective or nonselective school system are discussed from an empirical perspective in section 5.3.

5.2.2   Related Literature

With the shift to mixed-ability schooling in England and Wales, there commenced an ongoing and vitriolic debate about the perceived failure or success of the "comprehensive experiment" (Cox and Dyson 1969; Cox and Boyson 1975, 1977; Crook, Power, and Whitty 1999; Marks, Cox, and Pomian-Srzednicki 1983; Reynolds, Sullivan, and Murgatroyd 1987). Good quantitative empirical evidence on this issue is sparse and tends to concentrate on an assessment of the impact of the type of school attended rather than the schooling system experienced. This literature is somewhat mixed in its results (Fogelman 1983, 1984; Kerckhoff 1986; Harmon and Walker 2000; Jesson 2000; Dearden, Ferri, and Meghir 2003). In contrast with these studies, we are not directly interested in assessing the impact of specific school types, such as grammar schools, on educational achievement. Instead, we try to establish the *ex ante* impact of being part of a selective school system (whether in a secondary modern or a grammar school) on outcomes and, in particular, how the impact on educational achievement is distributed across pupils of differing ability.

This chapter builds on a previous study by the authors of the changing role of ability in determining educational outcomes (Galindo-Rueda and Vignoles 2005). It also links to a broader literature relating cognitive ability to various socioeconomic outcomes (see Cawley, Heckman, and Vytlacil 2001), as well as empirical evidence on the role of family background factors (such as parental income and social class) in determining educational attainment (Haveman and Wolfe 1995). The chapter also relates to the education-evaluation literature. See, for example, Meghir and Palme (2003), who investigated the educational and wage impact of a social experiment in Sweden, which simultaneously involved the abolition of the existing selective system and raised the school leaving age. There are also links to a wider literature on streaming within schools (Figlio and Page 2000). More directly related is a recent paper by Manning and Pischke (2006), who adopt a similar approach to ours in their investigation of the British comprehensive experiment and note the methodological problems in considerable detail.

5.3   Data

We use a unique longitudinal dataset, the National Child Development Study (NCDS),[6] which followed a complete cohort of individuals (all born in one week in March 1958) as they went through the education system and out into the labor market. This dataset is ideal for our purposes since it neatly spans the time period during which the selective system was being phased out and replaced by a comprehensive system. The NCDS has data on these children, their families, and their school environments at the ages of 7, 11, and 16. Further follow-up studies were undertaken in adulthood, and we have substantial data on these individuals' subsequent educational and labor-market outcomes. A major advantage of our data is that we have measures of each cohort member's early ability, with sets of cognitive test scores from ages 7 and 11. The age 7 test scores are particularly useful since they predate secondary school, and even more important, they predate the so-called 11 plus examination, which was the age 11 test used to determine entry into grammar or secondary modern school in the selective system. An important concern at the time was that the results of this examination reflected socioeconomic status rather than any real innate ability.

From the NCDS data, we know whether individuals were being educated in a selective-system school (either in a grammar school or in its counterpart, a secondary modern) at age 16 and for how long their school had been nonselective if they attended a comprehensive. This enabled us to construct two selection variables. First, we created an indicator for whether the individual was in a selective-system school (grammar or secondary modern) at age 16 (1974) or not. Second, we constructed a variable measuring the years spent in a selective school system between the ages of 11 and 16.[7] Key descriptive statistics are provided in table 5.1.

A number of issues arise if we use the individual's own school type as our measure of the selectivity of the education system experienced by the child. As discussed earlier, some "comprehensive" schools were located close to grammar schools. We risk misclassifying individuals in these comprehensives because they were actually experiencing a selective system owing to the effects of the *surviving* local grammar school. An alternative measure is the proportion of students in comprehensive schools in the LEA as a whole, which is also provided as part of the NCDS records. However, there was substantial variation within LEAs in the extent of selectivity. Given this, using an LEA-level indicator of the proportion of students in comprehensive schools will tend to produce attenuated estimates. Thus, we make use of both the individual's own school type *and* the LEA share in comprehensive schools to indicate the degree of selectivity in the child's local education system.

Our primary interest is in the potentially unequal impact of selective school systems for children of different ability to investigate the role of

Table 5.1
Descriptive statistics: NCDS members by schooling status in 1974 (age 16)

	In comprehensive school in 1974			In selective system: either grammar or secondary modern school in 1974		
	Mean	Standard deviation	Observations	Mean	Standard deviation	Observations
Schooling characteristics:						
Years of pre-16 selective schooling	1.247	1.500	4841	5.000	—	3976
Proportion LEA						
Noncomprehensive: 74	0.246	0.219	4823	0.511	0.211	3417
"Grammar" school				0.325	0.468	3976
"Secondary modern" school				0.675	0.468	3976
Selected individual characteristics:						
Ability index at 7 (missing baseline)						
Ability age 7 quintile = 1	0.163	0.369	4841	0.136	0.342	3976
Ability age 7 quintile = 2	0.165	0.371	4841	0.151	0.358	3976
Ability age 7 quintile = 3	0.155	0.361	4841	0.153	0.360	3976
Ability age 7 quintile = 4	0.148	0.355	4841	0.160	0.367	3976
Ability age 7 quintile = 5	0.132	0.339	4841	0.192	0.395	3976
Father's social class (unskilled baseline)						
Semiskilled manual	0.168	0.375	4841	0.153	0.359	3976
Skilled manual	0.451	0.497	4841	0.428	0.495	3976
Skilled nonmanual	0.091	0.288	4841	0.094	0.291	3976
Intermediate, managerial	0.134	0.340	4841	0.174	0.379	3976
Professional	0.037	0.188	4841	0.051	0.221	3976
Missing social class	0.047	0.213	4841	0.045	0.208	3976

	Mean	SD	N	Mean	SD	N
LEA secondary education features:						
LEA secondary school expenditure per student	1422.1	137.3	4841	1384.9	128.2	3976
LEA secondary pupils per teacher	17.119	1.170	4841	17.449	0.850	3976
General-election results (baseline: Labour victory):						
Conservative win MP 1974	0.304	0.460	4715	0.458	0.498	3976
Liberal win MP 1974	0.016	0.125	4715	0.007	0.086	3976
Other win MP 1974	0.009	0.009	4715	0.007	0.085	3976
Dependent variables:						
Math score at 11	-0.131	0.955	4188	0.161	1.030	3406
Reading score at 11	-0.127	0.948	4188	0.156	1.039	3406
Ability index at 11	-0.101	0.973	4188	0.124	1.019	3406
Math score at 16	-0.126	0.932	4457	0.149	1.055	3765
Reading score at 16	-0.087	0.997	4476	0.103	0.993	3782
Years of schooling or education	11.795	1.691	3293	12.231	2.048	2776
Achieved level 3 or higher	0.186	2.475	3442	0.268	0.443	2869

ability-based selection and the broader efficiency and equity questions. Our cognitive-ability variables therefore merit further discussion. Using a methodology similar to that of Cawley, Heckman, and Vytlacil (2001), we constructed a cognitive-ability measure based on test scores obtained at the age of 7 for the 1958 NCDS cohort. We undertook a principal-components analysis on the age 7 test scores (arithmetic, reading, copying designs, and "man-drawing" tests) to construct an index of cognitive ability, using the first principal component extracted.[8] Our interpretation of this variable is that of an index that allows us to rank each individual in terms of cognitive ability or early human capital. From a practical point of view, reducing the dimension of the available ability information at age 7 allows us to simplify considerably the analysis of interactions between ability and selective schooling, which is central to our study.

Additional controls used in this chapter include father's social class, parental schooling, household composition, and other measures of financial well-being (such as income). We also supplemented the data with information on the educational resources at the secondary school level in the child's LEA in 1974—in particular, the number of secondary-school pupils per full-time equivalent teacher, total secondary costs per student, and the teacher salary costs per pupil in secondary schools, together with the population share of secondary-school students in the local authority. We also merged in data from the 1971 census on the child's community or neighborhood (census enumeration district), including the proportion of unemployed, as well as the proportion working in agricultural, professional/managerial/nonmanual/manual/semiskilled jobs in the district, the proportion of owner occupiers, the proportion of council tenants, and the proportion of recent Commonwealth immigrants in the district.

The descriptive statistics in table 5.1 suggest that students in comprehensive schools have on average experienced slightly more than one year of schooling in the selective system, on the basis of the date in which their school turned comprehensive. Classifying students on the basis of the type of school attended is closely related to the density of noncomprehensive schools in the area. Approximately one-third of students classified as within the selective system are actually in the upper-tier grammar schools. This is higher than the fifth of students reported to be in grammar schools before the selective system began to be phased out. This implicitly suggests that (1) areas that delayed the phase-out process were likely to have a higher percentage of students passing the 11-plus test and (2) some of the students classified as being in comprehensive schools may actually have experienced a selective system if they were located in areas where grammar schools were still active.

Table 5.1 also shows that children in the selective system (either in secondary moderns and grammars) have higher ability levels and come from wealthier backgrounds. While one would expect grammar students to be more able, it is not clear a priori whether, on average, children in the selective system (including those in secondary moderns) would be more able. This again suggests that the shift from selective to comprehensive schooling may not have been random. Wealthier areas appear to have been slower to shift toward comprehensive schooling. Hence, whether a particular child was educated in a selective or nonselective school system would have been potentially endogenous, a matter discussed in the next section.

5.4   Estimation Strategy

Our objective is to assess the impact of selection in secondary education on an individual's educational outcomes. We can denote Y_1 as the potential educational outcome for an individual who has experienced a selective school system. The outcome for an individual who experienced a comprehensive system is Y_0.[9] If the other factors that may influence educational outcomes are similar across the two systems, including peer and area characteristics, the impact of selective schooling for an individual is thus $Y_1 - Y_0$.

The typical evaluation problem is to construct a valid counterfactual, providing a measure of what would have been the educational outcome for individuals who were not educated under a selective system had they been subject to selective schooling. The descriptive statistics in table 5.1 suggest that individuals who experienced comprehensive schooling are likely to differ from those in selective areas in many ways, some potentially correlated with educational outcomes. One possible approach to overcoming this problem is to control for a sufficiently wide set of characteristics W so that the expected potential outcome under a comprehensive system is independent of the actual system experienced.

$E[Y_0 \mid S = 1, W] = E[Y_0 \mid S = 0, W]$.

One might therefore regress educational outcome Y on a set of controls W and a variable indicating whether the child was subject to selective schooling S. Since the impact of selection is likely to vary according to values of W, interacting W and S will provide a richer description of the data and help us understand who benefits more and less from selective schooling. Within the standard regression framework, such effects can be captured by estimating

$$Y_i = W\alpha + S\beta + S'W\gamma + \varepsilon_i$$

through ordinary least squares. We are particularly interested in the impact of selective and nonselective schooling systems for differing-ability children, so our models control for the ability of the child as well as interactions between the ability and selection variables.

A less restrictive approach that we also adopt is to compute the non-parametric impact by means of matching, by pairing individuals in each system with very similar values of W. Rosenbaum and Rubin (1983) suggest matching based on propensity scores—that is, comparing individuals with the same probability $\pi(W) = \Pr[S = 1 \mid W]$ of being subject to selective schooling, to calculate the sample analogue of

$$E[Y_1 - Y_0 \mid S = 1] = E[Y_1 \mid S = 1] - E[E[Y_0 \mid S = 0, \pi]].$$

From the earlier discussion, it is clear that the success of this estimation strategy depends on the quality of the set of controls in W. Given that the treatment is theoretically area based, the focus should be on area-level characteristics. We thus include census-based socioeconomic characteristics at the level of the individual's enumeration district. We also control for LEA characteristics, including the level of educational resources.

Despite our efforts to compare like with like by means of matching methods and regression analysis, endogeneity may still bias our results. There may be unobserved characteristics that influence both the type of schooling experienced and educational outcomes. We adopt an instrumental variable strategy to try correct for the measurement-error problem induced by the misclassification of the treatment when an area, despite the presence of comprehensive schools, still operates a de facto selective system. We do so by instrumenting the school-based treatment with the proportion of noncomprehensive schools in the LEA.[10] This approach will identify the effect of experiencing education in a selective-system school as a result of living in an area with, say, a negligible presence of comprehensive schools.

5.5 Results

5.5.1 Selective Schooling in the 1958 Cohort

Table 5.2 reports results from a model of the determinants of the likelihood of experiencing a selective school system. The dependent variables considered are (1) attendance at age 16 of a school in the selective system (grammar or secondary modern), (2) the number of years of compulsory secondary schooling that NCDS cohort members are estimated to have spent in a selective school, and (3) the proportion of noncomprehensive schools in the area. Only a few selected characteristics are displayed, but all models control for the full set of individual, household, and area characteristics.

Relatively few of the explanatory variables are individually significant. The political affiliation of the child's constituency is the most robust determinant across specifications. Children in a Conservative constituency experienced on average 0.6 more years of selective schooling and live in areas with nearly a 6 percent higher share of noncomprehensive schools.

High-ability children at age 7 seem more likely to attend a school in the selective system and to have done so for longer (specifications 1 and 2) but do not seem to live in LEAs with a significantly higher proportion of noncomprehensive schools. The same applies to paternal schooling. Father's social class, on the contrary, appears to be more important for specification (3)—that is, in the model determining the likelihood of living in an area with a high proportion of noncomprehensive schools. There is also evidence of differential resourcing. Students in LEAs with higher levels of resources per secondary school student had a higher probability of attending a comprehensive school.

5.5.2 The Impact of Selective Schooling on Educational Attainment

Table 5.3 presents some results from our matching estimates of the effects of selective schooling on standardized math scores at age 16 and years of schooling, focusing on an overall selective-schooling effect, without disentangling the effects of specific school types within the selective system. These estimates compare the performance of the sample of students in both grammar and secondary modern schools against an appropriately reweighted average of the performance of students in comprehensive schools, using the estimated propensity to attend a noncomprehensive school as the matching characteristic.

Table 5.2
The determinants of selective schooling (selected coefficients)

Regressors	(1) Probit method In noncom-prehensive secondary school	(2) OLS method Secondary school years in noncom-prehensive	(3) OLS method Share of noncom-prehensive schools in LEA
Individual characteristics/background:			
Ability at age 7 (missing is baseline)			
Ability quintile = 1	−0.0025 (0.0244)	−0.0087 (0.1070)	−0.0156 (0.0123)
Ability quintile = 5	0.0867 (0.0239)**	0.2681 (0.0938)**	0.0044 (0.0122)
Female	0.0150 (0.0106)	0.0147 (0.0465)	0.0059 (0.0052)
Father professional (baseline: unskilled)	0.0254 (0.0414)	0.1460 (0.1720)	0.0520 (0.0213)*
Father's age left schooling	0.0102 (0.0043)*	0.0458 (0.0147)**	0.0031 (0.0025)
General-election results: 1974 (baseline Labour win):			
Conservative win	0.1130 (0.0413)**	0.6047 (0.1748)**	0.0569 (0.0235)*
Liberal win	−0.1599 (0.1241)	−0.3278 (0.4881)	0.0372 (0.0806)
Other win	−0.0092 (0.1454)	0.2037 (0.4078)	0.0362 (0.1212)
LEA characteristics:			
Average LEA secondary school costs per pupil	−0.0010 (0.0004)*	−0.0051 (0.0016)**	−0.0005 (0.0003)
Average LEA secondary school teachers salaries —cost per pupil	0.0015 (0.0010)	0.0029 (0.0037)	0.0013 (0.0008)
Average LEA secondary pupils per FT teacher	0.0816 (0.0427)	0.1156 (0.1236)	0.0549 (0.0275)*
Observations	8,252	8,252	7,734

Notes: Dependent variable in column headings. Robust standard errors, within parentheses adjusted for LEA clustering. *Significant at 5%, **significant at 1%. Other controls include full set of individual and household characteristics, Census 71 enumeration district composition. Selected coefficients presented, marginal effects reported in (1).

Table 5.3
Matching estimates of the effect of selective (noncomprehensive) schooling (decomposition by ability quintiles and selective school type)

	Math score at 16	Years of schooling completed
A. Full sample:		
Basic set of controls	0.137 (0.034)	0.221 (0.084)
Controlling for ability at age 11	0.079 (0.036)	0.117 (0.087)
B. By ability group at age 7:		
Low ability: quintile = 1	0.068 (0.051)	−0.042 (0.082)
Medium ability: quintile = 3	0.250 (0.061)	0.246 (0.161)
High ability: quintile = 5	0.288 (0.685)	0.734 (0.204)
C. By father's social class:		
Unskilled	0.082 (0.105)	−0.267 (0.274)
Semiskilled	−0.021 (0.078)	0.082 (0.149)
Skilled manual	0.075 (0.050)	0.096 (0.106)
Skilled nonmanual	0.324 (0.131)	0.204 (0.368)
Intermediate manager	0.292 (0.084)	0.453 (0.226)
Professional	−0.014 (0.225)	0.531 (0.639)
D. By ability and father's status:		
Low ability: low SES	−0.061 (0.059)	0.020 (0.078)
Low ability: high SES	0.009 (0.224)	−0.410 (0.665)
Medium ability: low SES	0.104 (0.045)	0.139 (0.176)
Medium ability: high SES	0.477 (0.141)	0.198 (0.437)
High ability: low SES	0.220 (0.105)	0.467 (0.256)
High ability: high SES	0.347 (0.147)	−0.059 (0.478)

Notes: Matching estimates calculated using nearest-neighbor matching estimator with *psmatch.ado* Stata routine. Propensity scores estimated for each sample using standard set of controls described in the text. Dependent variables are the standardized mathematics score at age 16 and the number of completed years of schooling. Panel A refers to full sample without and with ability controls at age 11 in addition to controls at age 7. Categories in panels B to D are self-explanatory. High SES includes children of professionals, managers, and other skilled workers.

The first row in panel A provides matching estimates for all students in our sample, from a model that controls for all the individual, household, and area characteristics discussed earlier, including ability levels at age 7. These estimates indicate a significant positive effect of selective schooling of 0.13 standard-deviation points for math and about one-fifth of a year of additional schooling. These estimates assume away selection on unobservables that may influence the educational outcomes considered. We have also checked that the degree of

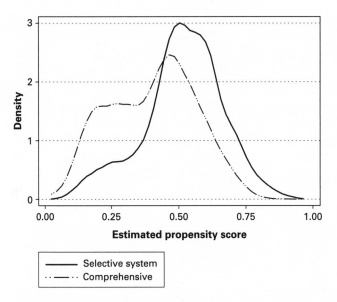

Figure 5.1
Distributions of propensity scores for attending school in selective system (comprehensive and noncomprehensive samples). *Note:* Kernel density estimates of predicted probability of attending school in selective system in 1974, using specification reproduced in table 5.2.

common support is reasonable (as shown by the distributions of the estimated propensity scores in figure 5.1) and ordinary balancing conditions. In the second row of panel A, we now control for ability at age 11 in the first-stage matching equation. The estimated effects are now half the size and are significant only for math scores. We come back to discuss this finding, but we can say that the reduced impact from selective schooling controlling for age 11 ability is partly explained by the incentive provided by the system for students to develop early the skills that at age 11 will already determine their allocation to a particular tier within the selective system.

In panels B to D, we investigate the possible heterogeneity of impacts by splitting our sample by ability and father's social class. While there is a clear indication that selection appears to be more beneficial for children who are in the upper end of the ability distribution, we do not find clear evidence of negative impacts at the lower end. In terms of social class, the impacts appear to be most powerful for the intermediate-skilled groups, instead of showing a monotonic relationship. When we look at specific combinations of ability and social-class levels, ability seems to be the dominant factor, but comparisons are difficult to make with our sample sizes.

We now try to correct for the potential measurement problems in the imputation of a selective school treatment from the type of school attended. In table 5.4, we compare basic OLS estimates with IV results where we instrument both the noncomprehensive dummy and the length of selective-schooling variables, using the share of noncomprehensive schools in the LEA. We consider the effect of our two school-based selection variables on the math score at age 16 and years of schooling. All models include controls for individual, family, and area-level characteristics.

The coefficients in panel A in table 5.4 are from a model that assumes an average, homogeneous impact across the whole population. While OLS estimates are strongly significant and positive, as found using a matching approach, the IV estimates are positive but do not reach full statistical significance, and hence we cannot reject the hypothesis of nil average impact.

In panel B, we consider the effect of selective schooling for the subsample of individuals in the top and bottom ability quintiles at age 7. The baseline OLS estimate of the impact of attending a noncomprehensive school is not significant. The interactions with the high-ability dummy are always positive and significant, suggesting the same type of heterogeneous effects found through matching estimates—that the selective school system appears to have positive benefits for the most able children. The IV estimates provide more of a mixed picture. For the first dependent variable (math scores), the baseline effects of attending a noncomprehensive school are positive but not entirely significant. The interactions with high ability are positive but not significant. The sum of baseline and interaction produces a positive significant result. For the second dependent variable (years of schooling), baseline effects are significant and negative, whereas the interactions with ability are significant, positive, and larger in absolute size.

These findings suggest tentatively that there were both winners and losers in the process of phasing out the selective system. Higher-ability pupils may have gained from the selective school system and by implication lost out when it was abolished. Lower-ability pupils in some specifications appear to have done marginally worse under the selective system and would therefore have gained somewhat by its abolition. It is also interesting that the negative effects of selective schooling are observed at the baseline for the model explaining years

Table 5.4
Regression estimates of the impact of selective schooling

	Mathematics				Completed years of schooling			
	(1) OLS	(2) IV	(3) OLS	(4) IV	(5) OLS	(6) IV	(7) OLS	(8) IV
Panel A. Full sample:								
Noncomprehensive	0.154 (0.030)**	0.070 (0.046)			0.500 (0.074)**	0.162 (0.109)		
Years in selective			0.035 (0.006)**	0.018 (0.012)			0.043 (0.012)**	0.041 (0.028)
Observations	7,220	7,220	7,220	7,220	5,678	5,420	5,420	5,420
Panel B. Highest- and lowest-ability quintiles, interaction effects:								
Noncomprehensive	0.049 (0.038)	0.127 (0.068)			-0.120 (0.071)	-0.395 (0.173)*		
High ability* noncomprehensive	0.188 (0.063)**	0.081 (0.136)			0.602 (0.136)**	0.734 (0.303)*		
Years in selective secondary school			0.005 (0.008)	0.031 (0.017)			-0.044 (0.016)**	-0.089 (0.040)*
High ability* years in selective			0.047 (0.014)**	0.020 (0.032)			0.124 (0.033)**	0.171 (0.073)*
Observations	2,304	2,304	2,304	2,304	1,704	1,704	1,704	1,704

Notes: OLS and IV estimates of the effect of attending grammar or secondary modern school (or the effect of number of years in either type of school) on standardized mathematics scores and completed years of schooling. IV estimates instrument the treatment variable with the proportion of noncomprehensive schools in LEA. Robust standard errors, adjusted for LEA clustering. *Significant at 5%, **significant at 1%. Panel A consists of full sample. Panel B includes only first and fifth quintiles of the ability distribution at age 7.

of schooling achieved but not for the model of math scores. This seems to point toward a distinction between the impact of selection for specific learning outcomes, such as math scores, and the impact more generally on educational aspirations and achievement, which were known to be lower at secondary modern schools.

5.5.3   Primary Schooling Incentives in a Selective Secondary Schooling System

In this section, we briefly discuss one of the possible channels through which selective secondary schooling has an effect on educational outcomes. As emphasized by results in table 5.3, estimates of the impact of selective schooling were dramatically reduced in models that controlled for attainment at age 11 (in models that were estimating the value added of secondary schools) compared to models that controlled only for ability at the beginning of primary schooling. One hypothesis is that this difference is explained by learning taking place between the ages of 7 and 11 throughout primary schooling. The key question is how can the extent of selection in secondary school influence primary-school outcomes?

In the selective school system, there is a clear incentive for individuals to meet the requirements for entry into grammar schools, as determined by the test taken at age 11. Pupils' ability to meet these requirements can be considered not as a fixed attribute but rather as something that can be influenced by means of educational efforts throughout primary school. A selective secondary-school system will thus induce a series of efforts in primary-school pupils, some of which may have long-lasting effects. In the light of this, the timing of the shift from a selective to a comprehensive system becomes a crucial factor because some of our cohort members may have accumulated skills related to the 11-plus examination in the expectation of an increased chance of being admitted into a grammar school. This expectation would have been absent from those students (and families) whose areas turned comprehensive in the early stages of the child's primary schooling.

Although we do not have information on the precise dates on which the selective system was phased out for each of the areas in which our cohort members lived, we do know, for students in comprehensive schools in 1974, the date on which their school became comprehensive. We use the latter as an imperfect measure of the former. We indicate in figure 5.2 the estimated change in the ability index between the ages of

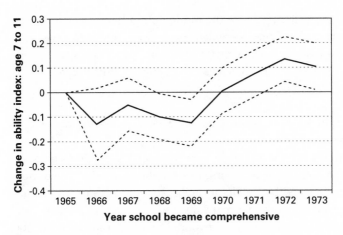

Figure 5.2
Phasing in of comprehensive schools and ability progression through primary school.
Notes: Estimated growth in ability score, measured by difference in first principal component of ability measures between ages of 7 (1965) and 11 (1969), by date the secondary school attended turned comprehensive. Expected value and confidence intervals
depicted, from regression on standard set of controls. Similar results obtained from
unconditional specification. Sample: 3,340 observations of students in comprehensive
schools in 1974.

7 and 11 by date of change in school selective status. We observe
greater pupil progress between ages 7 and 11 in areas that shifted to
comprehensive schooling later. We can thus infer that in areas that
had an earlier shift to comprehensive schooling there was a reduced incentive for pupils to exert particular effort in the lead up to age 11, as
compared with areas that shifted to comprehensive schooling later on.
Although the timing of the change in status could be also linked to
other factors driving this trend in pupil progress, it is possible to show
as in figure 5.3 that there are no comparable step changes in other
observable characteristics, including ability at age 7 as depicted. The
evidence supports the interpretation of positive impacts of selective
schooling through incentives for learning. It may be the case that a
comprehensive system provides incentives for alternative types of
pupil progression that are less focused on the possibly narrow measures of the 11-plus exams.

5.6 Policy Discussion and Conclusions

Many commentators have argued that the shift to mixed-ability schooling in England and Wales[11] (the "comprehensive experiment") failed,

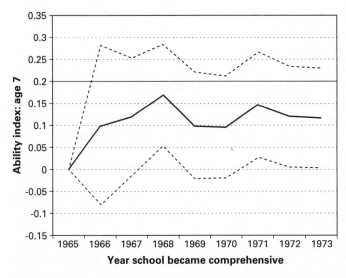

Figure 5.3
Phasing in of comprehensive schools and ability at age 7. *Notes:* Ability score at age 7 (1965), by date the secondary school attended turned comprehensive. Expected value and confidence intervals depicted. Sample: Students in comprehensive schools in 1974.

whereas others suggest it did not go far enough. Mixed-ability schooling, the former claim, has reduced educational achievement, particularly of the most able but less well off.

We have studied the educational performance of a cohort of students who went through school during the period in which the selective system was phased out, comparing students in the new comprehensive system against those in the old selective system. Our analysis has shown that the selective system had slightly positive average effects on key educational outcomes. Through a closer inspection, we have identified that high-ability students were most favored by selection, while depending on the specification, selection had nil or small negative effects on low-ability children. Given that the negative effects from selection are found only for years of completed schooling but not for test scores, we hypothesize that students assigned to secondary modern schools were particularly negatively influenced by the widespread expectation that they would not stay in school after the end of compulsory schooling. Furthermore, we cannot support the claim that poorer high-ability children were most negatively affected by the abolition of selective schooling, although the low numbers of individuals in our sample who are part of this group complicates judgements on this.

Our evidence suggests that the selective system provided strong incentives to the early development in a limited range of cognitive skills—namely, those that were tested and used in the age 11 examination used to assign students to different school types. Such effects appear to count for about half of the estimated impacts on later educational impacts. Incentive progression effects seem to be quite uniform across the distribution, but it is difficult to see how these (positive) incentives could have been maintained in the absence of differences in school characteristics and treatments.

Overall, our results tend to support the view that the UK selective system produced somewhat better average outcomes. However, they also show that this induced a more unequal distribution of educational outcomes, which appears to have been a key motivating factor in the decision to turn to a comprehensive system in many countries. Given these findings, how can we then reconcile them with the remarkable expansion of educational achievement since the 1960s in England and Wales? Have the standards achieved fallen even while the average years spent in education have risen? Evidence from our previous work (Galindo-Rueda and Vignoles 2005) indicated that, over time, early ability has started to play a lesser role in determining educational attainment, while family background appears to have become more important. In other words, the expansion of the education system appears to have disproportionately benefited less able (but wealthier) students. Can the dismantling of the selective grammar-school system explain these apparently contradictory trends?

A plausible hypothesis is that, coupled with an increasing trend in educational attainment, the shift to mixed-ability schooling may have reduced the gap in educational achievement between the most able and least able students. We do not claim that this particular system change can fully explain the various trends in educational attainment. Our research does, however, at least partly explain why the role of early cognitive ability in determining educational outcomes appears to have been reduced immediately after the abolition of the selective grammar-school system.

A key question that still needs to be resolved, after tested ability ceased to be the core factor determining the allocation of students to schools, is the nature of the new mechanisms used to deal with an apparent excess of demand for places in certain schools. In the light of the increasing role of family income and background, as has been documented by Blanden, Gregg, and Machin (2003), we strongly suspect that over a longer time period, the housing market may have eventually become the effective arbitrator between demand and supply. Distance to school is the key admission criterion to the majority of schools in the United Kingdom. This would have significant implications for our understanding of how the reform affected equality of opportunity.

Acknowledgments

We thank Jo Blanden, Steve Machin, Marco Manacorda, and Alan Manning for helpful comments and suggestions. Funding from a DfES/Treasury Evidence-Based Policy Fund grant is gratefully acknowledged. We would also like to thank participants at the PEPG/CESifo conference for their comments, particularly editors and referees. The usual disclaimer applies. The views expressed herein do not necessarily represent UK government policy.

Notes

1. A summary of the developments in the United Kingdom can be found in West and Pennell (1997).

2. During this period, the Scottish system was already fully comprehensive, while Northern Ireland remained selective. Our analysis is restricted to England and Wales.

3. CSEs were examinations that broadly catered for the 60th to 80th percentiles of the ability range, and students could take up to 10 different CSE subjects. CSE students tended to leave school at 16. However, many did go on to do vocational training.

4. Mixed-ability schools do not necessarily remove ability segregation within schools, as many schools tend to stream students into different classes on the basis of ability.

5. LEAs are somewhat akin to school districts in the United States. They are under local government political control and during the 1960s and 1970s had relatively high levels of autonomy in determining educational policy on the ground. They were responsible for most educational spending on primary and secondary schooling in the United Kingdom, although the majority of the money for education came from central government.

6. The data used in this chapter have been applied to other aspects of the relationship between socioeconomic background, cognitive ability, and socioeconomic outcomes (among many others, Breen and Goldthorpe 1999; Currie and Thomas 1999; Dearden 1999; Dearden, Machin, and Reed 1997; Feinstein and Symons 1999; Harmon and Walker 2000; McCulloch and Joshi 2000; Saunders 1997; Schoon et al. 2002).

7. We exclude from our analysis the small percentage of students in private (4 percent) and other schools (2 percent), such as those catering for children with special educational needs. We acknowledge that omitting private students can bias our results (overestimating of the effect of selection by social class) because the population of upper-class students in the state system under a comprehensive system may differ from that in the selective one.

8. Specification tests suggest that the first principal component is sufficient to control for the outcomes of interest in this chapter (see Galindo-Rueda and Vignoles 2005).

9. There is a substantial difference between our system-effects question and the potential effect of picking an individual from a selective area and putting her into a comprehensive one. The latter is of relatively marginal policy relevance compared to the former.

10. We have also attempted to tackle the more general endogeneity problem by pursuing the concept of political ideology, as measured by the political affiliation of the individual's consistency, as a possible source of exogenous variation. Such a strategy rests on the identifying assumption that affiliation does not directly interfere with the determinants of educational attainment, which is impossible to prove. It is indeed possible that areas favor a particular political representation on the basis of its own expected gains from having a selective or comprehensive system in place. Political affiliation would in that case be endogenous. Specific results are available on request.

11. See Gorman (1996) for a sociological discussion of these issues and the effect of curriculum change in Scotland.

References

Blanden, J., P. Gregg, and S. Machin. (2003). "Changes in Education Inequality." Discussion Paper, Centre for the Economics of Education, London School of Economics.

Breen, R., and J. Goldthorpe. (1999). "Class Inequality and Meritocracy: A Critique of Saunders and an Alternative Analysis." *British Journal of Sociology* 50(1): 1–27.

Cawley, J., J. Heckman, and E. Vytlacil. (2001). "Three Observations on Wages and Measured Cognitive Ability." *Labour Economics* 8(4): 419–442.

Central Advisory Council for Education (England). (1959). *15 to 18* (The Crowther Report). London: Her Majesty's Stationery Office.

Cox, C. B., and R. Boyson (eds.). (1975). *Black Paper 1975: The Fight for Education*. London: Dent.

Cox, C. B., and R. Boyson (eds.). *Black Paper 1977*. London: Maurice Temple Smith.

Cox, C. B., and A. Dyson (eds.). (1969). *Fight for Education: A Black Paper*. London: Critical Quarterly Society.

Crook, D. R., S. Power, and G. Whitty. (1999). *The Grammar School Question*. London: Institute of Education.

Currie, Janet, and D. Thomas. (1999). "Early Test Scores, Socio-economic Status and Future Outcomes." Working Paper No. 6943, National Bureau of Economic Research.

Dearden, L. (1999). "The Effects of Families and Ability on Men's Education and Earnings in Britain." *Labour Economics* 6(4): 551–567.

Dearden, L., J. Ferri, and C. Meghir. (2003). "The Effect of School Quality on Educational Attainment and Wages." *Review of Economics and Statistics* 84(1): 1–20.

Dearden, L., S. Machin, and H. Reed. (1997). "Intergenerational Mobility in Britain." *Economic Journal* 107(440): 47–64.

Department for Education and Science. (1965). *The Organisation of Secondary Education* (Circular 10/65). London: Her Majesty's Stationery Office).

Department for Education and Skills. (2004). *Statistics of Education: Schools in England*. London: Her Majesty's Stationery Office.

Feinstein, L., and J. Symons. (1999). "Attainment in Secondary School." *Oxford Economic Papers* 51(2): 300–321.

Figlio, D., and M. Page. (2000). "School Choice and the Distributional Effects of Ability Tracking: Does Separation Increase Equality?" Working Paper No. 8055, National Bureau for Economic Research.

Fogelman, K. (ed.). (1983). *Growing Up in Great Britain*. London: Macmillan.

Fogelman, K. (1984). "Problems in Comparing Examination Attainment in Selective and Comprehensive Secondary Schools." *Oxford Review of Education* 10(1): 33–43.

Galindo-Rueda, F., and A. Vignoles. (2005). "The Declining Relative Importance of Ability in Predicting Educational Attainment." *Journal of Human Resources* 40(2): 335–353.

Gorman, A. (1996). "Curriculum Standardization and Equality of Opportunity in Scottish Secondary Education: 1984–90." *Sociology of Education* 69(1): 1–21.

Harmon, C., and I. Walker. (2000). "Selective Schooling, School Quality and Labour Market Returns." *Economica* 67: 19–36.

Haveman, R., and B. Wolfe. (1995). "The Determinants of Children's Attainments: A Review of Methods and Findings." *Journal of Economic Literature* 33(4): 1829–1878.

Jesson, D. (2000). "The Comparative Evaluation of GCSE Value-Added Performance by Type of School and LEA." Discussion Paper 2000/52, University of York.

Kerckhoff, A. C. (1986). "Effects of Ability Grouping in British Secondary Schools." *American Sociological Review* 51: 842–858.

Kerckhoff, A. C., K. Fogelman, D. Crook, and D. Reeder. (1996). *Going Comprehensive in England and Wales: A Study of Uneven Change*. London: Woburn Press.

Manning, A., and S. Pischke. (2006). "Comprehensive versus Selective Schooling in England and Wales: What do we know?." IZA Discussion Paper 2072.

Marks, J., C. Cox, and M. Pomian-Srzednicki. (1983). *Standards in English Schools*. London: National Council for Educational Standards.

McCulloch, A., and H. Joshi. (2000). "Neighbourhood and Family Influences on the Ability of Children in the British National Child Development Study." *Social Science and Medicine* 53(5): 579–591.

Meghir, C., and M. Palme. (2003). "Ability, Parental Background and Education Policy: Empirical Evidence from a Social Experiment." Working Paper 03/05, Institute of Fiscal Studies.

Reynolds, D., M. Sullivan, and S. J. Murgatroyd. (1987). *The Comprehensive Experiment*. Lewes: Falmer Press.

Rosenbaum, P., and D. Rubin. (1983). "The Central Role of the Propensity Score in Observational Studies for Causal Effects." *Biometrika* 70(1): 41–55.

Saunders, P. (1997). "Social Mobility in Britain: An Empirical Evaluation of Two Competing Explanations." *Sociology* 31(2): 261–288.

Schoon, I., J. Bynner, H. Joshi, S. Parsons, R. Wiggins, and A. Sacker. (2002). "The Influence of Context, Timing, and Duration of Risk Experiences for the Passage from Childhood to Mid-adulthood." *Child Development* 73(5): 1486–1504.

Steedman, H. (1983). *Examination Results in Selective and Non-selective Schools: Findings from the National Child Development Study.* London: National Children's Bureau.

West, A., and H. Pennell. (1997). "Educational Reform and School Choice in England and Wales." *Education Economics* 5(3): 285–305.

6 The Optimal Timing of School Tracking: A General Model with Calibration for Germany

Giorgio Brunello, Massimo Giannini, and Kenn Ariga

6.1 Introduction

Most primary- and secondary-school systems in the developed world consist of an initial period of exposure to the same curriculum followed by diversification of curricula into separate tracks. In Europe, there are vocational and general or academic tracks, with allocation into tracks often based on previous performance or on ability tests (see Shavit and Muller 1998; Green, Wolf, and Leney 1999).[1] Tracking starts relatively early—after primary school in Germany and the Netherlands and later in France. In the United States, secondary schools are comprehensive, but it is common practice to separate students into different courses or course sequences (tracks) based on their level of achievement or proficiency as measured by some set of tests or course grades (see Gamoran 1987; Epple, Newlon, and Romano 2002). In Japan, stratification starts at the postcompulsory stage in upper secondary education, with elite schools at the top and vocational schools at the bottom of the hierarchy (see Ishida 1998).

In this chapter, we develop a simple model that determines the optimal timing of school tracking as the outcome of the trade-off between the advantages of specialization, which call for early tracking, and the costs of early selection, which call instead for later tracking. The optimal tracking time is the time that maximizes total output net of schooling costs. We calibrate the model for Germany and study how relative demand shifts toward more general skills and changes in the (exogenous) rate of technical progress affect the optimal tracking time as well as the allocation of students to schools.

Our simulations show that these exogenous changes increase the relative share of graduates from general schools, in line with the existing evidence on academic drift in German secondary schools, and induce an anticipation of the tracking time by close to 23 percentage points with respect to the baseline value, in sharp contrast with the observed delay taking place in German schools since 1970. We interpret the contrast between simulations and reality as evidence that actual policies have deviated from efficiency considerations, perhaps because of distributional concerns.

While our chapter focuses on efficiency, it also has implications for the relationship between schools and equal opportunity. It is often the case that students are sorted into different school tracks on the basis of their measured ability, which depends both on natural talent and on parental background. If individuals with a more privileged family background have higher opportunities to be allocated to the "better" track, the choice of the tracking time is not merely an issue of efficiency.

The road map of the chapter is as follows: in section 6.2, we discuss the relationship between technical progress and school design, and in section 6.3 we outline the key trade-off between specialization, misallocation, and skill obsolescence that generates an optimal tracking time. Section 6.4 describes the general model, and section 6.5 is devoted to the calibration for Germany. Conclusions follow.

6.2   Technical Change and School Design

International differences in school design have recently been associated in the economic literature to differences in economic performance. Krueger and Kuman (2004), for instance, have argued that the emphasis placed by Europe on specialized, vocational education may reduce the rate of technological adoption and lead to slower economic growth than in the United States, where the schooling system provides more general and comprehensive education. The broad idea is that general education is more suitable to induce (directed) technical change (see Acemoglu 2000). Since general education is more flexible and versatile, it also encourages organizational change and the adoption of high-performance holistic organizations in production (see Lindbeck and Snower 2000; Aghion, Caroli, and Penalosa 1999).

This literature looks at the effects of school design on technical and organizational change. It is natural to ask, however, whether and how these changes affect in turn endogenous school design. The timing of tracking has changed in several European countries after World War II. In the United Kingdom, there has been a shift in the mid-1960s from selection at 11 to selection at 16 (see Heath and Chieng 1998). In Germany, where tracking by ability starts relatively early, reforms in the 1970s have increased compulsory education from eight to nine years, in an effort to make the system more comprehensive (see Muller, Steinmann, and Ell 1998). In France, direct orientation to apprenticeships after two years of lower secondary school was abolished in the 1980s (Goux and Maurin 1998). All these reforms have gone in the direction of delaying tracking. Moreover, the fraction of the population in vocational secondary education compared to that in general secondary education has declined monotonically in most of postwar Europe (Bertocchi and Spagat 2003).

Technical progress leads to skill depreciation, and the degree of obsolescence is likely to be higher where skills are more specialized and tied to a specific set of techniques. While skills learnt in vocational schools can be easily transformed into the corresponding occupations in the labor market, they are less flexible and transferable than general skills (Shavit and Muller 1998). As argued by Aghion, Caroli, and Penalosa (1999, 1651), organizational change is skill biased, and nonhierarchical firms "rely on direct, horizontal communication among workers and on task diversification as opposed to specialization. They hence require multi-skilled agents, who can both perform varied tasks and learn from other agents' activities."

One implication of such organizational change is the relative demand shift toward more general and versatile skills (*upskilling*), which are better provided by general education.

6.3   The Trade-off between Specialization, Misallocation, and Skill Obsolescence

School tracking is associated to selection, and the key factor in the selection process is perceived ability.[2] Since ability at the time of the test depends both on nature and on nurture, pupils from better-educated households have, ceteris paribus, more opportunities to pass the test and be selected for the "best" track. Moreover, better-educated households tend to value the investment in education more highly and also do not face the liquidity constraints that could hamper investment (see Dustmann 2004).

In a world of imperfect information, selection conveys information about individual ability to the labor market. Tracking also leads to ability grouping, with higher-achieving students being separated from lower-achieving students. It is still an open issue whether separating students into different tracks leads to better educational outcomes than mixing students of different ability. Epple, Newlon, and Romano (2002) briefly review the empirical literature and conclude that, relative to the outcomes of mixed classes, students assigned to low tracks are hurt by tracking while those assigned to high tracks gain. Our model is consistent with these findings.

As shown by Hoxby (2001), peer effects have distributional effects, but no efficiency implications if individual outcomes, such as human capital, are affected linearly by the mean of peers' outcomes in that variable. Efficiency implications can be drawn only from models that are either nonlinear in peers' mean achievement or in which other moments of the peer distribution matter (Hoxby 2001, 2; see also Epple and Romano 1998).

In our model, the presence of nonlinear peer effects implies that tracking has a positive "specialization" effect.[3] In the absence of a countervailing factor, however, positive specialization would lead to immediate tracking. We identify one factor by noticing that the allocation of individuals to tracks is affected by noise in the selection process and that the relative importance of noise is higher the earlier the selection takes place. Misallocation owing to imperfect testing reduces both the quality of the signal offered by schools to the labor market and the peer effects in human-capital formation. As remarked by Judson (1998, 340; see also Allen and Barnsley 1993), "innate ability is measured with difficulty and with increasing clarity as education proceeds. Any test given will be a noisy signal, and the less education the person has had, the noisier the signal will be. Before primary school it is very difficult to discern levels of talent, but identification of talent is easier after a few years of primary school, still easier after high school, and so on."

The earlier selection is carried out, the higher the risk of misallocating individuals to the wrong track. We call this the *noise effect* of tracking. The trade-off between the positive specialization and negative noise effect generates an endogenous optimal tracking time.

Another countervailing factor is skill obsolescence. Skills accumulated in a system with early tracking are more specific than those acquired in a system with late tracking, and they depreciate faster in the presence of technical change.

The importance of ability tracking for school performance has already been studied in the literature, most recently by Epple, Newlon, and Romano (2002). These authors, however, ignore noise in the selection process and treat both the threshold ability required for the allocation of pupils to tracks and the tracking time as exogenous parameters. Allocation of individuals to tracks can be carried out either by prices (tuition fees) or by quantitative restrictions, such as tests. Selection by test implies that individuals with a test score higher than the selected threshold are admitted to the high track and individuals with a lower score are allocated to the low track. Fernandez (1998) shows that allocation by tests should be preferred to allocation by prices when individuals are liquidity constrained. In the absence of liquidity constraints, however, the two selection methods are equivalent.

In spite of the very simple structure of the model, its stochastic nature implies that we can offer relatively few analytical results. Therefore, we resort to calibration and focus on the German institutional setup to study how the optimal tracking time and the relative share of graduates from general schools vary with changes in the size of the peer effect, the noise in the selection process, the (exogenous) rate of technical progress, and the upskilling of labor from less to more general and versatile tasks.

6.4 The Model

6.4.1 Setup

Consider a simplified economy with an exogenous number of individuals and job slots. Each individual lives for two periods. In the first (preliminary) period she goes to school, and in the second period she is matched to a job slot supplied by a firm. The exogenous number of individuals is normalized to 1. There are a given number of public schools M, each with one teacher and $\frac{1}{M}$ students. The monetary cost Z of running each school does not vary with school design. In the rest of the chapter, we normalize this cost to zero for simplicity.

The assumption of public schools is quite accurate for most countries if we focus on primary to upper secondary education but is less accurate if we consider also tertiary education. While our model can be extended to include college, we prefer to focus our attention on primary and secondary education. In many developed countries, this coincides with compulsory education, which justifies our assumption of an exogenous length of time spent at school.

Let the period spent at school be equal to one unit, and define $\tau \in [0, 1]$ as the time when students are separated into tracks, or tracking time. Then τ is also the period spent in a comprehensive school, and $(1 - \tau)$ is the time spent in a stratified school. While a comprehensive school provides the same curriculum to everybody, in a stratified school students are allocated to two different tracks, H (high ability) and L (low ability), each with its own specialized curriculum. In the United States, the H and L tracks are segregated classes that coexist within the same comprehensive school. In most European countries, they correspond to general (academic) and vocational education.

When $\tau = 1$, all M schools are comprehensive for the entire period of time. When $\tau < 1$, the M schools are comprehensive for time length τ and are divided into MX classes or schools in the L track and $M(1 - X)$ classes in the H track for the rest of the time, where X is the percentage of pupils going to L tracks. By assumption, there is no further stratification within each type of school.

Risk-neutral individuals care only about (expected) wages and differ in their endowed ability, which cannot be observed by firms when recruitment takes place. While we can think of several types of ability, in this chapter we focus only on cognitive ability and assume that individuals differ in their endowment of this single type.[4] These differences reflect both nature and nurture. Conditional on nature, individuals with a better parental background (more educated parents, higher wealth) are likely to have better nurture and higher ability. Therefore, the observed distribution of ability reflects in part the inequality of opportunities.

Firms know only the school the individual has graduated from. Since ability cannot be observed, each individual is paid her expected productivity.[5] In this environment, firms make zero expected profits, and the efficient social outcome is produced by the school design, which maximizes total output net of schooling costs.[6]

When individual utility depends only on expected wages after school and admission to H and L schools is free and left to individual choice, all individuals should enroll in track H if the wage of graduates from these tracks is expected to be higher than the wage gained by L graduates. We assume that allocation of students to tracks is not based on free choice but on a noisy ability test: performance in the test higher than or equal to the required standard qualifies the candidate for the higher-ability track, and lower performance implies assignment to the lower-ability track. In practice, selection by test needs not be an entry exam but can be based on the quality of the leaving certificate from the previous school, on orientation and evaluation by teachers, and on selection during the first year after entry.

6.4.2 Schools

Using small letters for logarithms, let true ability $A \in (0, \infty)$ be log-normally distributed across individuals, and define $\alpha = ln(A) \sim N(0, 1)$. Let observed log ability θ when the test takes place be related to true log ability by

$$\theta = \alpha + \varepsilon, \tag{6.1}$$

where ε is an exogenous shock independent of α and normally distributed with mean zero and variance b^2. We capture the idea that the noise of the test increases the earlier the test is taken by letting

$$b = \mu(1 - \tau), \tag{6.2}$$

where μ is a suitable parameter.[7] It follows that observed ability is normally distributed with zero mean and variance $1 + b^2$. Since α and ε are both normally distributed, the conditional density ψ of α given θ is

$$\psi(\alpha \mid \theta) = \left(\frac{2\pi b^2}{1 + b^2} \right)^{-1/2} \exp \left[\frac{-\frac{1}{2} \left(\alpha - \frac{\theta}{1+b^2} \right)^2}{\frac{b^2}{1+b^2}} \right], \tag{6.3}$$

and the conditional mean is a linear function of observed ability θ (see Anderson and Moore 1979):

$$E[\alpha \mid \theta] = \frac{\theta}{1 + b^2}. \tag{6.4}$$

If observed log ability is positive, expected log true ability is higher the lower the variance of the noise. If, on the other hand, observed log ability is negative, expected log true ability falls as the variance of the noise declines.

If the government sets the test standard θ^* to allocate individuals to tracks, the expected log true ability of individuals is $E[\alpha \mid \theta \geq \theta^*]$ and $E[\alpha \mid \theta < \theta^*]$ in H and L tracks, respectively. Using the law of iterated projections, we get

$$E[\alpha \mid \theta \geq \theta^*] = E[E[\alpha \mid \theta] \mid \theta \geq \theta^*] = \frac{1}{1 + b^2} \frac{\int_{\theta^*} \theta \phi(\theta)\, d\theta}{1 - \Phi(\theta^*)}$$

$$= \frac{1}{1 + b^2} E[\theta \mid \theta \geq \theta^*] = m_h \tag{6.5}$$

and

$$E[\alpha \mid \theta < \theta^*] = E[E[\alpha \mid \theta] \mid \theta < \theta^*] = \frac{1}{1+b^2} E[\theta \mid \theta < \theta^*] = m_l. \qquad (6.6)$$

Since the unconditional mean of α is equal to zero by assumption, m_h and m_l are positive and negative, respectively. We establish the following remark:

Remark 6.1   The expected log true ability of pupils in H and L tracks is increasing in the threshold θ^*.

Proof   See section 6.7, appendix.

An increase in the selection standard θ^* eliminates from H tracks individuals in the lowest observed-ability group, who are allocated to L tracks, where they belong to the highest observed-ability group (see Betts 1998). Therefore, expected conditional observed ability of either group increases. Since expected conditional true ability increases with expected conditional observed ability, the former increases as well for both groups.

Each school combines individual ability with the effectiveness of teaching to produce human capital. Since by assumption the number and quality of schools and teachers are given, we posit that effectiveness varies with the average ability of the class (*peer effect*).[8] The abler the class, the more effective is instruction provided by a teacher of given quality. If an individual spends all of her first period in a comprehensive school ($\tau = 1$), her human capital at the end of the period is

$$H_c = A \exp[\beta E(\alpha)], \qquad (6.7)$$

where $\exp \beta E(\alpha)$ is the peer effect. In the selected specification, peer effects are convex, and their impact on individual human capital is higher for abler individuals. Therefore, winners in the H track win more than losers in the L track lose, and there are average gains from tracking. The (log) human capital accumulated in this type of schools is

$$h_c = \beta E(\alpha) + \alpha = \alpha. \qquad (6.8)$$

Next, consider schools stratified into tracks. Pupils in H tracks have an observed ability θ higher than θ^*. If they spend all their time in such tracks, their log individual human capital is

$$h_h = \beta E[\alpha \mid \theta \geq \theta^*] + \alpha = \beta m_h + \alpha > \alpha. \qquad (6.9)$$

Similarly, for L tracks we have

$$h_l = \beta E[\alpha \mid \theta < \theta^*] + \alpha = \beta m_l + \alpha < \alpha. \tag{6.10}$$

Notice that $h_h > h_c > h_l$. Therefore, an implication of tracking is that the human capital of high-ability students increases, while the expected human capital of low-ability students falls with respect to no tracking. This feature of the model is consistent with the existing empirical literature reviewed in the introduction.

Students spend an initial proportion τ of their time at school in mixed-ability classes and the complementary proportion $(1 - \tau)$ in stratified schools composed of two tracks. The individual log human capital at the end of the schooling period is

$$h_H = \tau h_c + (1 - \tau)h_h = \alpha + (1 - \tau)\beta m_h \tag{6.11}$$

if the student is assigned to the H track and likewise for students allocated to L tracks, except from the fact that we allow skills accumulated in the lower-ability track to depreciate at the rate g, where g is the rate of exogenous technical progress.[9]

The asymmetric obsolescence effects of technical progress can be justified as follows. First, ability lessens the adverse effect of technological change (see Galor and Moav 2000). Second, if we interpret skills developed in the L tracks as vocational, these skills are less flexible and adjustable than the general skills developed in the H track, and they depreciate faster. In the second period, the human capital of an individual who has enrolled in an L track is

$$H_L = H_c^\tau [H_l(1 - \delta g)]^{1-\tau},$$

where δ is a suitable parameter. Using logs and the approximation $ln(1 - x) \cong -x$,[10] we obtain

$$h_L = [\alpha + (1 - \tau)\beta m_l] - (1 - \tau)\delta g. \tag{6.12}$$

In the second period, graduates enter the labor market and are hired by firms, which observe the school type (the same type if schools are fully comprehensive, H or L type if schools are divided into tracks at some point in time) and infer ability from the observed type. Suppose that the graduate has spent all her education in a comprehensive school ($\tau = 1$). In this case, her expected human capital is

$$Eh_c = E(\alpha) = 0. \tag{6.13}$$

If the graduate has spent part of her time in a comprehensive school and part in an H track, her expected human capital is

$$Eh_H = E(h_H \mid \theta \geq \theta^*) = (1 - \tau)\beta m_h + E(\alpha \mid \theta \geq \theta^*)$$

$$= [1 + (1 - \tau)\beta]m_h \qquad\qquad (6.14)$$

because ability is time invariant and firms know that the graduate must have measured ability higher than θ^* to qualify for the H track. Similarly, for graduates of L tracks we have[11]

$$Eh_L = [1 + (1 - \tau)\beta]m_l - (1 - \tau)\delta g. \qquad\qquad (6.15)$$

Expected log human capital in either track varies with tracking time. Differentiation of (6.14) with respect to τ yields

$$\frac{\partial Eh_H}{\partial \tau} = -\beta m_h + [1 + (1 - \tau)\beta]\frac{2b\mu}{1 + b^2}m_h$$

$$- [1 + (1 - \tau)\beta]\frac{\mu}{1 + b^2}\frac{\partial E(\theta \mid \theta \geq \theta^*)}{\partial b}. \qquad (6.16)$$

Later tracking reduces the expected human capital of the high-ability group because students in this group spend less time together and have fewer opportunities to enjoy the positive peer effect. On the other hand, later tracking reduces the noise in the selection process, which positively affects human capital (second term on the right-hand side). Finally, later tracking also alters the conditional distribution of observed ability, with uncertain effects on expected human capital. Similarly, differentiation of (6.15) yields

$$\frac{\partial Eh_L}{\partial \tau} = -\beta m_l + [1 + (1 - \tau)\beta]\frac{2b\mu}{1 + b^2}m_l$$

$$- [1 + (1 - \tau)\beta]\frac{\mu}{1 + b^2}\frac{\partial E(\theta \mid \theta < \theta^*)}{\partial b} + \delta g. \qquad (6.17)$$

In the case of lower-ability students, later tracking reduces the negative peer effects ($m_l < 0$), with a positive effect on expected human capital.

6.4.3   Firms

The economy is populated by a given number of identical firms, which produce output by using two types of jobs or tasks, a G task and a V task. G tasks are general and require versatility and high ability. V tasks, on the other hand, are narrowly defined, vocational, and can be filled by less talented individuals. In the absence of tracking, both tasks can be filled indifferently by all graduates. With tracking, however, specialization makes graduates of H tracks more suitable for G tasks and graduates of L tracks a better match for V tasks. Therefore, tracking entails both the creation of different peer groups and specialized education.[12] For convenience, we normalize to 1 the number of firms. The Cobb-Douglas production technology is given by

$$y = a + \lambda(n_G + Eh_H) + (1 - \lambda)(n_V + Eh_L), \tag{6.18}$$

where a is the log of the technical level, y is log real output, $\lambda \in (0, 1)$, and n_G and n_V are the log of the number of employees in G and V tasks. Profit maximization yields

$$w_G = \ln \lambda + y - n_G; \quad w_V = \ln(1 - \lambda) + y - n_V, \tag{6.19}$$

where w is the log wage rate. Relative wages in this economy satisfy the following condition:

$$w_G - w_V = \ln \frac{\lambda}{(1 - \lambda)} + n_V - n_G. \tag{6.20}$$

Following Katz and Murphy (1992), $\ln \frac{\lambda}{(1-\lambda)}$ measures relative demand shifts in log quantity units, or upskilling. A demand shift toward more general tasks (a higher value of λ) can be met by an increase in relative wages, by an increase in the relative supply of general skills, or by a combination of both. Relative supply depends on the selection threshold θ^* and on the optimal timing τ, which are set by the government to maximize net output.

Figure 6.1 illustrates the structure of the model and divides the timing into school time and labor-market time. The shaded area corresponds to the time spent in a comprehensive school. The remaining time is spent in one of the two tracks, and each track leads to a job type in the labor market.[13]

6.4.4 The Optimal Policy
When schools are comprehensive ($\tau = 1$), graduates have the same expected human capital and can fill indifferently either task. Since perfect competition in the labor market guarantees that $w_G - w_V = 0$, relative employment is simply

$$n_G - n_V = \ln \frac{\lambda}{(1 - \lambda)}. \tag{6.21}$$

Labor supply is defined by

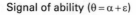

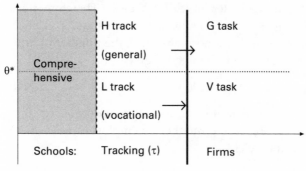

Figure 6.1
The structure of the model

$$ln(N_G + N_V) = 0. \tag{6.22}$$

Therefore, $n_G = ln\,\lambda$ and log output y_c (where the subscript c is for comprehensive) is

$$y_c = y = a + \lambda\,ln\,\lambda + (1 - \lambda)\,ln(1 - \lambda). \tag{6.23}$$

With selection, there are $1 - \Phi(\theta^*)$ graduates from the H track and $\Phi(\theta^*)$ graduates from the L track, and log output y_s (where the subscript s is for stratified) can be rewritten as

$$y_s \equiv \chi(\tau, \theta^*, \lambda, g, \mu, \delta)$$
$$= a + \lambda\,ln[1 - \Phi(\theta^*)] + (1 - \lambda)\,ln\,\Phi(\theta^*)$$
$$+ [1 + (1 - \tau)\beta][\lambda m_h + (1 - \lambda)m_l] - (1 - \lambda)(1 - \tau)\delta g. \tag{6.24}$$

The government maximizes net output by selecting the optimal values of τ and θ^*. The first-order conditions are

$$\chi_\tau(\tau, \theta^*, \lambda, g, \mu, \delta) : -\beta[\lambda m_h + (1 - \lambda)m_l] + (1 - \lambda)\delta g$$
$$+ [1 + (1 - \tau)\beta]\frac{2\mu b}{1 + b^2}[\lambda m_h + (1 - \lambda)m_l]$$
$$- [1 + (1 - \tau)\beta]\frac{\mu}{1 + b^2}\left[\lambda\frac{\partial E[\theta\,|\,\theta \geq \theta^*]}{\partial b} + (1 - \lambda)\frac{\partial E[\theta\,|\,\theta < \theta^*]}{\partial b}\right]$$
$$+ \left[\frac{1 - \lambda}{\Phi} - \frac{\lambda}{1 - \Phi}\right]\frac{\mu b\Phi}{1 + b^2}\left(1 - \frac{E[\theta^2\,|\,\theta < \theta^*]}{1 + b^2}\right) = 0 \tag{6.25}$$

$$\chi_{\theta^*}(\tau, \theta^*, \lambda, g, \mu, \delta) : -\frac{\lambda\phi}{1-\Phi} + \frac{(1-\lambda)\phi}{\Phi}$$

$$+ [1 + (1-\tau)\beta]\left[\lambda\frac{\partial m_h}{\partial \theta^*} + (1-\lambda)\frac{\partial m_l}{\partial \theta^*}\right] = 0. \qquad (6.26)$$

We establish

Lemma 6.1   The threshold $\theta^* \in (-\infty, \infty)$ is finite.

Proof   Since $N_G = 1 - \Phi(\theta^*)$ and $N_V = \Phi(\theta^*)$, the threshold needs to be a finite number to guarantee positive output.

Because θ^* is finite, remark 6.1 can be used in (6.26) to yield

$$-\frac{\lambda\phi}{1-\Phi} + \frac{(1-\lambda)\phi}{\Phi} < 0.$$

This condition can be rewritten as

$$\frac{\lambda}{(1-\lambda)} > \frac{1-\Phi}{\Phi} = \frac{N_G}{N_V}, \qquad (6.27)$$

which implies from (6.20) that $w_G - w_V > 0$. Therefore, with tracking and selection, the graduates of H tracks (which have higher average observed and true ability) are paid in equilibrium a higher wage than the graduates of L tracks. We use this result to establish the following lemma:

Lemma 6.2 $[\lambda m_h + (1-\lambda)m_l]$ is positive.

Proof   See section 6.7, appendix.

This lemma implies that, at the optimal value of the selection threshold θ^*, a linear combination of the expected abilities of H and L graduates, with weights equal to the relative wage bill of each group, is higher than the expected ability of graduates of a comprehensive school, which is equal to zero by definition. We call this the *specialization effect* of tracking. The first-order condition with respect to τ is composed of five terms. The first term is negative and captures the fact that later tracking reduces the gains from specialization. The second term is positive because later tracking is associated with lower depreciation of vocational skills. The third term is positive because later tracking reduces the noise in the selection process. The last two terms capture the changes in the conditional distribution of θ as τ varies and can take either sign. In the absence of noise, $\mu = 0$, and (6.25) boils down to

$$-\beta\{[\lambda E[\theta \mid \theta \geq \theta^*] + (1 - \lambda)E[\theta \mid \theta < \theta^*]]\} + (1 - \lambda)\delta g = 0. \qquad (6.28)$$

Without skill depreciation, the left-hand side is negative, and optimal τ is equal to zero. In the absence of noise and depreciation, the positive effects of specialization prevail, and tracking starts from the beginning of the schooling period. On the other hand, in the absence of peer effects ($\beta = 0$), the left-hand side is positive, and the optimal tracking time is $\tau = 1$ (no tracks). We can establish the following.

Proposition 6.1   Tracking is optimal if the depreciation effect is small.

Proof   See section 6.7, appendix.[14]

Corollary 6.1   If tracking is optimal, $\tau^* \in (0, 1)$ when the noise parameter μ is sufficiently large.

Proof   See section 6.7, appendix.

Proposition 6.2   When an interior solution (τ, θ^*) exists, the effect of an acceleration in the rate of TFP growth g on the optimal tracking time τ is positive.

Proof   See section 6.7, appendix.

Proposition 6.1 is key because it establishes conditions for an efficient solution with $\tau < 1$ to exist. Corollary 6.1 shows that, if the noise of the test is large enough and proposition 6.1 holds, an internal solution for tracking time τ exists. An acceleration of growth increases the depreciation of skills provided by vocational schools. The optimal government response consists of delaying stratification. Unfortunately, because of the complexity of (6.25), the two propositions and the corollary are the only analytical results that can be derived from the model. Therefore, we turn to calibration and illustrate the properties of the model by focusing on the German system of early tracking.

6.5   Calibration

Stratification by ability in Germany starts at age 10, when pupils are allocated to the H track (*Gymnasium*) or to the L track (*Hauptschule* and *Realschule*). While education in the H track is general, the L track leads in most cases to vocational education and training (see Schnepf 2002). The calibration of the model requires that we assign numerical values to the parameters β, δ, and λ. Starting with β, we need to recognize that most available empirical evidence on the size of peer effects is based on U.S. data. In a recent survey of the U.S. empirical literature, Hoxby (2001) reports that the estimated value of β ranges between 0.15 and 0.4. We assume that these estimates can also be applied to Germany and take a conservative view by setting $\beta = 0.2$.[15]

Next consider parameter δ. We start from the working assumption that average working life during the second period lasts 30 years and take from Nickell and Layard (1999) the 1976 to 1992 average annual rate of total factor productivity growth in the private sector in Germany, which is equal to 0.0191. We use ECHP data for Germany[16] for the period 1994 to 2000 and identify G tasks with professionals, technicians, and clerks and V tasks with craft workers and plant and machine operators. We select male workers from ages 25 to 59 employed full time in the private sector and fit for each occupational group the following Mincerian equation:

$$\ln w = \alpha + \beta X + \gamma AGE + \eta AGE^2 + u,$$

where w is the hourly wage, X a vector of standard controls, and AGE is individual age. The fitted regression is used to predict the age wage profile at ages 29 and 59, respectively. Defining

$$Z_j^i = \bar{\gamma} AGE_j^i + \bar{\eta} AGE_j^{i2}$$

as the fitted wage for age i, $i = 29, 59$, and occupational group j, $j = H, L$, the ratio

$$\frac{\frac{Z_L^{59}}{Z_L^{29}}}{\frac{Z_H^{59}}{Z_H^{29}}} = \omega$$

can be considered as a proxy of the depreciation of L skills after 30 years in the labor market, relative to H skills. Our estimates suggest that $\omega = 0.862$. The value of δ must be such that the relative value of human capital in L tracks after 30 years of use is equal to ω. Therefore, we estimate δ by solving

$$(1 - 0.0191\delta)^{29} = 0.862,$$

which yields $\delta = 0.267$. Since one single period in the model corresponds to 30 years of working life, it is not appropriate to use in the

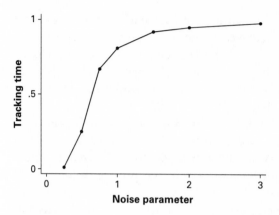

Figure 6.2
Changes in the tracking time τ as the noise parameter μ increases (with the peer-effect parameter $\beta = 0.2$)

calibrations the annual rate of productivity growth, which refers to a single year. We define the average rate of technical progress over 30 years, g_{30}, as the rate that produces in a single year of depreciation the average value of human capital over 30 years of working life and solve

$$1 - 0.267g_{30} = \frac{1 + (1 - 0.267 * 0.0191) + \cdots (1 - 0.267 * 0.0191)^{29}}{30},$$

which yields $g_{30} = 0.264$.

With a Cobb-Douglas production function, λ is the share on the total wage bill of the wages paid out to workers in G jobs. Therefore,

$$\lambda = \frac{W_G N_G}{WN}.$$

We use the 2000 wave of ECHP and estimate that the value of λ for Germany is 0.625. With these values of the key parameters in hand, we illustrate in figures 6.2 to 6.5 how the optimal tracking time τ and the optimal selection threshold θ^* adjust to variations in the peer effect β and in the noise parameter μ. In figures 6.2 and 6.3, we plot the optimal values of τ and θ^* by keeping β constant and by allowing μ to vary between 0 and 3. In figures 6.4 and 6.5, we set instead μ to 0.495, the value that would produce as an internal solution for τ equal to the observed value, and allow β to vary between 0 and 1.

Figure 6.2 shows that as μ increases from zero, the optimal value of τ also increases and converges fairly rapidly to its upper value, where

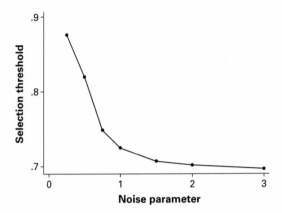

Figure 6.3
Changes in the threshold θ^* as the noise parameter μ increases (with the peer-effect parameter $\beta = 0.2$)

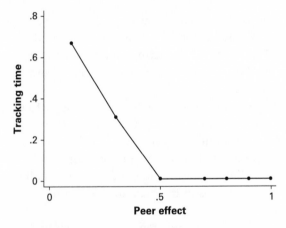

Figure 6.4
Changes in the tracking time τ as the peer-effect parameter β increases (with the noise parameter $\mu = 0.495$)

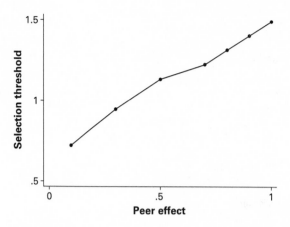

Figure 6.5
Changes in the optimal threshold θ^* as the peer-effect parameter β increases (with the noise parameter $\mu = 0.495$)

schools are fully comprehensive. Figure 6.3 shows that the increase in τ as μ rises is accompanied by a reduction in the optimal threshold θ^*. Finally, figures 6.4 and 6.5 show that an increase in the size of the peer effect, given the noise in the test, reduces the optimal tracking time and increases the selection threshold.

In particular, it takes a value of the peer effect equal at least to 0.5 to make tracking from the start optimal. These figures suggest that optimal τ and θ^* tend to move in opposite directions: later tracking is associated to less selective tests for access to H tracks and consequently to a higher share of students in these tracks. Therefore, the two policy instruments turn out to be substitutes in the maximization of total net output.

The calibration of β and λ leaves two endogenous variables τ and θ^* and an additional parameter μ that measures the relative variance of the noise in the test with respect to the variance of true talent, α. Clearly, it is difficult to pin down μ.[17] Rather than trying to do this, we assume that the actual value of τ in Germany is equal to the optimal value and solve (6.25)–(6.26) for θ^* and μ. Since tracking time is likely to be persistent and vary slowly over time, we feel that this working hypothesis is reasonable.

The actual value of τ for Germany is 0.31 and is computed as the ratio of the total years of schooling spent in a comprehensive system, before selection takes place (four years) to the total years of schooling from primary school to upper secondary education (13 years). The cor-

Table 6.1
Simulation results (percentage deviations from the baseline)

	Threshold θ^*	Tracking time τ	Human capital H track Eh_H	Human capital L track Eh_L	Employment G jobs N_G
−25% rate of technical progress g_{30}	0.70	−16.10	0.10	0.80	0
+10% demand shift parameter λ	−13.10	−12.90	−10.60	−6.50	18.10
+10% peer effect parameter β	2.80	−29.03	3.30	−0.20	−0.50
+10% noise parameter μ	−2.10	38.71	−2.80	0.50	1.40

responding value of μ turns out to be 0.495. The value of the selection threshold and the percentage of students enrolled in H tracks associated to the assigned parameters and to the actual value of τ are 0.812 and 0.221, respectively. The latter value is very close to the percentage of high school graduates from general tracks reported by the OECD for Germany in 1995 (0.23) (OECD 1997), which suggests that our calibration baseline is not far from observed values.

Next, we turn to simulations and consider the following experiments: (a) a 25 percent decline in the rate of productivity growth, a proxy of the rate of technical progress g_{30}, which corresponds to the decrease experienced by (West) Germany between the early 1980s and the late 1990s (see Gust and Marquez 2002); (b) a 10 percent increase in the relative demand shift parameter λ, a good approximation of the increase in the actual wage bill share of nonproduction workers between 1970 and 1990 (see Berman and Machin 2000); (c) a 10 percent increase in the peer effect β; (d) a 10 percent increase in the noise parameter μ. The results are reported in table 6.1.[18] The figures in the table are percentage deviations from the baseline solution described above.

The optimal tracking time τ is affected negatively by the decline in the rate of productivity growth g_{30} (as predicted by proposition 6.1) and by the relative demand shift toward more general and versatile jobs (measured by λ). More in detail, we find that a 25 percent reduction in g_{30} triggers a 16.1 percent decline in the optimal tracking time. We also find that a 10 percent increase in λ reduces tracking time by 12.9 percent. If we simulate the combined effect of g and λ on τ, we obtain that the optimal tracking time should decline by 22.6 percent.

Starting from four years of comprehensive school before selection into tracks, which corresponds to the German situation in the early 1970s, these simulations imply that the optimal tracking time should have been reduced further by the end of the century to about three years of comprehensive school to accommodate the slowdown of productivity growth and the relative demand shift toward more general and versatile jobs. In practice, however, during this period "reforms have attempted to narrow the gap between the *Hauptschule* and the other tracks through prolongation of compulsory education from eight to nine years and by introducing additional subjects into the curriculum" (Muller, Steinmann, and Ell 1998, 145). These reforms can be interpreted as a prolongation of the comprehensive period and as a delay of the tracking period.

We see two ways to reconcile our simulations with the observed trends in German school design. The most natural way is to argue that either the size of peer effects has declined or the noise in the selection process has increased, perhaps as a consequence of the substantial inflow of immigrants. As shown in table 6.1, the efficient tracking time τ is very sensitive to changes in these two parameters. The other way is to interpret the current trends as deviations from the efficient policy, driven perhaps by distributional and equity concerns.

If the observed equilibrium is a political equilibrium driven by majority voting, tracking can be delayed if the majority of students are in the vocational track. The pressure of majority could also affect the optimal selection threshold because a higher threshold improves both peer groups, lowering the human capital only of those who are forced in the lower track.[19]

Our simulations also show that the relative share of graduates from general tracks, which depends on the strictness of the selection criterion θ^*, is marginally affected by changes in g_{30} but varies significantly with changes in λ. In particular, a 10 percent increase in λ is expected to reduce significantly the admission threshold and to increase by 18.1 percent the share of H graduates. We conclude from this that the widespread academic drift, which characterizes both Germany and other developed countries, can be interpreted as the response of school design to the relative demand shift toward more general and versatile skills.[20]

Table 6.1 also reports the impact of each simulation on the expected individual human capital in each track. We find that a 10 percent increase in parameter λ leads to a significant reduction in the expected human capital associated to either track. Since upskilling increases the relative size of the academic track, individuals with relatively lower ability are admitted to this track, which reduces average human capital. Similarly, the lower track loses the individuals with highest ability and ends up with lower average human capital. Relative wages can go either way because the higher value of λ is compensated by the increase of N_G.

6.6 Conclusions

We have presented a simple model of endogenous tracking in secondary schools. In the model, tracking has two features: the time spent in separate tracks and the relative size of each track, which depends on the difficulty of the admission test. Optimal tracking is the outcome of the trade-off between the advantages of specialization and the costs of early selection and skill obsolescence. We calibrate the model for Germany and simulate how endogenous school design should vary with the significant changes in the rate of technical progress and in the relative demand for skilled and versatile jobs that occurred in Germany during the last 20 years of the century.

Our calibrations generate the academic drift in secondary schools, observed in Germany and elsewhere, as the outcome of the upskilling process associated to technological change. They also show that the tracking time in Germany should have been anticipated because of upskilling and the slowdown in productivity growth, but this is not what has happened in Germany in the past 20 years. We speculate that either other key parameters have changed in the required direction—a reduction in the size of peer effects or an increase in the noise of the test—or that the observed policies have deviated from efficiency considerations, perhaps because of distributional concerns.

Our simple model can be best viewed as a first step in the modeling of endogenous tracking. To be simple, a model requires assumptions. Some of the assumptions used in the chapter can be removed or modified in future research. For instance, we have assumed a frictionless labor market and no uncertainty about the future allocation of general and vocational tasks. Removing these assumptions would allow us to consider the possibility of mismatch between the supply and the demand of skills and to discuss important issues such as overeducation.

Moreover, when the future is uncertain and labor-market frictions do not allow an instantaneous adjustment of demand and supply, an additional reason to delay tracking is the option value of waiting.

We have focused in the chapter on efficiency issues and have restricted attention to policies that maximize net output. It would be interesting to contrast this approach with an approach based on the concept of political equilibrium. We have speculated in the chapter that the pressure of majority voting could affect significantly both the tracking time and the selection threshold.

Finally, we have restricted attention to secondary schools and ignored college choice. The introduction of college in the model complicates things in a number of ways. First of all, we need to consider that a relevant percentage of students do not enroll in college. Second, the sequence of comprehensive and stratified education typical of compulsory education can be modified in an interesting way because students from vocational tracks can enroll in colleges providing general education and thereby reduce their specialization. We plan to consider these and other extensions of the model in future research.

6.7 Appendix

Proof of Remark 6.1

$$\frac{\partial m_h}{\partial \theta^*} = \frac{1}{1+b^2} \frac{\phi(\theta^*)}{1-\Phi(\theta^*)} \{E[\theta \mid \theta \geq \theta^*] - \theta^*\}$$

is positive because the expression within brackets is positive. Similarly,

$$\frac{\partial m_l}{\partial \theta^*} = \frac{1}{1+b^2} \frac{\phi(\theta^*)}{\Phi(\theta^*)} \{\theta^* - E[\theta \mid \theta \leq \theta^*]\}$$

is also positive.

Proof of Lemma 6.2 The expression $[\lambda m_h + (1-\lambda)m_l] > 0$ can be written as

$$\lambda \int_{\theta^*} \theta f(\theta) \, d\theta \int^{\theta^*} f(\theta) \, d\theta + (1-\lambda) \int^{\theta^*} \theta f(\theta) \, d\theta \int_{\theta^*} f(\theta) \, d\theta > 0.$$

Adding and subtracting from the left-hand side of the above expression

$$\lambda \int^{\theta^*} \theta f(\theta)\, d\theta \int^{\theta^*} f(\theta)\, d\theta$$

and using the facts that $E(\theta) = 0$ and $m_l < 0$, we can rewrite it as

$$(1 - \lambda)[1 - \Phi(\theta^*)] < \lambda \Phi(\theta^*),$$

which corresponds to (6.27) in the main text.

Proof of Proposition 6.1   Assume that $\tau \Rightarrow 1$ in the limit (no tracking). As τ converges to 1, $w_G = w_V$ and

$$\frac{\Phi(\theta^*)}{1 - \Phi(\theta^*)} = \frac{1 - \lambda}{\lambda},$$

so that (6.26) turns positive and the selection threshold increases while remaining a finite number. Next, it is convenient to rewrite

$$\lambda m_h + (1 - \lambda)m_l = \frac{E[\theta \mid \theta \le \theta^*]}{1 + b^2} \left[1 - \lambda - \lambda \frac{\Phi(\theta^*)}{1 - \Phi(\theta^*)}\right]$$

by using

$$E[\theta \mid \theta \ge \theta^*] = \frac{E(\theta) - \Phi(\theta^*)E[\theta \mid \theta \le \theta^*]}{1 - \Phi(\theta^*)}$$

and $E(\theta) = 0$. It follows that in the vicinity of $\tau = 1$ the moving average $\lambda m_h + (1 - \lambda)m_l$ is equal to zero, which makes sense in the absence of tracking. Recall that in the vicinity of $\tau = 1$, the variance b^2 tends to zero, and the distribution of observed ability θ converges to the distribution of true ability α, which is independent of b and τ. Therefore, in the vicinity of $\tau = 1$, the first-order condition (6.25) boils down to $\chi_\tau = (1 - \lambda)\delta g$. Notice that $(1 - \lambda)\delta g$ must be small for the approximation in (6.12) to be correct. Finally, write total net output in implicit form as $\chi = \chi(\tau, \theta^*(\tau))$. Then optimal timing in the vicinity of $\tau = 1$ is given by

$$\frac{\partial \chi}{\partial \tau}_{|\tau \cong 1} = \chi_\tau + \chi_{\theta^*} \frac{\partial \theta^*}{\partial \tau}.$$

The first element on the left-hand side is positive but small. The second element has two parts. The first part is positive because of (6.26) and

$$\frac{\Phi(\theta^*)}{1 - \Phi(\theta^*)} = \frac{1 - \lambda}{\lambda}.$$

The second part is negative because

$$\chi_{\theta^*} = -\beta\left[\lambda\frac{\partial m_h}{\partial\theta^*} + (1-\lambda)\frac{\partial m_l}{\partial\theta^*}\right].$$

Since χ_τ is positive but small and $\chi_{\theta^*}\frac{\partial\theta^*}{\partial\tau}$ is negative, we can have that

$$\frac{\partial\chi}{\partial\tau}\bigg|_{\tau\cong 1} < 0,$$

which guarantees that tracking ($\tau < 1$) can be optimal.

Proof of Corollary 6.1 We need to show that

$$\frac{\partial\chi}{\partial\tau}\bigg|_{\tau\cong 0} = \chi_\tau + \chi_{\theta^*}\frac{\partial\theta^*}{\partial\tau} > 0$$

in the vicinity of $\tau = 0$. We start by noticing that

$$\chi_\tau(\tau,\theta^*)|_{\tau=0} = (1-\lambda)\delta g + \frac{(2+\beta)\mu^2 - \beta}{1+\mu^2}[\lambda m_h + (1-\lambda)m_l]$$

$$- [1+\beta]\frac{\mu}{1+\mu^2}\left[\lambda\frac{\partial E[\theta\,|\,\theta\geq\theta^*]}{\partial b} + (1-\lambda)\frac{\partial E[\theta\,|\,\theta<\theta^*]}{\partial b}\right]$$

$$+ \left[\frac{1-\lambda}{\Phi} - \frac{\lambda}{1-\Phi}\right]\frac{\mu^2\Phi}{1+\mu^2}\left(1 - \frac{E[\theta^2\,|\,\theta<\theta^*]}{1+\mu^2}\right)$$

because $b|_{\tau\cong 0} = \mu$. If we allow μ to be large enough, the above expression tends to

$$\chi_\tau(\tau,\theta^*)|_{\tau\cong 0} = (1-\lambda)\delta g + (2+\beta)[\lambda m_h + (1-\lambda)m_l] + \left[\frac{1-\lambda}{\Phi} - \frac{\lambda}{1-\Phi}\right]\Phi.$$

Since when μ is large the second line in (6.26) vanishes,

$$\left[\frac{1-\lambda}{\Phi} - \frac{\lambda}{1-\Phi}\right]\Phi$$

tends to zero, and the above expression becomes positive. Similarly, χ_{θ^*} goes to zero as μ becomes large. Therefore,

$$\frac{\partial\chi}{\partial\tau}\bigg|_{\tau\cong 0} > 0$$

when the noise of the test is sufficiently large.

Proof of Proposition 6.2 Total differentiation of the first-order conditions when μ is constant yields

$$\chi_{\tau\tau}\partial\tau + \chi_{\tau\theta^*}\partial\theta^* = -\chi_{\tau g}\partial g - \chi_{\tau\lambda}\partial\lambda$$

$$\chi_{\theta^*\tau}\partial\tau + \chi_{\theta^*\theta^*}\partial\theta^* = -\chi_{\theta^*g}\partial g - \chi_{\theta^*\lambda}\partial\lambda$$

so that by Cramer's rule we obtain

$$\frac{\partial\tau}{\partial g} = \frac{-\chi_{\tau g}\chi_{\theta^*\theta^*} + \chi_{\theta^*g}\chi_{\tau\theta^*}}{\varDelta},$$

where

$$\varDelta = \chi_{\tau\tau}\chi_{\theta^*\theta^*} - \chi_{\tau\theta^*}\chi_{\theta^*\tau}$$

is positive if the second-order conditions for a maximum hold. The second-order conditions also imply that $\chi_{\tau\tau} < 0$ and $\chi_{\theta^*\theta^*} < 0$. Moreover, $\chi_{\theta^*g} = 0$ and $\chi_{\tau g} > 0$, which guarantee the result.

Acknowledgments

We are grateful to the editors, two anonymous referees, Gianni De Fraja, Kyota Eguchi, Fumio Hayashi, Charlotte Lauer, Paolo Manasse and the audiences in Milan, Kyoto, Rome (Tor Vergata), and Tokyo and at the CESifo/Harvard PEPG Conference on the economics of education in Munich for comments and suggestions. A special thanks to Richard Romano for his very constructive comments and for providing a detailed proof of proposition 6.1. The usual disclaimer applies.

Notes

1. Vocational education is directly related to a specific occupation, with a substantial part of the curriculum devoted to learning practical skills to be used immediately after graduation. General education has no immediate connection with any occupation but provides basic knowledge that can be used to learn different occupations (see Bertocchi and Spagat 2003).

2. In Germany, "the decision about school track is taken by both parents and the local educational authorities...but children's measured ability remains the most important factor determining the selection process. This takes the form of a primary school recommendation for a secondary school track, generally based on a pupil's marks in the core subjects of German and mathematics" (Schnepf 2002, 8).

3. Specialization does not require peer effects. An alternative route is to assume that the productivity of schooling is higher in more homogeneous classes (see Bedard 1997).

4. See Brunello and Giannini (2004a, 2004b) for models with two ability types.

5. This assumption simplifies the model considerably. In principle, firms could learn more about individual ability by using recruitment tests. Bishop (1992) argues that in the United States such tests are not widely implemented because of a legal environment that discourages potential discriminatory practices.

6. This design also maximizes a utilitarian welfare function.

7. The specification (6.2) should be considered as a convenient linearization of the relationship between the size of the noise and the time when selection occurs. The true relationship need not be linear.

8. Zimmer and Toma (2000); Hoxby (2001); Zimmermann (2003). Hanushek et al. (2003) is a nonexhaustive list of recent contributions on peer effects.

9. Since we are only concerned with the relative effect of technical change on vocational and general skills, we find it convenient to normalize the obsolescence of general skills to zero.

10. This approximation is reasonable since δg is small.

11. Casual observation of schooling around the world suggests that primary education and often lower secondary education are comprehensive, with tracking starting later on. In principle, however, we could have tracking from the start followed by a period of comprehensive schooling. Suppose, for instance, that tracking lasts for the period $(1 - \tau)$, followed by comprehensive schooling for the remaining period τ. Assuming that firms have information on the entire school curriculum, expected human capital would be as in (6.14) and (6.15), and so would be depreciation. The only key difference between tracking first and tracking later is that noise and misallocation in selection are higher when tracking starts earlier on.

12. While most theoretical contributions on tracking emphasize peer effects, our contribution is the first to introduce the combination of peer effects and specialized education.

13. We thank Kyota Eguchi for providing the figure.

14. We are indebted to Richard Romano for suggesting the proposition and especially for providing a proof.

15. As a caveat, we notice that there are empirical studies suggesting that there are no peer effects (see, for instance, Hanushek, Kain, and Rivkin 2002).

16. The ECHP data (release 2003) are available at the Department of Economics, University of Padova, contract 4/99.

17. One possibility is to use the actual share of students who move from one track to another. In principle, the higher this share the higher the noise in the allocation test. As shown by Schnepf (2002), however, the German system is fairly rigid, and only a small proportion of students switch tracks—with many misallocated individuals remaining in the assigned track.

18. In each simulation, we solve explicitly for θ^* and perform a detailed grid search for τ to find the pair that maximizes total net output.

19. We are grateful to Richard Romano for suggesting these points to us.

20. Academic drift is discussed in detail by Green, Wolf, and Leney (1999).

References

Acemoglu, D. (2000). "Technical Change, Inequality and the Labor Market." Working Paper No. 7800, National Bureau for Economic Research.

Aghion, P., E. Caroli, and G. Penalosa. (1999). "Inequality and Economic Growth: The Perspective of the New Growth Theories." *Journal of Economic Literature* 37(4): 1615–1660.

Allen, J., and R. Barnsley. (1993). "Streaming and Tiers: The Interaction of Ability, Maturity and Training in Systems with Age Dependent Recursive Selection." *Journal of Human Resources* 28(3): 649–659.

Anderson, B., and J. Moore. (1979). *Optimal Filtering*. Englewood Cliffs, NJ: Prentice-Hall.

Bedard, K. (1997). "Educational Streaming, Occupational Choices and the Distribution of Wages." Mimeo, McMaster University.

Berman, E., and S. Machin. (2000). "Skill-Biased Technology Transfer around the World." *Oxford Review of Economic Policy* 16(3): 12–22.

Bertocchi, G., and M. Spagat. (2003). "The Evolution of Modern Education Systems." *Journal of Development Economics* 73: 559–582.

Betts, J. (1998). "The Impact of Educational Standards on the Level and Distribution of Earnings." *American Economic Review* 88(1): 266–275.

Bishop, J. (1992). "The Impact of Academic Competencies on Wages, Unemployment and Job Turnover." *Carnegie Rochester Conference Series on Public Policy* 37: 127–194.

Brunello, G., and M. Giannini. (2004a). "Selective Schools." *Bulletin of Economic Research* 56(3): 207–226.

Brunello, G., and M. Giannini. (2004b). "Stratified or Comprehensive? The Economic Efficiency of School Design." *Scottish Journal of Political Economy* 51(2): 173–194.

Dustmann, C. (2004). "Parental Background, Secondary School Track Choice, and Wages." *Oxford Economic Papers* 56(2): 209–230.

Epple, D., and R. Romano. (1998). "Competition between Private and Public Schools, Vouchers and Peer Group Effects." *American Economic Review* 88(1): 33–60.

Epple, R., E. Newlon, and R. Romano. (2002). "Ability Tracking, School Competition, and the Distribution of Educational Benefits." *Journal of Public Economics* 83(1): 1–48.

Fernandez, R. (1998). "Education and Borrowing Constraints: Tests vs. Prices." Working Paper No. 6588, National Bureau for Economic Research.

Galor, O., and O. Moav. (2000). "Ability-Biased Technological Transition, Wage Inequality, and Economic Growth." *Quarterly Journal of Economics* 115(2): 469–497.

Gamoran, A. (1987). "The Stratification of High School Learning Opportunities." *Sociology of Education* 60: 135–155.

Goux, D., and E. Maurin. (1998). "From Education to First Job: The French Case." In Y. Shavit and W. Muller (eds.), *From School to Work*. Oxford: Oxford University Press.

Green, A., A. Wolf, and T. Leney. (1999). "Convergence and Divergence in European Education and Training Systems." Bedford Way Papers, Institute of Education, University of London.

Gust, C., and J. Marquez. (2002). "International Comparisons of Productivity Growth: The Role of Information Technology and Regulatory Practice." International Finance Discussion Paper 727, Board of Governors of the Federal Reserve System.

Hanushek, E., J. Kain, J. Markman, and S. Rivkin. (2003). "Does Peer Ability Affect Student Achievement?" *Journal of Applied Econometrics* 18(5): 527–544.

Hanushek, E., J. Kain, and S. Rivkin. (2002). "New Evidence about *Brown v. Board of Education*: The Complex Effects of School Racial Composition on Achievement." Working Paper 8741, National Bureau for Economic Research.

Heath, A., and S. Y. Cheung. (1998). "Education and Occupation in Britain." In Y. Shavit and W. Muller (eds.), *From School to Work*. Oxford: Oxford University Press.

Hoxby, M. C. (2001). "Peer Effects in the Classroom: Learning from Gender and Race Variation." Working Paper 7867, National Bureau for Economic Research.

Ishida, H. (1998). "Educational Credentials and Labor Market Entry Outcomes in Japan." In Y. Shavit and W. Muller (eds.), *From School to Work*. Oxford: Oxford University Press.

Judson, R. (1998). "Economic Growth and Investment in Education: How Allocation Matters." *Journal of Economic Growth* 3(4): 337–359.

Katz, L., and K. Murphy. (1992). "Changes in Relative Wages, 1963–1987: Supply and Demand Factors." *Quarterly Journal of Economics* 107(1): 35–78.

Krueger, D., and D. Kumar. (2004). "Skill-Specific Rather Than General Education: A Reason for U.S.-Europe Growth Differences?" *Journal of Economic Growth* 9(2): 167–207.

Lindbeck, A., and D. Snower. (2000). "Multitask Learning and the Reorganization of Work." *Journal of Labor Economics* 18(3): 353–376.

Muller, W., S. Steinmann, and R. Ell. (1998). "Education and Labor Market Entry in Germany." In Y. Shavit and W. Muller (eds.), *From School to Work*. Oxford: Oxford University Press.

Nickell, S., and R. Layard. (1999). "Labor Market Institutions and Economic Performance." In O. Ashenfelter and D. Card (eds.), *Handbook of Labor Economics* (vol. 3). Amsterdam: North Holland.

Oakes, J. (1994). "Educational Matchmaking: Academic and Vocational Tracking in Comprehensive High Schools." RAND, Santa Monica, CA.

Organization for Economic Cooperation and Development. (1997). *Education at a Glance*. Paris: OECD.

Schnepf, Sylke V. (2002). "A Sorting Hat That Fails? The Transition from Primary to Secondary School in Germany." Innocenti Working Paper No. 92, UNICEF, Florence.

Shavit, Y., and W. Muller. (1998). *From School to Work*. Oxford: Oxford University Press.

Zimmer, R., and E. Toma. (2000). "Peer Effects in Private and Public Schools across Countries." *Journal of Policy Analysis and Management* 19(1): 75–92.

Zimmermann, C. (2003). "Peer Effects in Academic Outcomes: Evidence from a Natural Experiment." *Review of Economics and Statistics* 85(1): 9–23.

III

Solutions B: Refocus Resources?

7   Some U.S. Evidence on How the Distribution of Educational Outcomes Can Be Changed

Eric A. Hanushek

Distributional issues are seldom far from the minds of U.S. educational policymakers. At a minimum, information is readily available on the proportion of students who fail to achieve some level of proficiency on standardized tests. Attention to such issues has even been written into U.S. federal law with the No Child Left Behind Act of 2001. But observing differences in performance and knowing what to do about them are not the same thing. Indeed, a variety of researchers and policymakers have argued that the schools cannot be expected to have much impact on the existing distribution of educational outcomes. The theme developed here is that many discussions have confused the potential for impact with current results based on the existing organization of schools.

This chapter assesses recent evidence on schools' potential impact on both the level and pattern of student achievement. The central quantitative estimates rely on a consistent set of analyses of the Texas Schools Project that my colleagues—principally Steven Rivkin and John Kain—and I have conducted. These estimated impacts, which range across a variety of separate areas of policy concern, provide powerful evidence of the influence of schools on achievement, but the results are seldom jointly considered in contemplating policy.

The starting point of this discussion is a review of observed outcomes of U.S. schooling as they have evolved over time. Since the beginning of regular testing, focus has centered on the significant variations in student performance identified by race. Yet policy initiatives have appeared to have relatively minimal impact on the test variation.

Research has also provided somewhat disheartening findings, suggesting the limited impact of schools. The accumulated evidence has not provided much in the way of systematic findings that suggest obvious policies for the improvement of student achievement.

The goal of this work is assessing the leverage that public policy can have to change the current patterns of achievement disparities. The central focus is racial differences in achievement, although other dimensions are also considered. While the discussions are closely related to how overall performance can be improved, differences arise with distributional issues.

This discussion begins with a review of these different strands of research put into the context of a common database and school system. It is difficult to make clear statements about much of the prior discussion of factors that impact achievement because data and modeling issues become completely intertwined with the analytical results. This discussion does not attempt to provide a thorough discussion of relevant existing work—a Herculean task given the breadth and depth of research that has now developed. Instead, it focuses directly on analyses of student performance in Texas that permit a consistent evaluation of outcomes. Texas is itself interesting because it is a large and diverse state that permits a variety of detailed analyses of performance. More important, by focusing on a single state with a common methodological approach, the magnitudes of various achievement factors can be compared directly.

The analysis suggests that the common interpretation of the evidence is much too pessimistic because there are actions of schools that have considerable potential for change. Concentrating on the white-black achievement gap, the analysis suggests that improving the quality of teachers and their assignment and altering the peer composition in schools can produce noticeable changes in achievement gaps.

7.1 School Outcome Differences, Research, and Policy

Most school-policy discussions go back and forth between consideration of overall performance and consideration of the distribution of outcomes. The backdrop for this chapter—which emphasizes distributional, or equity, concerns—is what has been happening in terms of overall performance. If there is a concern about an equity-efficiency trade-off, it would be important to compare movements in one dimension with those in the other.

Figure 7.1 provides the overall performance of U.S. 17-year-olds on the National Assessment of Educational Progress (NAEP). NAEP provides a consistent national testing of a random sample of students in different subjects, so it is possible to observe any changes in perfor-

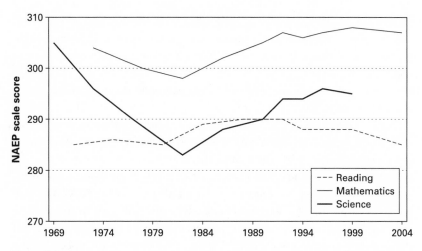

Figure 7.1
Trends in NAEP performance by subject, 17-year-olds

mance over time.[1] The remarkable thing about this picture is that performance appears roughly flat for over three decades. This constancy is particularly remarkable given the effort expended (measured in terms of resources) to improve the performance.

This flat achievement profile has been maintained in the face of substantial policy efforts to change it. Probably the most obvious policy change has been continued increases in the funding and resources of schools. The commonly discussed policy instruments—reducing pupil-teacher ratios, retaining more teachers, and having more educated teachers—have been systematically employed over the past decades. Between 1960 and 2000, U.S. pupil-teacher ratios fell by a third, teachers with a master's degree and over doubled to above 50 percent, and average experience increased (see Hanushek 2003). These actions are expensive, and real spending per pupil more than tripled between 1960 and 2000.

The simple picture thus is that school policy has not been directed primarily at overall student performance (at least as seen by outcomes). Thus, it is also useful to see what happened in terms of the distribution of outcomes. This discussion concentrates largely on racial differences in performance patterns, although income differences are also discussed below.

Over a long period, differences in school attainment by race and family background have been the subject of analysis. The large discrepancies in quantity of schooling for blacks and whites are easily seen from decennial census data (e.g., Smith and Welch 1989; Jaynes and Williams 1989; Neal 2006). Analyses of the differences in schooling also pointed to potential quality differences, arising partly from segregated schools but also from differences in local schooling outside of states that had de jure segregation of schools. The evidence on such differences centered on data about such things as credentials of teachers, length of the school year, and spending differences among the schools attended by blacks and those attended by whites.

The attention to the quality issue was elevated, however, by a massive government report, *Equality of Educational Opportunity*, commonly referred to as the "Coleman Report" after its principal author (Coleman et al. 1966). This report was mandated by the Civil Rights Act of 1964, which instructed the U.S. Office of Education to report on the lack of educational opportunity by reason of race or ethnicity. To address this issue, the Coleman research team turned attention to school outcomes through testing some 600,000 students in the United States in 1965.

The analysis vividly underscored huge differences in the achievement of students by race and background. A simple summary of the magnitude of differences comes from equating test scores to grade-level equivalents. If white twelfth graders in the urban Northeast (in 1965) were the standard for the knowledge that a twelfth grader should have, black twelfth-grade students also in the urban Northeast were achieving at the ninth-grade level, and black twelfth-grade students in the rural South were achieving at the seventh-grade level. Surprisingly, however, the magnitude of these differences never received much attention, perhaps because most of the discussion revolved around their analysis of the determinants of achievement (below).

The achievement differences have been consistent across studies. For example, when disaggregated by race, the SAT tests showed differences of approximately one standard deviation. The SAT relied on voluntary test taking for a changing group of students, however, and thus the interpretation is somewhat ambiguous.

The clearest picture nonetheless again comes from the National Assessment of Educational Progress. Figure 7.2 displays the average performance gap between whites and blacks in the different subject areas at age 17. Across each of the tests there is a very consistent pattern: racial gaps tended to shrink noticeably during the 1980s and then to be flat or to widen somewhat during the 1990s. If anything, the white-

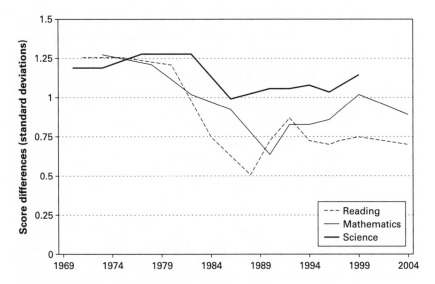

Figure 7.2
White-black differences in NAEP scores, 17-year-olds

black gap expanded some in the 1990s (even though the white-Hispanic gap, not shown, narrowed some).[2]

Much has been made of the narrowing of the black-white achievement gap including a widely cited conference book (Jencks and Phillips 1998). The one-time nature of the test-score convergence, however, was not anticipated and has received less attention than the significant closing of the gaps that occurred over a decade ago.

The resource patterns described previously were not explicitly directed at disadvantaged students or at the racial and ethnic gaps in performance. Nonetheless, throughout this period the level of performance overall did not increase (see figure 7.1), suggesting that it was not just resources going to majority students. Moreover, there was indeed a general tendency to focus money on disadvantaged students with spending on the schools of the disadvantaged (particularly inner-city schools) surpassing that others (National Center for Education Statistics 2004). During this period, the federal government also expanded its role in providing compensatory funds for disadvantaged students under the Elementary and Secondary School Act of 1965.[3] This targeted funding was also accompanied by federal support of preschool programs for disadvantaged students under the Head Start program.

The fact that substantial resources had been put into improving schools and specifically into raising the performance of disadvantaged students with no results has led to some discouragement about the efficacy of school programs to improve equity. Decades of attempts to add programs and improve the schools for disadvantaged students have shown little impact except perhaps for those in the late 1970s.

This aggregate situation was reinforced and extended by the analysis in the 1966 Coleman Report and subsequent work. The Coleman Report is commonly viewed as the first attempt to judge systematically the factors that affect student outcomes. The background is straightforward. While the U.S. Office of Education was instructed to report on inequality of educational opportunity, it did not have any common metric for assessing the importance of different resources that might enter into achievement differences. If, for example, it surveyed schools and found that one group had better science laboratories but its teachers had less experience than another group, which students were better off?

To deal with this issue, the Coleman team pursued a statistical analysis of the determinants of student performance—an introductory foray into what is now commonly referred to as *educational production function analysis*. The Coleman Report came out with the stunning conclusion that the most important factor in achievement was parents and that schools played a much less important role. In fact, in terms of impact, the ordering of influences was family, peers, and finally schools. This led to two very common statements in policy debates. First, by far the most important influence on achievement cannot be readily treated by public policy because we are not prepared to intervene in the family except in extreme circumstances. Second, schools do not make a difference.

The Coleman Report has been heavily criticized for its methodology.[4] Nonetheless, many of the basic findings of the Coleman Report have been confirmed—namely, many of the measured attributes of teachers and schools, following the approach of the report, have not been systematically related to student performance (see the review in Hanushek 2003). A wide variety of statistical analyses have failed to find descriptors of schools and teachers that are consistently associated with improved student achievement.

The interpretation of the results from the Coleman Report and subsequent work is very important and guides the remainder of this discussion. Specifically, finding that a series of measures of teacher characteristics do not systematically influence performance is not the same as finding that teachers do not matter. Since the publication of the Coleman Report, there has been a continued confusion between measurement and effectiveness.

The issue of measurement pervades all of the discussions and is the heart of the various analyses that we have undertaken. In simplest terms, accurately identifying the influences of both schools and peers is highly dependent on having satisfactory measures of the range of various influences.

The policy leverage to deal with equity and performance issues in schools resides in altering the operations of schools and, perhaps, affecting the composition or peer groups. Therefore, it is crucial that these influences are accurately identified and estimated. Specifically, much of new work on achievement differences concentrates on issues of causal relationships. One concern with much of the past research into student performance is that it has not accurately identified factors that directly affect performance but instead has obtained biased estimates owing to misspecification of the underlying models. Thus, a key element in the ensuing work is to identify reliably factors that are causally related to achievement.

7.2 Texas Schools

The analysis here is based on the experiences in the state of Texas. It is useful to understand the nature of Texas and the schools in Texas. With some 3 million students, Texas is the second-largest state.[5] White and Hispanic students each make up slightly over 40 percent of the student population, with blacks being about 15 percent. The state combines both heavily urbanized areas and very rural areas; 15 districts are in the top 100 districts of the nation in terms of student population. Its spending in 2000 was $6,288 per student, or 91 percent of the national average. Performance on the NAEP tests in both math and reading is approximately the level of the national average.

The analysis here relies on state administrative records for student performance and school characteristics. The cornerstone of the analysis of teacher quality is the unique stacked panel dataset constructed by the Texas Schools Project of the University of Texas at Dallas. The data on students, teachers, schools, and other personnel come from administrative records on individual students and teachers collected by the Texas Education Agency (TEA) and follow several entire cohorts of students. Each cohort contains some 200,000 students, and depending on the specific analysis, individual students are followed for up to five years. The student data contain a number of student, family, and program characteristics including race, ethnicity, gender, and eligibility for a free or reduced-price lunch (the measure of economic disadvantage) and Title I services. Students are also observed when they switch schools and can be followed across all public schools in Texas. Teacher and administrative personnel information include characteristics such as race/ethnicity, degrees earned, years of experience, certification test results, tenure with the current district, role, and campus.

Student performance is assessed by the Texas Assessment of Academic Skills (TAAS), which was administered each spring to eligible students enrolled in grades three through eight. These criterion-referenced tests evaluate student mastery of grade-specific subject matter in reading and mathematics.

The relative performance of students in Texas is seen from table 7.1, which provides performance by family income and race/ethnicity for the cohort of fifth-grade students in 1995. TAAS score are normalized for the state to have a mean of zero and a standard deviation of one. However, following most of the analyses employed here, students in special education or limited English proficiency (LEP) programs along

Table 7.1
Student performance in Texas by race/ethnicity/income

	Proportion of students	Mean fifth-grade TAAS math	Mean sixth-grade TAAS math
Total	1.00	0.14	0.20
By eligibility for free or reduced price lunch:			
Eligible	0.40	−0.16	−0.09
Not eligible	0.60	0.33	0.39
Race/ethnicity:			
White	0.58	0.34	0.41
Black	0.13	−0.37	−0.26
Hispanic	0.29	−0.08	−0.04

Notes: Data for fifth-grade students in 1995. Mean achievement scores are standardized to mean zero and variance one for the entire grade cohort in Texas. The data exclude special education and students identified as having limited English ability, thus yielding the nonzero mean for the population.

with students lacking information on gains over time are excluded, so that the average performance of the remaining students is 0.14. In this sample, math performance of white students exceeds that of blacks by 0.71 standard deviation and of Hispanics by 0.42. Students eligible for free or reduced-price lunch fall almost one-half standard deviation below those not eligible.

These data, following individual students over time and across schooling experiences, permit unique analyses of the determinants of achievement. The question is whether the gaps in performance are affected by public policy and, if so, by how much.

7.3 Teacher Quality

Since the Coleman Report, answers to questions about the impact of schools have been surrounded by a series of difficult methodological problems. To understand the basic nature of these, we begin with a simple description of student achievement and then proceed to consider ways of analyzing it.

Today's achievement is influenced not just by current family, school, and peer interactions but also by those of the past that establish the base for any current learning. This fundamental relationship is captured by equation (7.1) that describes achievement (A) for student i in grade G, in school s:

$$A_{iGs_t} = \underbrace{X_{iGs_t}\beta_G + S_{Gs_t}\delta_G + \bar{P}_{(-i)Gs_t}\lambda_G}_{\text{current inputs}}$$

$$+ \underbrace{\sum_{\tau=1}^{G-1} X_{i,G-\tau,s_{t-\tau}}\beta_g + \sum_{\tau=1}^{G-1} S_{i,G-\tau,s_{t-\tau}}\delta_{G-\tau} + \sum_{\tau=1}^{G-1} \bar{P}_{(-i),G-\tau,s_{t-\tau}}\lambda_{G-\tau}}_{\text{cumulative past inputs}}$$

$$+ \sum_{\tau=1}^{G} e_{i,G-\tau,s_{t-\tau}}, \tag{7.1}$$

where $\bar{P}$ measures peer behavior, X and S are vectors of relevant family background and school inputs, respectively, and the subscript $(-i)$ indicates that peer measures omit attributes of student i. Because it is useful for developing the estimation issues, this representation separates current and past influences.[6]

Clearly, simply estimating relationships between the current level of achievement and the current inputs has little chance of accurately separating the various influences on achievement. Almost certainly, current inputs are correlated with past inputs, leading to obvious problems.

The now standard approach of analyzing the growth in student achievement, as in equation (7.2), substantially reduces the problem, but not all concerns are eliminated:

$$\Delta A_{iGs_t} = A_{iGs_t} - A_{iG-1s_{t-1}}$$

$$= X_{iGs_t}\beta_G + S_{Gs_t}\delta_G + \bar{P}_{(-i)Gs_t}\lambda_G + e_{iGs_t}. \tag{7.2}$$

One still needs good measures of the inputs $(X, S, \text{and } \bar{P})$. In the presence of either mismeasured or left-out inputs, the remainder of the estimation is going to be problematic.[7]

By far the most important issue is the specification of school and teacher inputs. The approach that we have pursued is the semiparametric estimation of teacher and school effects. In a simple formulation, consider

$$\Delta A_{iGs_t} = X_{iGs_t}\beta_G + S^*_{iGs_t}\delta_G + \bar{P}_{(-i)Gs_t}\lambda_G + \sum_{j=1}^{N} t_j T_{ijG} + e_{iGs_t}, \tag{7.3}$$

where $T_{ijG} = 1$ if student i has teacher j in grade G and $= 0$ otherwise. $S^*_{iGs_t}$ represents school factors other than individual teachers. In this, we include individual teacher fixed effects, and t_j is a natural measure of teacher quality that is based on effectiveness of individual teachers in raising student achievement.[8]

This formulation circumvents problems of identifying the separate components of teachers but does not necessarily provide unbiased estimates of teacher quality. First, several selection issues related to the matching of teachers and students are important. Because of the endogeneity of community and school choice for families and of administrator decisions for classroom placement, the unmeasured influences on achievement are potentially not orthogonal to teacher quality. In particular, students with family background and other factors conducive to higher achievement will tend to seek out better schools with higher-quality teachers. Administrative decisions regarding teacher and student classroom assignments may amplify or dampen the correlations introduced by such family choices. The matching of better students with higher-quality teachers would tend to increase the positive correlations produced by family decisions, while conscious efforts to place more effective teachers with struggling students would tend to reduce them.

Second, another source of correlation between teacher quality and student circumstances results from the matching of teachers with schools. Teacher preferences for better working conditions and higher-achieving, nonpoor, nonracial/ethnic minority students in addition to higher salaries potentially introduce a positive correlation between teacher quality and family contribution to learning (Hanushek, Kain, and Rivkin 2004b). Note, however, that failure to hire the best available candidates would reduce the magnitude of this relationship (see Ballou 1996). Within districts, the assignment practices tend to give the newest teachers the lowest priority in terms of deciding where to teach.

Our general approach to separating the effects of teachers, discussed with the empirical results, is to remove student, school, and school-by-grade fixed effects. This strategy, made possible by our stacked panel data on performance, provides a very general way of dealing with the severe selection and measurement issues.

7.3.1 Potential Influence

To provide bounds for the potential impact of teacher quality, we can look at two different general estimates of the impact of schools and teachers on student performance. These use very different approaches to estimate quality differences and thus the potential for using direct policy interventions.

Method 1 is the most conservative (Rivkin, Hanushek, and Kain 2005). It focuses entirely on the within-school variation in student performance that is related to teacher-quality differences. Looking just within schools eliminates the potential bias from school selection by students and their parents. By aggregating student-performance gains across classrooms within each grade, the potential impact of purposeful classroom placement is also circumvented. Finally, individual and school fixed effects are removed—allowing for the influences of family and school factors (other than teachers) in a very general manner. It then directly estimates the variance in teacher quality by considering the variance in average student outcomes over grades in each school and the ways that this relates to teacher turnover. Because this approach assumes, for example, no changes in teacher effectiveness across years, because it ignores any between-school variance in quality, and because of its treatment of measurement error, this approach produces a lower bound on the variance of school quality.

The estimates of teacher quality for teachers of fifth, sixth, and seventh graders indicate that one standard deviation in teacher quality translates into at least a 0.10 standard deviation higher annual growth in student achievement.[9]

Method 2 relies on the direct matching of students and teachers for one large urban district in Texas (Hanushek et al. 2005). By following students and teachers over time, we can estimate the mean achievement gain of students in each classroom. These raw estimates tend to be overestimates because the variance in classroom gains will include a component of measurement error that is possibly amplified by the impact of remaining selection effects and of school organization and leadership.[10] However, by also investigating variations in teacher effectiveness within schools, it is possible to control for selection across schools by students and teachers. Direct estimates of teacher effectiveness come from extracting the common component of teacher differences across years.

Based on the learning across classrooms for teachers in grades four to eight within one large Texas district, we obtain estimates of the standard deviation of teacher quality of approximately 0.15.[11]

These differences in teacher quality ignore differences that might exist in the quality of teachers across districts. Fortunately, we have another method for developing the across-district differences in quality. Our analysis of student mobility (Hanushek, Kain, and Rivkin 2004a) identified the average gains in achievement that accrued from moving to a new district. If moves were generally predicated on seeking out improved schooling for children, the gains would indicate how teachers were distributed across schools. Our estimate of the difference in achievement (.025 standard deviation) is, however, an underestimate of the variation in average quality as many moves will reflect other purposes, such as job location or housing-quality choice.

Combining the within-school and between-school estimates of quality suggests a range of teacher-quality differences of 0.125 to 0.175 standard deviation. In other words, moving one standard deviation across the teacher-quality distribution—say, from the median to the 84th percentile—is associated with differences in annual student-achievement growth of 0.125 to 0.175 standard deviation. This provides an indication of how different teachers and schools can be in terms of annual achievement growth. For any student a run of good or bad teachers would clearly accumulate to yield substantial differences in the level of achievement—a point we return to below.

7.3.2   Current Distribution

The prior estimates characterize how much leverage exists if policies were put into place either to rearrange existing teachers or to alter the hiring of teachers. An alternative perspective is consideration of the magnitude of existing differences across race or income groups. In other words, can the distribution of existing teachers be part of the explanation for currently observed achievement differences?

The easiest summary comes from the large urban district that was employed in the prior estimation. While most discussions of differences in teacher and school quality point to differences across districts, a lower bound on differences would come from looking at just the within-district differences.

Unfortunately, our methodology does not permit reliable assessment of any teacher-quality differences between black and white students. Black students disproportionately have black teachers, so it would be interesting to look at differences in quality of black and white teachers. Yet it is difficult to distinguish between differences in preparation of students taught by black and white teachers and differences in the distribution of teachers across the district. Specifically, within our general methodology, inclusion of student fixed effects can correct for any sorting of students by teachers, but it also restricts comparisons to students who have been observed with both black and white teachers. Thus, there is inherent ambiguity about any quality among teachers by race.[12]

7.4   Peer Influences

The second avenue for schools to influence performance is through the impact of peers in the school. The neighborhood and school determine a circle of friends and acquaintances. If these other students influence attitudes and behaviors, they can directly affect schooling outcomes.

Analysis of peer influences is, nonetheless, very difficult. The difficulty in this is making sure that the observed relationship really reflects the causal impact of peers—and not just other factors that tend to coincide with differences in peers. Three general and significant issues arise in doing this analysis.

First, most studies of the effects of peers rely on data about student outcomes and peer groups that are naturally generated by schools. But these observations of schooling circumstances are the result of the choices of schools (and implicitly peers) that are made by individual families and, to some extent, by school administrators. Thinking initially of the choices of families, which often come through residential location choices, we can be quite certain that they are not random. These choices, while frequently motivated by a number of factors beyond schools, such as incomes or job locations, will reflect the preferences and opportunities facing individual families. This simple fact—that there is a purposeful element in the individual choices of families—implies that some of the outcomes for student performance may result from attributes of families that are unobserved while they enter into their decisions. For example, the parents most motivated about the schooling of their children may both provide the best family environment for learning and pay particular attention to their choices of school location. In such a case, it is frequently difficult to sort out the separate influences on student performance and to identify the impact of peers per se, particularly when parents at a school tend to make similar choices. Similarly, school administrators often make both resource decisions and classroom-composition decisions with some underlying purpose in mind. They might attempt to place their best teachers with students most in need or to group students according to an estimate of their entering abilities.

Second, the ability to distinguish the separate effects of individual and school factors from those of peers depends crucially on observing and measuring the significant inputs into student performance. The typical analysis, however, does not have perfect measures of either family background or of school inputs. For example, from the perspective of family inputs into achievement, researchers typically have just a few crude measures of background available—and often lack even basic characteristics like the education level of parents. Similarly, the details of school quality and school inputs may be known only imperfectly. On the other hand, the consistency of choice of schools across families implies that there is a strong tendency for similar parents to select a common school, and there is an additional likelihood that school quality affects peers in a similar way as the individual student. As a result, measures of peer backgrounds and performance may provide reasonably accurate surrogates for the individual's characteristics (which are measured with error). Even when peers have no true impact, for example, they may appear significant just because the peer measurements effectively provide additional information about the individual student.

Finally, one must sort out causal influences. It is not sufficient to know that, say, peer characteristics are associated with individual characteristics and performance. One needs to know whether this association results from peer attributes and interactions causing the observed differences in student performance. The reason for this is also straightforward. To ascertain the impacts of peers and of possible alterations in the composition of peers, it is necessary to capture the amount of difference that the peers cause achievement differences as opposed simply to selecting peers with certain characteristics or to residing together because of common decision-making processes. This issue of causation pervades most analyses of student performance but is most acute when analyzing peers.[13] The inherent tendency for peers with similar attributes and motivations to cluster together makes associations of performance across peers very likely and builds in difficulties in inferring the causal aspects of the various associations.[14]

These issues are introduced to underscore the uncertainty that surrounds much of the discussion of peer influences. Our approach throughout this analysis is to exploit our stacked panel data to deal with the significant measurement issues. With the stacked panel data, we can generally remove individual fixed effects, allowing for very general background and ability factors through individual specific growth rates. We also quite generally remove school-by-grade differences in curriculum, leadership, student aging patterns, and so forth—things that might be correlated with the grade level.

7.4.1   Potential Influence

7.4.1.1   Race or Ethnicity   The landmark legislatively mandated civil rights report on the *Equality of Educational Opportunity* (Coleman et al. 1966) and its offshoot (U.S. Commission on Civil Rights 1967) provide empirical evidence that racial isolation harms academic achievement. Subsequent work by Crain and Mahard (1978), Boozer, Krueger, and Wolkon (1992), and Grogger (1996) also finds that school racial composition affects academic, social, and economic outcomes. In contrast, Cook and Evans (2000) conclude that desegregation has little if any effect on mathematics and reading achievement in elementary school, and Rivkin (2000) finds no evidence that exposure to whites increased academic attainment or earnings for black men or women in the high school class of 1982. Overall, there remains considerable disagreement about the nature and magnitude of benefits of desegregation efforts, let alone about their costs (see, for example, the reviews in Crain 1970; Armor 1995; and Schofield 1995).[15]

The contrasting findings and lack of consensus concerning the importance of school racial composition emanate in large part from the difficulty of isolating the causal impact of peer characteristics.

In Hanushek, Kain, and Rivkin (2002), we estimate the impact of racial composition on blacks, whites, and Hispanics in ways consistent with the previous modeling discussion. Specifically, we adopt the very general fixed-effect approach to eliminating the bias from mismeasured other inputs.

We find small and insignificant impacts of school racial composition on whites and Hispanics, but there are strong impacts of the black composition of schools on the performance of blacks. The magnitude of the proportion black coefficient for blacks of -0.25 suggests that a 10 percentage-point reduction in percentage black would raise annual achievement growth by 0.025 standard deviations. These estimated effects apply to the growth of annual achievement and thus accumulate across grades, implying a substantial role for school racial composition in the determination of the racial achievement gap.

7.4.1.2 Socioeconomic Status (SES)

Much of the attention to socioeconomic status has concentrated on issues of neighborhood poverty and, particularly, the ways that concentrations of poverty affect individual outcomes. This discussion of neighborhood poverty emphasizes employment and crime outcomes, although some gets into schooling.[16] For example, Mayer (1991) finds that socioeconomic status (and racial composition) of the school affects high-school completion of both whites and blacks—but measures of characteristics of schools other than student-body composition are missing.

The direct analysis of achievement effects of low-income peers (Hanushek, Kain, Markman, and Rivkin 2003) does not indicate that poverty concentrations have a significant negative effect on student performance. While the income measure is relatively imprecise, these results suggest that prior estimation of the effect of poverty concentrations in schools have not uncovered causal influences.

7.4.1.3 Peer Ability The analysis of peer ability and achievement has been particularly problematic from a statistical viewpoint.[17] Students in a common classroom have many shared educational experiences, so that the quality of questions or the amount of disruption affects all of the students. From an analytical viewpoint, each student contributes to the classroom experience and is simultaneously affected by those same experiences. Moreover, common factors such as an impact of a particularly good teacher will heighten the common experiences and, if teacher quality is not well measured, lead to biases in understanding peer influences. These situations make it virtually impossible to separate out the effects of current classroom behavior on individual achievement. The import of this is largest when considering the influence of other students' ability and achievement on learning.

If we distinguish between the ability of peers and their current behavior, however, it is possible to gain some insights. By measuring peer ability by their prior achievement levels, any direct relationship of current interactions, teacher quality, and the like is broken, and it is possible to gain some insights into how the level achievement of other students influences individual performance.

Attempts to estimate peer effects on educational achievement in this way have been relatively limited. Hanushek (1972, 1992) finds no peer-achievement effects when looking at achievement growth in individual classrooms. On the other hand, Henderson, Mieszkowski, and Sauvageau (1976), Summers and Wolfe (1977), and Zimmer and Toma (2000) report positive influences of higher-achieving peers at least for some students. Summers and Wolfe (1977) find stronger effects of peers for low-income students. Consideration of ability tracking in schools likewise has yielded mixed results (e.g., see Oakes 1992; Argys, Rees, and Brewer 1996).

Our own attempt to investigate peer ability yields ambiguous results. Our initial work suggested that the level of achievement of others in the classroom has a small but significant influence on performance (Hanushek et al. 2003). It also suggested that any effect is relatively constant across achievement levels.[18] However, after developing a more detailed description of the racial composition of schools (Hanushek, Kain, and Rivkin 2002), we found no impact of student achievement. In part, our approach aggregates performance across classrooms in a grade—a necessity because of data availability but a useful approach for assessing selection effects. This aggregation may be particularly important, however, in the case of ability differences, since classroom interactions likely to be a central issue.

In sum, our best estimates do not support a strong influence of peer achievement on learning, but difficulties in the estimation leave some uncertainty.

7.4.1.4 Student Mobility Student moves are associated with lower achievement, but the more interesting impact of mobility is the externality for other students. The relevance of this is that schools with higher mobility rates tend to have a less coherent structure of instruction. The possibility that turnover affects nonmovers as well as movers is raised by many, including Alexander, Entwisle, and Dauber (1996) and Kerbow (1996), though neither study attempts to estimate the turnover externality.

Our estimation again relies on our fixed-effects strategy, removing both school-by-grade and school-by-year terms and then observing how students react to varying amounts of annual mobility (Hanushek, Kain, and Rivkin 2004a). A high mobility rate lessens the amount of learning, even for students who themselves do not move. The magnitude of the coefficient for overall proportion new students in the more complete specifications suggests that a one standard-deviation increase in the proportion of students who are new to the school (an 11 percentage-point change) would reduce achievement by over 0.013 standard deviation. While a single-year effect of this magnitude is not large, the sum total of 10 or 12 years of high turnover will have a substantial cumulative effect on learning for those students who attend high-turnover schools year after year.

7.4.2 Current Distribution

The previous section describes a variety of potential influences on student achievement and, particularly, on racial or economic divisions and provide insights into some of the divisions in performance identified at the beginning. In terms of the peer effects, outcomes for different groups can diverge when there are different reactions to peer inputs or when the distribution of peers differs even with the same impact. This section discusses how the peer factors may or may not contribute to distributional impacts.

The magnitude of the black composition effects is significant and represents both fundamental forces behind peer impacts. First, black students react to racial composition to a much greater extent than whites and Hispanics. Second, the typical black student (regardless of achievement quartile) has 30 percent more black classmates than the typical white and has 25 percent more black classmates than would be obtained with a completely even distribution of blacks across the state. This difference combines with the race-specific impact of composition such that equalizing the black distribution throughout the entire state for just grade five would be consistent with an increase in black achievement growth of 0.06 standard deviation.[19]

School mobility provides the second significant example of peer influences that have direct distributional impacts. The income difference in school turnover rates is 1.5 percentage points, and the black/white difference is 6.2 percentage points. Higher school turnover reduces annual achievement gains for lower-income students by roughly 0.005 standard deviation relative to higher-income students; blacks lose roughly 0.015 standard deviation relative to whites. Hispanics, by a similar calculation, would lose 0.005 standard deviation relative to whites because they attend schools with higher student mobility rates. These annual differences would cumulate as blacks, Hispanic, and low-income students continue to attend high-mobility schools.

On the other hand, there is not much evidence that peer ability or the socioeconomic mixing of schools has much impact. Both of these investigations are, nonetheless, subject to greater uncertainty. The only available measure of socioeconomic status is the imprecise characterization of eligibility for free or reduced-price lunch. Nonetheless, it does not appear that the distribution of students by socioeconomic status has had much impact on the currently observed distribution of student outcomes. Similarly, while there is some uncertainty about the magnitude of any peer-ability impacts, our best estimates indicate that this aspect of peers is not having much influence on the distributional issues.

7.5   School Resources and Other Inputs

While the previous discussion has concentrated on issues of teacher quality as identified by student performance, the traditional perspective on both performance and distribution has focused more on characteristics of schools and teachers. Specifically, an enormous amount of policy attention has gone into analysis of the experience, degrees, and credentialing of teachers along with the class sizes that students face.

The discussion of school inputs has been controversial (see Hanushek 2003). Input characteristics nonetheless remain an important part of the debate for three reasons. First, they are the object of much policy consideration and debate. Second, relative to the distributional discussions here, a frequent hypothesis has been that disadvantaged students, variously defined by income or race, are more sensitive to variations in inputs. Thus, simply ensuring the same level of inputs could have beneficial effects for distributional outcomes. Third, teachers themselves have preferences for the schools at which they teach.[20] In a systematic way, teachers appear to seek out schools with higher-achieving students and fewer minority students.

Part of the controversy about school inputs has related to issues of causality and the possible contamination of unmeasured student and school characteristics. For example, if class sizes are set in a compensatory manner such that more educationally disadvantaged students are placed in smaller classes, one would see a positive correlation of the level of achievement and class sizes. Thus, commonly available estimates of the impact of class size might give a misleading view of the leverage that can be had.

Various approaches have been pursued to circumvent these problems, particularly in the area of class size. These include attempts to isolate exogenous variations in class size (Angrist and Lavy 1999; Hoxby 2000; Woessmann and West 2005). They also include the use of random assignment experiments (Word et al. 1990; Krueger 1999). In each instance, however, the efforts to isolate the causal impact have also been accompanied by other complications having to do with the quality of the underlying data, thus leading to uncertainty about the results.

An alternative within the framework of our work is to control more directly for various influences that might be correlated with the inputs of note to isolate their impact. Consider class-size policy and its potential interaction with estimation. If schools actively decide class size on the basis of student need and if student need is not accurately assessed in the analysis, standard estimation will yield significant bias. Our approach follows the development above. We investigate student-achievement growth, allow for individual specific growth rates through fixed effects, and incorporate generalized measures of school inputs with grade-by-school fixed effects. We then consider how the variations in class size that occur over and above these—largely through demographic variations across time—influence achievement.

Similarly, we investigate other measured teacher and school inputs after allowing for systematic variation in factors affecting achievement growth.

Our investigation of school performance in Texas confirms large parts of the past analyses of inputs but also sheds further light onto the distributional issues here. The analysis in Rivkin, Hanushek, and Kain (2005) suggests four important findings. First, among the traditional measured inputs, the most important is early career teaching experience. Teachers in their first few years of teaching do worse than those later in their careers, with the most important impact during the first year of teaching. In other words, regardless of subsequent performance, rookie teachers on average do more poorly in the classroom than they will later. Second, class size has a significant but very small impact on student performance. Third, there is no evidence that disadvantaged students, identified by parental income, are more sensitive to school inputs than more advantaged students. Finally, other common inputs including teacher degrees, scores on teacher-certification tests, and teacher certification in general do not have a systematic impact on student performance.

Perhaps the most important of these findings from a distributional perspective is the finding about early career performance of teachers. The impact of the initial year of experience appears to be approximately 0.1 standard deviation of student growth (that is, student growth is on average one-tenth of a standard deviation lower during a teacher's first year).[21] This impact is potentially important when put into the context of the mobility of teachers. Since teachers appear to seek out schools with higher achievement levels and lower percentages of disadvantaged and minority students (Hanushek, Kain, and Rivkin 2004b), there is a concern that this induces minority students to face more rookie teachers. In our samples, however, there is only a modest difference in the proportion of teachers with one to three years of experience (0.16 for whites, 0.19 for blacks, and 0.20 for Hispanics), and the net impact is just 0.001 to 0.002 s.d. on the gaps with blacks and Hispanics.

7.6 Distributional Policy

One way to draw together the previous evidence is to summarize the major factors identified both as having an impact on student performance and as potentially entering into the observed distribution of outcomes. Table 7.2 provides the two dimensions of the key factors discussed above in the dimension of white-black achievement gaps. First, based on both the impact and the distribution of underlying characteristics, there is a rough calculation of how much the annual differences in underlying achievement factors contribute to the relatively higher performance of white students. Second, the potential impact reflects simply the estimate of how "distributionally sensitive" changes in each factor will affect the gap—that is, the potential strength of any policies aimed directly at improving distribution. The previous discussion is meant to highlight the various dimensions of policy choices that affect distributional issues. For example, while the importance of family background has been well understood since the Coleman Report, governmental intrusion into families has never been a substantial part of the policy agenda.[22] On the other hand, altering both the resources and organization of schools and the characteristics of student peers has been on the policy agenda. The suspicion has long been, however, that policy is impotent and that achieving a significant closing of the gaps through policy manipulations is not possible.

Table 7.2 provides the quantitative summary of the consistent estimation of various effects on the racial distribution of student outcomes.[23] The table, which directly follows the previous presentation in the text, gives an immediate picture of where leverage is greatest. Teacher quality can dramatically change student outcomes: a one standard-deviation improvement in teacher quality (measured in terms of variations in average classroom gains) can yield somewhere between 0.125 and 0.175 standard-deviation change in student achievement. (The range of estimates reflects the underlying approach to assessing differences in teacher quality, as described earlier.) Similarly, the racial composition of the school and the student mobility rate in a school have large impacts on distribution—reflecting the different impacts on black and white students.

The prior analysis focuses on the data for distributional considerations. The large and unmistakable variations in performance by race and income have been the object of an enormous amount of concern and policy attention. The full impact of policy interventions aimed at dealing with distributional issues depends on both the magnitude of any policy and its impact on different groups.

A distinguishing characteristic of policies aimed at distribution is the potential interaction with policies aimed at overall performance and efficiency. One class of policies considers simple redistribution of exist-

Table 7.2
Estimated current influence and potential influence on white-black achievement gaps

	Analytical sources	Annual contribution to current gap (white-black gap)	Potential annual impact
Teacher quality:			
Total quality[a]	Rivkin, Hanushek, and Kain (2005); Hanushek et al. (2005); Hanushek, Kain, and Rivkin (2004a)	−.025 to 0.08	0.125 to 0.175
Peer influences:			
Racial composition[b]	Hanushek, Kain, and Rivkin (2002)	0.038	−0.14 to −0.25
Peer SES	Hanushek et al. (2003)	—	—
Peer ability	Hanushek et al. (2003)	—	—
Student mobility[c]	Hanushek, Kain, and Rivkin (2004a)	0.06	−0.18 to −0.3
School resources/other inputs:			
Teacher experience[d]	Hanushek et al. (2005)	0.001	−0.10
Class size[e]	Rivkin, Hanushek, and Kain (2005)	—	0.0 to −0.01 per student
Teacher degree level	Hanushek et al. (2005)	—	—
Teacher certification	Hanushek et al. (2005)	—	—

a. Teacher quality is measured in terms of standard deviations of the teacher distribution, where, for example, 0.1 indicates that one standard deviation of teacher quality implies 0.1 s.d. higher growth in student achievement.

b. Racial composition indicates the impact of a higher proportion of black students on achievement growth of black students, where, for example, −0.14 indicates that 10% more black students (0.1) translates into 0.014 s.d. lower student annual achievement growth. The current gap is calculated as the impact of moving from the existing unequal distribution across schools to an equalized distribution.

c. School mobility indicates the impact of a higher proportion of student moves on student achievement growth, where, for example, −0.18 indicates that 10% higher student turnover (0.1) translates into 0.018 s.d. lower student annual achievement growth. The range on potential impact depends on the level of mobility before and during the school year.

d. Teacher experience is measured by teachers in their first three years of experience. The potential impact indicates that having a first-year teacher is associated with 0.1 s.d. lower student-achievement growth.

e. Class size effects give the change in performance predicted for a one student change in class size. Estimates vary by grade level with the largest impacts for grade four and smallest for grade seven.

ing resources. Thus, for example, if we take the current set of teachers as constant and simply redistribute them on the basis of student characteristics, it suggests the possibility of a zero-sum game: those who get higher achievement are offset by those who get lower achievement. Policies such as these might readily be justified if the existing distribution of resources, say, favors the otherwise advantaged group. They might also be justified if there is no existing inequity in distribution, but there is general agreement to weight the disadvantaged more heavily. The key element, however, is that actions to improve the distribution of outcomes—and the equity between groups—affect others, and thus it becomes a political question.

The example of the current distribution of teachers that favors higher-income white students is one obvious situation. Here policy aimed at achieving a more equitable distribution of teachers may have great political appeal.[24] But the evidence indicates substantial ability to alter the situation. The white-black gap of 0.7 s.d. (table 7.2) could, by our estimates, be eliminated if blacks systematically got teachers one standard deviation above the mean or at the 85th percentile for four to six years in a row. Having a teacher at the 70th percentile for this period would cut the gap in half. Clearly, these would imply substantial improvements in the quality of teachers within our urban district, but the results underscore the point that correcting the gaps is not impossible.[25]

Table 7.2 shows that the current gaps in performance do not result from differences in having inexperienced teachers. On the other hand, policies that simultaneously kept the good teachers in heavily disadvantaged schools and cut down on the necessity of hiring new teachers would be beneficial.

A potentially more fortuitous situation would be one where disadvantaged students were more sensitive to certain inputs than more advantaged students. For example, if disadvantaged students reacted more strongly to small class sizes, a policy of providing smaller class sizes for disadvantaged students would simultaneously meet two objectives—improving overall achievement by obtaining a more efficient distribution of inputs and working to reduce any distributional differences in outcomes. (If more advantaged students reacted more strongly, the distributional issues would be made even larger.)

This situation occurs in two places across the Texas schools: racial composition and school mobility. First, black achievement responds adversely to increased proportions of black students, but neither whites nor Hispanics are similarly affected. The estimates in table 7.2 show that these effects are truly substantial. The difference in achievement growth given the current distribution of blacks compared to an equal distribution across the entire state is 0.038 standard deviation. This growth difference accumulates across time, suggesting that it is a direct contributor to the existing racial gap. At the same time, it is not entirely clear what can be done about the racial composition of schools from a policy standpoint. Most of the racial concentration in the schools results from black concentrations within certain districts. Within most districts, the distribution of the black population across schools is quite even—the result of school-desegregation actions following *Brown v. Board of Education* (Rivkin 2000). There is no legal basis for moving students across district boundaries (Armor 1995), and even if there were a basis, much of the distribution is also complicated by regional patterns of settlement in Texas. The possibility of opening up housing in suburban areas could accomplish part of this, although the policy consensus needed for such actions is difficult to achieve.

Second, blacks are more sensitive to mobility rates in their schools and also attend schools with higher mobility rates than whites. Therefore, if policies can stabilize the schools for black students, substantial gains could be possible. To date, few policies that try to affect either the level of mobility or the impact of mobility have been developed. Nonetheless, because of the magnitude of these effects, some increased attention would seem warranted.

The summary of this consideration of distributional issues is simple. The large gaps in performance by race and income can be affected by policies. The policies that might work, however, differ substantially from the existing set of common initiatives. Equalizing standard teacher inputs or reducing class sizes for disadvantaged students has little hope of lessening the observed achievement gaps simply because these factors do not systematically affect outcomes. On the other hand, substantial leverage exists through actions to alter the quality of teachers for disadvantaged students. Further, some peer aspects of schools— namely, the racial composition and the levels of student mobility— have substantial impacts on existing gaps and, if the effects could be lessened, offer another avenue for improving equity in the schools. Little policy attention has been given, however, to these aspects of peer composition.

The prior discussion has also taken a "benevolent-dictator" view of policy. If one actually wished to affect any of the changes discussed, it would be necessary to consider the underlying politics of the situation. How could the changes be accomplished? These are large and truly important issues.

Additionally, the discussion has largely taken the current system—with its operations and possibilities—as given. In a variety of other analyses, however, it has been clear that substantial inefficiency exists (see the summary in Hanushek 2003). An alternative way to view the entire issue revolves around improving the entire system. If, in fact, something could be done to improve the overall performance of the system, policies that also improved the equity would be easier to accomplish. In other words, redistributing a larger pie is generally easier than redistributing a constant-size pie through zero-sum policies.

Although they go beyond the scope of this chapter, it is worth noting some of the choices that have a reasonable chance of improving the schools. The basic notion is to change the incentives that are relevant to the schools. If, contrary to the current situation, rewards are given for improving performance, it is much more likely that we will move in the direction of better results.

The two leading candidates for reform include a combination of improved accountability for school performance and enhanced parental choice of schools (see Hanushek and Raymond 2005; Peterson 2003). These options offer the possibility of spurring innovation and change that provide real improvements in student performance—and thus the possibility that a larger pie can also be used to improve the equity of the system.

Notes

1. Testing is conducted at ages 9, 13, and 17. The trend data employed here are designed to provide a direct summary of how performance changes through time.

2. Scores at age 17 are the product of schooling received over the prior 10 years. Looking at the achievement gaps for 13-year-olds shows that the gains seen during the 1980s for the oldest students have their antecedents in the 1970s. Most recently, the achievement gap for nine-year-olds narrowed in reading and math. Some popular statements have attributed this narrowing to increased national accountability and particularly the introduction of the federal No Child Left Behind Act of 2001. Nonetheless, no formal analyses have yet to be conducted.

3. This act, when most recently renewed, became the No Child Left Behind Act of 2001.

4. Bowles and Levin (1968); Cain and Watts (1970); Hanushek and Kain (1972).

5. Overall state data can be found in U.S. Department of Education (2003).

6. Presentation of achievement solely in terms of school experiences, ignoring preschool experiences, is done solely for expositional ease. Given our estimation strategy, it has no effect on the results.

7. Specifying the underlying achievement relationship in terms of the simple difference in achievement is one of several alternative forms (see Hanushek 1979). This formulation assumes that there is no depreciation of prior effects over time (Rivkin 2005). The primary alternative estimation puts lagged achievement on the right-hand side of the equation. A coefficient on lagged achievement of one indicates that the simple difference model in the text is correct, while a coefficient less than one indicates some depreciation. In estimation that relaxes the form in the text, the qualitative results shown here are very similar, although the precise quantitative results will vary (Hanushek and Rivkin 2006).

8. For previous analyses of this sort, see, among others, Hanushek (1971, 1992), Murnane (1975), Armor et al. (1976), Murnane and Phillips (1981), Aaronson, Barrow, and Sander (2007), and Rockoff (2004). Rivkin et al. (2005) address the various selection factors and provide a lower bound on the variations in teacher quality specified in this way.

9. In the specific estimates, while we concentrate most on math performance, we obtain an estimate of 0.09 s.d. for reading and 0.11 s.d. for math.

10. One important aspect of that analysis is making adjustments for characteristics of the student-achievement tests. The tests concentrate on performance at the lower end. Because of this, it is easier to get large changes in performance at the lower end of the test. For the analysis, achievement gains are standardized to the gains of others within each decile of the test score.

11. The estimation in Hanushek, Kain, O'Brien, and Rivkin (2005) considers estimates obtained from within-school and within-district comparisons. It also concentrates on standardized gains (see previous note). The bound on the estimates presented here translates gains into raw gains and uses the within-district estimates (which include variations across schools for the district).

12. We do find that there are positive effects to matching student and teacher race (Hanushek et al. 2005).

13. For example, it is common to employ income measures to proxy differences in family background that might be important for student learning or other outcomes, but there are serious questions about whether the relevant causal factor is income per se or some other attributes that are related to income (cf. Mayer 1997).

14. An additional problem, that we do not dwell on here, is the reciprocal relationship between the individual student and peers. The underlying idea behind peer influences is that the others in a classroom and school affect the character of learning. But if that is true, then it is natural to believe that the individual student also affects all of her classmates— implying that the direction of causation for any observed association is unclear. This problem, which is crucial in some kinds of analyses, proves to be difficult to deal with in many studies. This issue, sometimes referred to as the *reflection problem*, is described technically in Manski (1993) and Moffitt (2001).

15. The findings in areas other than achievement are even more difficult to characterize, in part because the quality of the underlying research is quite mixed. In reviewing reviews of desegregation effects on nonachievement outcomes, Schofield (1995, 607, 609) concludes that "desegregation has no clear-cut consistent impact" on African American

self-concept or self-esteem and that "the evidence taken as a whole suggests that desegregation has no clearly predictable impact on student intergroup attitudes". While each of these conclusions is heavily qualified, the research makes it clear that the currently available evidence does not indicate that these wider outcomes are places of systematic impact.

16. Discussions of a wide range of issues related to neighborhood-poverty concentrations can be found in Jencks and Peterson (1991), Jargowsky (1997), and O'Regan and Quigley (1999). More recent investigations relying on randomization of people who leave bad neighborhoods can be found in Rosenbaum (1995), Rosenbaum and Popkin (1991), Katz, Kling, and Liebman (2001), and Ludwig, Duncan, and Hirschfield (2001).

17. The chief problem has revolved around the simultaneous determination of achievement by all students in the classroom. Formal statements of the problem can be found in Manski (1993) and Moffitt (2001).

18. A common policy thread has been that low-achieving students benefit from being in classes with high-achieving students but that high-achieving students are unaffected by classroom composition. If this were the case, heterogeneous classroom groupings would provide the best policy because it would maximize performance of low achievers at no cost. This presumption has been challenged, however, suggesting that detracking or tracking is a zero-sum game where losers balance winners (Argys, Rees, and Brewer 1996).

19. When these results are translated into potential national effects, as measured by the national gaps on the National Assessment of Educational Progress (NAEP), it is estimated that past changes in racial composition of U.S. schools could account for a substantial portion—if not all—of the past closing of the racial achievement gap that occurred in the 1980s (Hanushek 2001).

20. Several early analyses suggest that teachers systematically search out schools with a more affluent population (Greenberg and McCall 1974; Murnane 1981). Those analyses motivate the general discussion here.

21. This estimate is obtained from two very different approaches. In the analysis of the lower bound on teacher quality in Rivkin, Hanushek, and Kain (2005), indirect estimation—through considering the impact on the variance in student achievement of teacher turnover and experience—is very consistent with the direct production function estimates. Also, after estimating the year-by-year performance on individual teachers in the large Texas district used in the quality estimation (Hanushek et al. 2005), virtually identical estimates are obtained.

22. At various times, some thought has been given to such ideas as improving the quality of parenting, although there is little evidence that any of these policy initiatives has been very successful.

23. A similar set of calculations using a different estimation approach is found in Hanushek and Rivkin (2006).

24. Even here, complications of alternative policy goals enter. In many U.S. urban areas, upper-income white families have moved out of the central city and into surrounding suburban areas. This movement has put fiscal pressure on cities as their tax bases erode and has led central cities to seek ways to make themselves attractive to middle-income families. Ensuring quality schools is often identified as the most important approach.

25. Note that the district has just 15 percent white students, so it is not feasible simply to move good teachers from whites to blacks. There are insufficient numbers of high-quality teachers currently with white students to yield the gains for blacks.

References

Aaronson, D., L. Barrow, and W. Sander. (2007). "Teachers and Student Achievement in the Chicago Public High Schools." *Journal of Labor Economics* 25(1): 95–135.

Alexander, K. L., D. R. Entwisle, and S. L. Dauber. (1996). "Children in Motion: School Transfers and Elementary School Performance." *Journal of Educational Research* 90(1): 3–12.

Angrist, J. D., and V. Lavy. (1999). "Using Maimondides' Rule to Estimate the Effect of Class Size on Scholastic Achievement." *Quarterly Journal of Economics* 114(2): 533–575.

Argys, L. M., D. I. Rees, and D. J. Brewer. (1996). "Detracking America's Schools: Equity at Zero Cost?" *Journal of Policy Analysis and Management* 15(4): 623–645.

Armor, D. J. (1995). *Forced Justice: School Desegregation and the Law.* New York: Oxford University Press.

Armor, D. J., P. Conry-Oseguera, M. Cox, N. King, L. McDonnell, A. Pascal, E. Pauly, and G. Zellman. (1976). *Analysis of the School Preferred Reading Program in Selected Los Angeles Minority Schools.* Santa Monica, CA: Rand Corp.

Ballou, D. (1996). "Do Public Schools Hire the Best Applicants?" *Quarterly Journal of Economics* 111(1): 97–133.

Boozer, M. A., A. B. Krueger, and S. Wolkon. (1992). Race and School Quality since Brown v. Board of Education. *Brooking Papers: Microeconomics.* M. N. Baily and C. Winston. Washington, DC: Brookings Institution.

Bowles, S., and H. M. Levin. (1968). "The Determinants of Scholastic Achievement: An Appraisal of Some Recent Evidence." *Journal of Human Resources* 3(1): 3–24.

Cain, G. G., and H. W. Watts. (1970). "Problems in Making Policy Inferences from the Coleman Report." *American Sociological Review* 35(2): 328–352.

Coleman, J. S., E. Q. Campbell, C. J. Hobson, J. McPartland, A. M. Mood, F. D. Weinfeld, and R. L. York. (1966). *Equality of Educational Opportunity* [the Coleman Report]. Washington, DC: U.S. Government Printing Office.

Cook, M. D., and W. N. Evans. (2000). "Families or Schools? Explaining the Convergence in White and Black Academic Performance." *Journal of Labor Economics* 18(4): 729–754.

Crain, R. (1970). "School Integration and Occupational Achievement of Negroes." *American Journal of Sociology* 75(4, Part II): 593–606.

Crain, R. L., and R. E. Mahard. (1978). "Desegregation and Black Achievement: A Review of the Research." *Law and Contemporary Problems* 42(3): 17–53.

Greenberg, D., and J. McCall. (1974). "Teacher Mobility and Allocation." *Journal of Human Resources* 9(4): 480–502.

Grogger, J. T. (1996). "Does School Quality Explain the Recent Black/White Wage Trend?" *Journal of Labor Economics* 14(2): 231–253.

Hanushek, E. A. (1971). "Teacher Characteristics and Gains in Student Achievement: Estimation Using Micro Data." *American Economic Review* 60(2): 280–288.

Hanushek, E. A. (1972). *Education and Race: An Analysis of the Educational Production Process*. Lexington, MA: Lexington Books.

Hanushek, E. A. (1979). "Conceptual and Empirical Issues in the Estimation of Educational Production Functions." *Journal of Human Resources* 14(3): 351–388.

Hanushek, E. A. (1992). "The Trade-off between Child Quantity and Quality." *Journal of Political Economy* 100(1): 84–117.

Hanushek, E. A. (2001). "Black-White Achievement Differences and Governmental Interventions." *American Economic Review* 91(2): 24–28.

Hanushek, E. A. (2003). "The Failure of Input-Based Schooling Policies." *Economic Journal* 113(485): F64–F98.

Hanushek, E. A., and J. F. Kain. (1972). "On the Value of 'Equality of Educational Opportunity' as a Guide to Public Policy." In Frederick Mosteller and Daniel P. Moynihan (eds.), *On Equality of Educational Opportunity*. New York: Random House.

Hanushek, E. A., J. F. Kain, J. M. Markman, and S. G. Rivkin. (2003). "Does Peer Ability Affect Student Achievement?" *Journal of Applied Econometrics* 18(5): 527–544.

Hanushek, E. A., J. F. Kain, D. M. O'Brien, and S. G. Rivkin. (2005). "The Market for Teacher Quality." Working Paper No. 11154, National Bureau of Economic Research.

Hanushek, E. A., J. F. Kain, and S. G. Rivkin. (2002). "New Evidence about *Brown v. Board of Education*: The Complex Effects of School Racial Composition on Achievement." Working Paper No. 8741, National Bureau of Economic Research.

Hanushek, E. A., J. F. Kain, and S. G. Rivkin. (2004a). "Disruption versus Tiebout Improvement: The Costs and Benefits of Switching Schools." *Journal of Public Economics* 88(9–10): 1721–1746.

Hanushek, E. A., J. F. Kain, and S. G. Rivkin. (2004b). "Why Public Schools Lose Teachers." *Journal of Human Resources* 39(2): 326–354.

Hanushek, E. A., and M. E. Raymond. (2005). "Does School Accountability Lead to Improved Student Performance?" *Journal of Policy Analysis and Management* 24(2): 297–327.

Hanushek, E. A., and S. G. Rivkin. (2006). School Quality and the Black-White Achievement Gap. Working Paper No. 12651, Cambridge, MA: National Bureau of Economic Research.

Henderson, V., P. Mieszkowski, and Y. Sauvageau. (1976). *Peer Group Effects and Educational Production Functions*. Ottawa: Economic Council of Canada.

Hoxby, C. M. (2000). "The Effects of Class Size on Student Achievement: New Evidence from Population Variation." *Quarterly Journal of Economics* 115(3): 1239–1285.

Jargowsky, P. A. (1997). *Poverty and Place: Ghettos, Barrios, and the American City*. New York: Russell Sage Foundation.

Jaynes, G. D., and R. M. Williams. (1989). *A Common Destiny: Blacks and American Society*. Washington, DC: National Academy Press.

Jencks, C., and P. E. Peterson (eds.). (1991). *The Urban Underclass*. Washington, DC: Brookings Institution.

Jencks, C., and M. Phillips (eds.). (1998). *The Black-White Test Score Gap*. Washington, DC: Brookings Institution.

Katz, L. F., J. R. Kling, and J. B. Liebman. (2001). "Moving to Opportunity in Boston: Early Results of a Randomized Mobility Experiment." *Quarterly Journal of Economics* 116(2): 607–654.

Kerbow, D. (1996). "Patterns of Urban Student Mobility and Local School Reform." *Journal of Education for Students Placed at Risk* 1(2): 147–169.

Krueger, A. B. (1999). "Experimental Estimates of Education Production Functions." *Quarterly Journal of Economics* 114(2): 497–532.

Ludwig, J., G. J. Duncan, and P. Hirschfield. (2001). "Urban Poverty and Juvenile Crime: Evidence from a Randomized Housing-Mobility Experiment." *Quarterly Journal of Economics* 116(2): 655–679.

Manski, C. F. (1993). "Identification of Endogenous Social Effects: The Reflection Problem." *Review of Economic Studies* 60: 531–542.

Mayer, S. E. (1991). "How Much Does a High School's Racial and Socioeconomic Mix Affect Graduation and Teenage Fertility Rates?" In C. Jencks and P. E. Peterson (eds.), *The Urban Underclass*. Washington, DC: Brookings Institution.

Mayer, S. E. (1997). *What Money Can't Buy: Family Income and Children's Life Chances*. Cambridge, MA: Harvard University Press.

Moffitt, R. A. (2001). "Policy Interventions, Low-Level Equilibria, and Social Interactions." In S. D. and H. P. Y. (eds.), *Social Dynamics*. Cambridge, MA: MIT Press.

Murnane, R. J. (1975). *Impact of School Resources on the Learning of Inner City Children*. Cambridge, MA: Ballinger.

Murnane, R. J. (1981). "Teacher Mobility Revisited." *Journal of Human Resources* 16(1): 3–19.

Murnane, R. J., and B. Phillips. (1981). "What Do Effective Teachers of Inner-City Children Have in Common?" *Social Science Research* 10(1): 83–100.

National Center for Education Statistics. (2004). *The Condition of Education 2004*. Washington, DC: U.S. Department of Education.

Neal, D. (2006). Why Has Black-White Skill Convergence Stopped? In E. A. Hanushek and F. Welch (eds.), *Handbook of the Economics of Education*, Volume 1. Amsterdam: Elsevier.

O'Regan, K. M., and J. M. Quigley. (1999). "Accessibility and Economic Opportunity." In C. Winston, J. A. Gomez-Ibanez, and W. Tye (eds.), *Essays in Transportation Economics*. Washington, DC: Brookings Institution.

Oakes, J. (1992). "Can Tracking Research Inform Practice? Technical, Normative, and Political Considerations." *Educational Researcher* 21(4): 12–21.

Peterson, P. E. (ed.). (2003). *Our Schools and Our Future: Are We Still at Risk?* Stanford, CA: Hoover Institution Press.

Rivkin, S. G. (2000). "School Desegregation, Academic Attainment, and Earnings." *Journal of Human Resources* 35(2): 333–346.

Rivkin, S. G. (2005). Cumulative Nature of Learning and Specification Bias in Education Research, Amherst College.

Rivkin, S. G., E. A. Hanushek, and J. F. Kain. (2005). "Teachers, Schools, and Academic Achievement." *Econometrica* 73(2): 417–458.

Rockoff, J. E. (2004). "The Impact of Individual Teachers on Student Achievement: Evidence from Panel Data." *American Economic Review* 94(2): 247–252.

Rosenbaum, J. E. (1995). "Changing the Geography of Opportunity by Expanding Residential Choice: Lessons from the Gautreaux Program." *Housing Policy Debate* 6(1): 231–269.

Rosenbaum, J. E., and S. J. Popkin. (1991). "Employment and Earnings of Low-Income Blacks Who Move to Middle-Class Suburbs." In C. Jencks and P. E. Peterson (eds.), *The Urban Underclass*. Washington, DC: Brookings Institution.

Schofield, J. W. (1995). "Review of Research on School Desegregation's Impact on Elementary and Secondary School Students." In J. A. Banks and C. A. McGee Banks (eds.), *Handbook of Research on Multicultural Education*. New York: Macmillan.

Smith, J. P., and F. Welch. (1989). "Black Economic Progress after Myrdal." *Journal of Economic Literature* 27(2): 519–564.

Summers, A. A., and B. L. Wolfe. (1977). "Do Schools Make a Difference?" *American Economic Review* 67(4): 639–652.

U.S. Commission on Civil Rights. (1967). *Racial Isolation in the Public Schools*. Washington, DC: Government Printing Office.

U.S. Department of Education. (2003). *Digest of Education Statistics, 2002*. Washington, DC: National Center for Education Statistics.

Word, E., J. Johnston, H. P. Bain, B. D. Fulton, J. B. Zaharies, M. N. Lintz, C. M. Achilles, J. Folger, and C. Breda. (1990). *Student/Teacher Achievement Ratio (STAR), Tennessee's K–3 Class Size Study: Final Summary Report, 1985–1990*. Nashville: Tennessee State Department of Education.

Woessmann, L., and M. R. West. (2005). "Class-Size Effects in School Systems around the World: Evidence from between-Grade Variation in TIMSS." *European Economic Review* 50(3): 695–736.

Zimmer, R. W., and E. F. Toma. (2000). "Peer Effects in Private and Public Schools across Countries." *Journal of Policy Analysis and Management* 19(1): 75–92.

8

The Effectiveness of Human-Capital Policies for Disadvantaged Groups in the Netherlands

Edwin Leuven and Hessel Oosterbeek

8.1 Introduction

Governments around the world emphasize that investment in education is important for the future prosperity of their citizens. Yet simply increasing public (and private) expenditures on education is probably not a sensible policy. It is crucial to allocate resources efficiently, and an efficient allocation of the education budget requires knowledge about the effectiveness of separate interventions and policies. There is an inadequate supply of such knowledge because the number of convincing evaluations of education interventions is limited.

This chapter summarizes some recent evaluation studies of education interventions in the Netherlands. The common element in all studies is that they build on a quasi-experimental identification strategy. The distinctive feature of quasi-experimental methods is that the assignment of the observed units (in our case, students or schools) to treatment and comparison groups can be argued to mimic random assignment. As a result, very equal students (or schools) are treated very unequally. The different studies also are explicit about the assumptions required to give the estimated effects a causal interpretation, and these assumptions are relatively unrestrictive. Because of this, these studies produce fairly convincing results.

Another common element of the studies is that they pay special attention to the effects for disadvantaged pupils. For some of these interventions, this is inevitable since they are especially targeted toward disadvantaged groups. Other interventions are not targeted toward a specific group, but we consider their effects on different groups of students.

The evaluation studies reviewed in this contribution deal with the following policy measures and interventions: class-size reduction, extra resources for personnel, extra resources for computers, lowering the compulsory school-attendance age, and increasing the compulsory school-leaving age. Four of these interventions have been put into operation by the Dutch ministry of education. Class sizes in primary schools have been reduced, extra funding was given for personnel and computers, and substantial resources are nowadays spent on raising the qualifications of early school leavers. Only proposals to lower the compulsory school-attendance age (from age five to age four) were not begun by the government. Ironically, our results indicate that the intervention that was not put into practice is the most promising one in terms of its effect on achievement of disadvantaged students. For the other interventions, which the government proceeded to expand, substantial positive effects can be ruled out.

The next section summarizes the methods and findings of these studies. For (technical) details, we refer to the respective research papers. The aim of this summary is twofold. The first purpose is to present a number of interesting and policy-relevant research outcomes. While the studies certainly do not cover the entire spectrum of possible interventions, the results indicate that not all interventions are equally effective. As a by-product, the summary of recent research demonstrates different methods to attain credible identification of the effects of policies. We return to these issues in the final section.

8.2 Summary of Evaluation Studies

8.2.1 Effect of Extra Time in School on Early Test Scores

The age at which pupils are allowed or required to start school differs across countries and within countries over time. In Scandinavian countries, the typical school-attendance age is seven. It is six in most OECD countries (including Canada, Belgium, France, Germany, Italy, Spain, and a majority of states in the United States) and five in the United Kingdom and New Zealand. At the lower end of the spectrum is the Netherlands, where children are allowed to start attending school at the age of four.

Whereas the cross-country variation reveals that the school starting age is a policy variable, little is known about the effects of starting at a younger age on achievement. Several studies point to substantial positive effects of early childhood education programs (Currie 2001; Garces, Thomas, and Currie 2002). These studies deal, however, with targeted programs for special groups. Effects of such programs need not be informative about the effects of additional time in regular education.

The key problem for identification of the effect of extra time in school is to have a credible source of exogenous variation in time in school, which is unrelated to factors such as innate ability and parents' aspirations. In an interesting study, Cahan and Cohen (1989) estimate the effect of extra time in school on early test scores in Israel. As in many other countries, a whole-year cohort starts school at the same day. By comparing achievement of students in adjacent grade levels, Cahan and Cohen are able to separate the effect of extra time in school from the effect of age on achievement. Their key finding is that the effect of an extra year in school is about twice as large as the effect of being one year older. Some other related studies fail to disentangle the effect of starting school at a different age and making the achievement test at a different age.

Leuven et al. (2004b) investigate the effect of extra time in school on early test scores by exploiting two specific features of the Dutch regulations with regard to primary-school enrollment. The first feature is that a child is allowed to enroll in school immediately after his or her fourth birthday. This is different from the situation in most other countries, where typically all children of the same cohort start on the same day. The second feature is that a school-year cohort consists of the children born between October 1 of a year and September 30 of the next year. As a result, children turning age four before, in, and after the summer holiday are placed into the same class. Together, these two features generate—conditional on age variation in the maximum number of school days a child can have attended at any given date during his or her school career.

Leuven et al. (2004b) report significantly positive effects of extra time in school on language and arithmetic scores in grade two for disadvantaged pupils.[1] Minority pupils, as well as Dutch pupils with less educated parents, benefit from the opportunity to spend more time in school. The effect is substantial; one more month of potential school enrollment increases early test scores by 6 percent of a standard deviation. To illustrate, the difference in average test scores of a school without any disadvantaged student and a school with only minority pupils amounts to one standard deviation.[2] Nondisadvantaged pupils do not benefit from the opportunity of extra time in school at a young age.

The chapter argues that the reported effect of extra potential time in school is a lower bound of the effect of extra actual time in school.

A way to increase the actual amount of time in school is to lower the compulsory school-attendance age. The results suggest that we may expect beneficial effects from lowering the compulsory school-attendance age for children with disadvantaged backgrounds. This assumes, however, that the effects obtained for compliers carry over to the situation in which students are forced to enroll at a younger age. This, in turn, assumes that parents, who currently do not send their children to school as soon as it is allowed, make a wrong decision from the perspective of maximizing achievement of their offspring.

This finding on the possible effect of lowering the compulsory school-attendance age is interesting in light of recent policy discussions in the Netherlands. Some years ago, the vice minister of education proposed lowering the compulsory school-attendance age from five years to four years. But when the cabinet to which this vice minister belonged was replaced by a new cabinet, one of the first actions of the new minister of education was to withdraw this proposal. According to the new minister, the proposed change would interfere too much with parents' freedom to choose.

8.2.2 Effects of Class-Size Reduction on Achievement in Primary Schools

The effect of class size on achievement has attracted substantial attention from researchers. This is a prime example of a case where simply comparing achievement of pupils placed in small and large classes is likely to give biased estimates of the causal effect. The bias can go either way. If parents who are more interested in their offsprings' achievement opt for schools with smaller classes, a naïve comparison is likely to overestimate the true effect of class size on achievement. If, instead, schools place their more problematic pupils in smaller classes, the same comparison will probably produce an underestimate of the effect of interest.

The results of the STAR field experiment conducted in the mid-1980s in the state of Tennessee are well known. Pupils and their teachers in kindergarten through third grade were randomly assigned to classes of different sizes. A careful analysis of the results is reported in Krueger (1999) (see also Krueger and Whitmore 2001). The main finding is that pupils who have been assigned to smaller classes perform better than the pupils placed in larger classes, both in terms of short-term outcomes and in terms of longer-term outcomes. Pupils from disadvantaged backgrounds seem especially to benefit from being placed in smaller classes.

Two reasons limit the external validity of the results of the STAR experiment. First, as is argued by Hoxby (2000), teachers are aware of their assignment to the treatment or control group, and they may realize that continuation of the program depends on the program's success. This may give teachers in the treatment group an incentive to exert more effort and at the same time give teachers in the control group an incentive to slow down. Second, the experiment was conducted in the mid-1980s in Tennessee. Results are not necessarily valid for other populations or periods. The average treatment effect of smaller classes is positive, but the fact that disadvantaged students benefit more already shows that there are heterogeneous treatment effects. Krueger (1999, 526, figure II) illustrates this by showing the distribution of average treatment effects within schools. For a large number of schools, the point estimate of the treatment effect has the wrong sign. Together, these two facts illustrate that the overall positive impact of smaller classes depends on the composition of the pupil population and of the schools. In another context (state, country, and period), the composition may be different, such that the average treatment effect is larger or smaller than the effects reported in the STAR experiment.

A study that does not suffer from the concern of participants being aware of the experimental setting is Angrist and Lavy (1999). That paper uses a regression discontinuity design resulting from specific features of the funding rules applying to primary schools in Israel. According to the so-called Maimonides' rule, an extra teacher is added to a grade level as soon as the number of pupils at the grade level exceeds a multiple of 40. Therefore, average class size is expected to equal 40 when the school has 40 pupils at the grade level, while it is expected to equal $20\frac{1}{2}$ when the school has 41 pupils at the grade level. By comparing the achievement of pupils in schools just above and just below the cutoffs, a credible estimate of the causal effect of class size on achievement is obtained. The identifying assumptions are that parents cannot choose schools based on their position around the cutoff and that no other special events happen precisely at the grade-level size of 40. Like Krueger (1999), Angrist and Lavy find positive effects of smaller classes, and effects are larger at schools with higher proportions of disadvantaged pupils. Hoxby (2000), in contrast, finds no positive effect of class-size reduction; she can even rule out modest effects.

In a recent study, Woessmann and West (2006) estimate class size effects for 11 different countries. They find positive effects of class-size reduction in two countries. For the other countries, they do not find such effects. For four countries, they can rule out effects as small as 1 percent of a standard deviation for a one-pupil change in class size.

Given these positive results of class-size reduction, it is interesting and important to investigate whether similar effects are realized in other countries. Inspired by Angrist and Lavy's study, Dobbelsteen, Levin, and Oosterbeek (2002) conducted a similar type of analysis using features of the Dutch funding scheme for primary schools (and Dutch data). The Dutch funding scheme, too, has discontinuities in the relation between number of pupils (at the school level) and teacher formation. The discontinuities are less pronounced than those in Israel. The disadvantage of this is that the size of the treatment is much smaller, making it more difficult to identify effects with sufficient precision. The advantage is that the size of the discontinuities in the Dutch funding scheme is fairly close to the reductions in class size that have been implemented in the Netherlands in recent years.

Dobbelsteen et al. report separate effects of class size on language and arithmetic in grades four, six, and eight (grade eight is the last year of primary school, when pupils are age 11 or 12). Most of the point estimates based on instrumental variable techniques are positive, implying that pupils in smaller classes perform worse than pupils in larger classes. The factors underlying this counterintuitive conclusion are further explored by including an extra variable in the achievement regressions. This extra variable measures for each pupil the (absolute) number of pupils in the class that has almost the same level of ability (measured by IQ). This variable intends to measure the peer effects that are predicted by social cognitive learning theories (cf. Bandura 1986; Schunk 1987). According to these theories, pupils benefit most from peers that have about the same level of cognitive ability. The variable "number of similar classmates" has the positive sign predicted by the learning theories, while at the same time inclusion of the variable reduces the positive class-size effect. Hence, the nonnegative and sometimes even positive relation between class size and achievement in Dutch primary schools can—at least partially—be attributed to the fact that reduction of class size also reduces the (expected) number of pupils in the class with a similar level of competence. This reduction apparently limits a pupil's scope to learn from her classmates.

While the results reported above are interesting, it should be stressed that the analysis is only exploratory. It attempts to find an explanation for the positive class-size effects. The results with respect to the effects of the "number of similar classmates" should be interpreted with caution because no attempt has been made to purge these effects for endogeneity.

In a follow-up study, Levin (2001) uses the same specifications but now uses quantile regression techniques. This produces effect estimates at different percentiles of the conditional achievement distribution. Effects are reported for the 10th, 25th, 50th, 75th, and 90th percentiles, again separately for language and arithmetic and for grades four, six, and eight. The results obtained without inclusion of the number of similar classmates reveals an erratic pattern. Sometimes the estimated effect of class size on achievement is larger at lower percentiles; sometimes the opposite holds. When the number of similar classmates is included, the pure class-size effect remains irregular. More clear-cut are the results with regard to the effect of the number of similar classmates. For all grade levels, Levin reports a significant and monotonic decrease in the estimated peer effect when estimated at higher levels of the conditional achievement distribution. This implies that pupils who are in the lower tail of the conditional achievement distribution benefit more from being placed in classes with pupils of similar ability.

8.2.3   Effect of Extra Funding for Personnel for Schools with Minority Students

In an attempt to improve the performance of schools with a large share of minority students, the Dutch ministry of education decided in 2000 to give extra funding to primary schools with at least 70 percent minority students. All schools with at least 70 percent minority students received the same extra funding of about 13,000 guilders per teacher.[3] This amount was spread over two years and is slightly less than 10 percent of the annual personnel costs of a school. Schools could spend the additional resources the way they wanted, as long as it contributed to improving teachers' working conditions. Schools with less than 70 percent minority students (including schools with 69.9 percent minority students) were not eligible for the subsidy. To prevent strategic behavior from the schools, the share of minority students was based on the composition of the student population some years prior to the announcement of the policy in 2000.

This feature of the policy creates two different groups: schools with at least 70 percent minority students and schools with less than 70 percent minority students. Leuven et al. (2004a) use this feature to evaluate the effects of this policy. By restricting the analysis to schools close to the cutoff, it is likely that there are no systematic differences between the two groups. Leuven et al. restrict the analysis to schools with at least 60 percent and at most 80 percent minority students. This choice of bandwidth balances the trade-off between having more comparable schools and having more observations. Assuming that there are no systematic differences just around the cutoff point, this subsidy scheme is like an experiment that assigns schools randomly to the two groups. The fact that schools around the cutoff are similar in observed characteristics supports, but does not prove, that these schools are also similar in unobserved characteristics. The empirical analysis also controls for the direct effect of the share of minority students on achievement. This is an example of a policy that treats almost identical cases very differently.

As outcome measure, the study takes the scores of students in eighth grade for language, arithmetic, and information processing at a nationwide test. In the Netherlands 80 percent of primary schools participate in this test, which is considered to be important and which is known as the Cito-test (Cito is the name of the institute that develops the test and used to be the acronym for Centraal Instituut voor Testontwikkeling). Results are used to allocate students to different levels of secondary schools. Secondary schools of higher levels require specific minimum levels of performance on this test. Moreover, the average score on this test of the students of a school is used in procedures to assess the performance of schools. This all implies that doing well on the test is important for both students and schools. Outcome measures are available for 1999, 2000, 2002, and 2003. The first two are preintervention measures; the last two are postintervention measures. As a result, the analysis focuses on changes in achievement rather than levels of achievement.

Between the payments of the first and last payment of the subsidy, Beerends and Van der Ploeg (2001) interviewed schools' headmasters about the subsidy. The results of these interviews show that around 90 percent of the extra funding schools received are spent in accordance with the ministry's intentions. Hiring and recruitment of extra personnel, extra payments of personnel, and extra facilities appear to be the main components. Ten percent of the extra funding was not spent immediately but was added to schools' reserves. It is noteworthy that evaluating the effectiveness of the scheme was also attempted. This was done by asking to headmasters of the treated schools whether the scheme had an effect. Over 80 percent of the respondents gave an affirmative answer. This method does not meet the minimum standards of a proper evaluation study.

Leuven et al.'s choice of achievement as a relevant outcome measure reflects the view that ultimately extra personnel, extra payments, and extra facilities should translate into higher achievement by students. This seems reasonable given that extra resources were directed to schools with large shares of disadvantaged students; these students are regarded as disadvantaged because they perform worse (especially on the nationwide test).

None of the effect estimates differ significantly from zero. However, the reported estimates are quite precise, so that even modest positive effects can be excluded. For instance, for language the study can rule out effects in excess of 3 percent of a standard deviation with 95 percent probability.

For the interpretation of this result, it is important to realize that the main funding scheme for primary schools in the Netherlands already channels a substantial amount of compensatory resources to schools with large proportions of disadvantaged students. In this main funding scheme, minority students enter with a weight of 1.9 relative to a unit weight for a nondisadvantaged student. This implies that schools with at least 70 percent minority students already receive over 50 percent more resources than a school with no disadvantaged students. The results from the evaluation study suggest that a level of resource adequacy has been reached (or surpassed).

8.2.4 Effect of Extra Funding for ICT for Schools with Disadvantaged Students

A twin of the intervention just described is a subsidy scheme that provided a fixed amount of 209 Dutch guilders per student to all schools with a share of at least 70 percent disadvantaged students. Disadvantaged students cover minority students and students with lower-educated parents as the two main categories. Schools with less than 70 percent disadvantaged students (again including schools with 69.9 percent disadvantaged students) were not eligible for the subsidy. To prevent strategic behavior by the schools, the share of disadvantaged students was based on the composition of the student population some years prior to the announcement of the policy in 2000. This intervention is also evaluated in Leuven et al. (2004a).[4]

This design of the policy creates two different groups: schools with 70 percent or more disadvantaged students and schools with less than 70 percent disadvantaged students. The study again restricts the analysis to schools with at least 60 percent and at most 80 percent of the targeted type of students. Again assuming that there are no systematic differences just at the cutoff point, this subsidy scheme is like an experiment that assigns schools almost randomly to the two groups. The empirical analysis also controls for the direct effect of the share of disadvantaged students on achievement. Again, very similar cases are treated very dissimilarly.

Outcome measures are once more the scores of students in eighth grade for language, arithmetic, and information processing at the Cito final test. Test results are available for 1999, 2000, 2002, and 2003. The first two are preintervention measures; the last two are postintervention measures. As a result, the study focuses on changes in achievement rather than levels of achievement.

All estimation results reported in Leuven et al. (2004a) are negative, and in some cases they are significantly different from zero. This holds especially for language and arithmetic. The extra funding for ICT seems to have adverse effects on students' achievement. Leuven et al. also report results from a questionnaire sent to schools in the 65 to 75 percent interval. The questionnaire included items concerning the computer per student ratio, the age of the computers, and the intensity of computer use in general and for language and arithmetic in particular. The results reveal no significant differences in the computer per student ratio and age of computers. In both the treatment and control groups, this ratio is on average 1:5, which is high compared to the standard of 1:10 in primary schools. There is, however, a significant difference in the amount of school time that students use a computer. Students in the treated schools spend on average 50 minutes per week more using a computer than students in the control group. Part of this extra time is used for language and arithmetic instruction. Hence, extra resources for computers and software increase school time using a computer and reduce test scores.

The negative findings on computer usage on test scores found in this Dutch study are consistent with findings from two other recent studies.

Angrist and Lavy (2002) evaluate the effects of a program in which the Israeli state lottery funded new computers in elementary and middle schools in Israel. They use several estimation strategies and find a marginally significant negative effect of the program-induced use of computers on the fourth-grade math scores. For eighth graders and for scores on Hebrew, the estimated effects are mostly negative although not significantly different from zero. Rouse, Krueger, and Markman (2004) study the effects of the instructional computer program Fast For-Word (FFW). They find no evidence that the use of FFW results in gains in language acquisition or actual reading skills. The time spent using FFW was in addition to the amount of time that students spent in regular reading instruction. Although Rouse et al. do not find negative effects, broader use of computers in instruction is likely to substitute regular instruction. If computer-based learning is less effective than more traditional forms of classroom teaching, negative effects cannot be ruled out.

8.2.5   Effects of Extending Lower Vocational Programs from Three to Four Years

It is often argued that low-skilled workers should receive more general education or training because it equips them better to participate in the so-called knowledge economy. An important question is to what extent such targeted education programs for low-skilled groups are effective.

Several recent studies report results that are related to this question. Aakvik, Salvanas, and Vaage (2003) use an increase in the amount of compulsory schooling from seven to nine years in Norway to identify the wage effect of an extra year of schooling. For an extra year of the lowest level of vocational education, a return of 0.7 percent is reported. Meghir and Palme (2003) evaluate a social experiment in Sweden. One ingredient of the experiment was an increase in the number of years of compulsory schooling from seven or eight to nine years. The results suggest that the extra education obtained by those with low ability did not significantly affect their earnings. Oreopoulos (2003) analyzes changes in school-leaving laws for the United States, Canada, and the United Kingdom, thereby concentrating on the effects for dropouts. In the United Kingdom, students with less than high school experienced an earnings increase of 5.2 percent as a consequence of the reform. Increasing the minimum school-leaving age has substantial positive effects on the number of years of schooling of dropouts in the United States and on the highest grade attended by dropouts in Canada. Also, the wage effects for dropouts in both countries are substantial.[5]

In the mid-1970s, the Dutch government implemented a reform that did exactly what the current proposals aim to do. Until then, lower vocational education programs had a length of either three or four years. The reform extended the length of all three-year programs to four years and left the programs that already took four years unchanged. The focus of the extra year had to be on general skills rather than on vocational skills. This change in the program length was accompanied by an increase of compulsory education in the Netherlands from 9 to 10 years, thereby raising the minimum school-leaving age from 15 to 16.

Oosterbeek and Webbink (2004) evaluate the effect of the increased program length on the wages of graduates of the extended courses. They use a difference-in-differences (DD) approach, where the graduates of the lower vocational courses that did not change in length form the control group. The analysis is related to previous studies that have exploited changes in compulsory school laws to obtain credible estimates of the wage effect of an extra year of schooling.

Oosterbeek and Webbink fail to find a significantly positive effect of this reform. Their best estimate is -0.018 with a standard error of 0.019, thereby excluding positive effects of 0.02 or more with 95 percent probability. This result cannot be explained by the fact that it took some period to fully implement the change. The result may be biased owing to changes in the composition in the control group. In that case, the results are likely to provide upper bounds of the true effect. The different results for the simple difference specifications and the DD specifications suggest that previous results based on simple difference specifications are biased.

The findings seem to be at odds with the many studies that report highly significant and substantial returns to a year of schooling. Explanations for this may be that the extra year of schooling did not change the highest degree obtained and that it is conceivable that the old three-year program was spread out more thinly over the new four-year program. Pischke (2003) offers comparable explanations for his finding of no adverse earnings effect from less time in school. Oosterbeek and Webbink's finding is consistent with that of Pischke and also with the results reported by Meghir and Palme (2003) and Aakvik, Salvanas, and Vaage (2003), who also report negligible effects for groups comparable with the group affected by the reform we study.

The findings of Oosterbeek and Webbink suggest that individuals attending lower vocational programs do not benefit (in terms of later wages) of additional general education. This finding contrasts sharply with current policy initiatives that aim to provide young people with minimum levels of general skills. The results relate to a different period of time and a different situation, which limits their external validity. Yet the results at least cast some doubt on the effectiveness of the current initiatives.

8.3   Discussion and Conclusion

The previous section summarizes the results from evaluation studies of five different education interventions. All evaluations are based on some quasi-experimental design. These designs produce results, which have a high degree of internal validity. That is, one can validly conclude from these studies that the differences in outcomes are caused by the differences in treatment (cf. Meyer 1995, 152). The possibility that the findings are corrupted by one of the usual threats to internal validity like omitted variables, trends in outcomes, simultaneity, selection, or attrition seems negligible. Table 8.1 lists the key features of each of the studies.

An important limitation of the results is, however, the extent to which they generalize to other contexts. The fact that Dutch primary schools with around 70 percent of disadvantaged students fail to transform extra resources for computers into higher test scores does not prove that extra resources for computers would have no effects in schools that have no disadvantaged students. The Dutch findings about the negative effects of extra resources for computers, however, get more weight when complemented with the other recent findings from other countries and other contexts. At the same time, the Dutch findings give more weight to these other studies as well.

When we limit attention to the Dutch context, the evaluations of the five interventions paint a clear picture. Extra resources, for personnel or for computers, for schools with a high share of disadvantaged students have no impact on students' achievement. Class-size reduction on the scale recently implemented in Dutch primary education has no beneficial impact on pupils' achievement. An extension of the length

Table 8.1
Summary of effects

Intervention	Outcome variables	Average effects	Disadvantaged groups	Effect(s) for disadvantaged groups
Lowering school starting age by one month	Early language and math scores	0.024 (0.016) s.d. (language); 0.022 (0.016) s.d. (math)	Dutch pupils with low-educated parents; Minority pupils	0.062 (0.034) s.d. (language); 0.061 (0.034) s.d. (math); 0.060 (0.028) s.d. (language); 0.071 (0.029) s.d. (math)
Increasing class size by one pupil	Language and math scores in grades 4, 6, 8	−0.261 (0.270) percentile points (language 6th grade) to 0.857 (0.367) percentile points (math 8th grade)	Low-achieving pupils (25th percentile)	−0.245 (0.424) percentile points (language 6th grade) to 1.050 (0.414) percentile points (math 6th grade)
Extra resources for personnel	Language, math, and information processing scores in grade 8		Minority pupils	−0.055 (0.043) s.d. (language); −0.023 (0.047) s.d. (arithmetic); −0.035 (0.043) s.d. information processing
Extra resources for computers	Language, math, and information processing scores in grade 8		Dutch pupils with low-educated parents; minority pupils	−0.079 (0.030) s.d. (language); −0.061 (0.033) s.d. (arithmetic); −0.032 (0.030) s.d. information processing
Extending lower vocational program	Earnings after 20 years		Students in lower secondary vocational programs	−0.018 (0.019) percentage earnings change

of lower vocational programs with an extra year of general training that took place in the mid-1970s appears to have no positive impact on earnings of graduates 20 years later. The only intervention that has a clear beneficial effect is to allow young children from disadvantaged families to attend school at a younger age. This policy recommendation concurs with Heckman's (1999) advice to start investing in human capital at a young age. In his view, an important element are dynamic complementarities in skill formation ("skill begets skill"). This view is further developed in Cunha et al. (2005). They argue that skill attainment at one stage of the life cycle raises skill attainment at later stages of the life cycle (self-productivity) and that early investment facilitates the productivity of later investment (complementarity).

The summary of findings has also an important methodological edge. Two of the five interventions could be evaluated with a convincing approach owing to specific features of the implemented policy. The personnel subsidy for primary schools treats schools with at least 70 percent minority students very differently from schools with less than 70 percent minority students. The computer subsidy for primary schools treats schools with at least 70 percent disadvantaged students very differently from schools with less than 70 percent disadvantaged students. In both cases, the specific design of the policy offers a neat research design, but in both cases this was not intentional. The policymakers were not aware of the evaluation opportunities they created. This gives rise to two recommendations. First, it seems likely that more policies with discontinuous treatments have been implemented without the intention to use this for evaluation. Researchers should utilize these features whenever possible. Second, the examples show that it is possible to implement policies that treat very similar cases rather differently. Neither in the case of the personnel subsidy nor in the case of the ICT subsidy have there been any complaints from schools, teachers, parents, or their organizations about unequal treatment. Policymakers should consider taking advantage of this by including such features in the designs of new programs. These features can then be exploited to evaluate the policy.

8.4 Appendix

Table 8.2 briefly describes the data sources used in the research papers summarized in this contribution.

Table 8.2
Data sources

Evaluation study	Name(s) of data sources	Population	Year(s) outcome measured	Type of data collection
School-attendance age	PRIMA	2nd graders	1994, 1996, 1998, 2000	Achievement tests + questionnaires
Class-size reduction	PRIMA	4th, 6th, and 8th graders	1994	Achievement tests + questionnaires
Extra funding for personnel	CITO + administrative data	8th graders in schools with 60% to 80% minority students in 1998	2002–2003	Nationwide exit exam + administrative data
Extra funding for ICT	CITO + administrative data	8th graders in schools with 60% to 80% disadvantaged students in 1999	2002–2003	Nationwide exit exam + administrative data
Extending lower vocational school	Labor force survey	Birth cohorts 1953 to 1963 who enrolled in lower vocational school	1995	Questionnaires

Notes

1. An appendix to this chapter gives a brief description of the various data sources on which the underlying research papers are based.

2. Dutch education policy distinguishes between two main groups of disadvantaged students: nonminority students with less educated parents and minority students. In the funding scheme of primary schools, schools receive 25 percent extra funding for a non-minority student with less educated parents, and 90 percent extra funding for a minority student. In the near future, this system is about to change to a scheme that compensates on the basis of measured language deficiencies at a young age.

3. The official exchange rate before the guilder was taken out of circulation was 2.2 guilders for 1 euro.

4. The evaluation of the extra funding for personnel uses information of schools with 60 percent to 80 percent minority students (group A). The evaluation of the extra funding for ICT uses information of schools with 60 percent to 80 percent disadvantaged students (group B). All schools in group A also receive the ICT-subsidy because schools with 60 percent to 70 percent minority students also have at least 10 percent nonminority students with low-educated parents. On the other hand, virtually no school in group B received the personnel subsidy because schools with 70 percent to 80 percent disadvantaged students typically have less than 60 percent minority students. Consequently, the

personnel subsidy is evaluated in a situation in which all schools (treatment and control) also receive the ICT-subsidy, and the ICT-subsidy is evaluated in a situation in which no school (treatment and control) receive the personnel subsidy.

5. Related are also the studies by Harmon and Walker (1995), Vieira (1999), and Pischke (2003).

References

Aakvik, A., K. Salvanas, and K. Vaage. (2003). "Measuring Heterogeneity in the Returns to Education in Norway Using Educational Reforms. Discussion Paper No. 815, IZA.

Angrist, J. D., and V. Lavy. (1999). "Using Maimonides' Rule to Estimate the Effect of Class Size on Scholastic Achievement." *Quarterly Journal of Economics* 114: 533–575.

Angrist, J. D., and V. Lavy. (2002). "New Evidence on Classroom Computers and Pupil Learning." *Economic Journal* 112: 735–765.

Bandura, A. (1986). *Social Foundations of Thought and Action: A Social Cognitive Theory.* Englewood Cliffs, NJ: Prentice Hall.

Beerends, H., and S. van der Ploeg. (2001). "Onderzoek vergoeding schoolspecifieke knelpunten." Report OA-230, Regioplan.

Cahan, S., and N. Cohen. (1989). "Age versus Schooling Effects on Intelligence Development." *Child Development* 60: 1239–1249.

Cunha, F., J. Heckman, L. Lochner, and D. Masterov. (2005). "Interpreting the Evidence of Life Cycle Skill Formation." Working Paper No. 11331, National Bureau for Economic Research.

Currie, J. (2001). "Early Childhood Interventions." *Journal of Economic Perspectives* 15: 213–238.

Dobbelsteen, S., J. Levin, and H. Oosterbeek. (2002). "The Causal Effect of Class Size on Scholastic Achievement: Distinguishing the Pure Class Size Effect from the Effect of Changes in Class Composition." *Oxford Bulletin of Economics and Statistics* 64: 17–38.

Garces, E., D. Thomas, and J. Currie. (2002). "Longer-term Effects of Head Start." *American Economic Review* 92: 999–1012.

Harmon, C., and I. Walker. (1995). "Estimates of the Economic Return to Schooling for the United Kingdom." *American Economic Review* 85: 1278–1286.

Heckman, J. J. (1999). "Policies to Foster Human Capital." Working Paper No. 7288, National Bureau for Economic Research.

Hoxby, C. M. (2000). "The Effects of Class Size on Student Achievement: New Evidence from Population Variation." *Quarterly Journal of Economics* 115: 1239–1285.

Krueger, A. B. (1999). "Experimental Estimates of Education Production Functions." *Quarterly Journal of Economics* 115: 1239–1285.

Krueger, A. B., and D. Whitmore. (2001). "The Effect of Attending a Small Class in the Early Grades on College-test Taking and Middle School Test Results: Evidence from Project STAR." Economic Journal 111: 1–28.

Leuven, E., M. Lindahl, H. Oosterbeek, and D. Webbink. (2004a). "The Effect of Extra Funding for Disadvantaged Pupils on Achievement." Review of Economics and Statistics, forthcoming.

Leuven, E., M. Lindahl, H. Oosterbeek, and D. Webbink. (2004b). "The Effect of Potential Time in School on Early Test Scores." Working paper.

Levin, J. D. (2001). "For Whom the Reductions Count: A Quantile Regression Analysis of Class Size and Peer Effects on Scholastic Achievement." Empirical Economics 26: 221–246.

Meghir, C., and M. Palme. (2003). "Ability, Parental Background and Education Policy: Empirical Evidence from a Social Experiment." Working Paper 5/03, IFS, London.

Meyer, B. D. (1995). "Natural and Quasi-Experiments in Economics." Journal of Business and Economics Statistics 13: 151–161.

Oosterbeek, H., and D. Webbink. (2004). "Wage Effects of an Extra Year of Basic Vocational Education." Economics of Education Review, forthcoming.

Oreopoulos, P. (2003). "Do Dropouts Drop Out Too Soon? International Evidence from Changes in School-Leaving Laws. Working Paper No. 10155, National Bureau for Economic Research.

Pischke, J.-S. (2003). "The Impact of Length of the School Year on Student Performance and Earnings: Evidence from the German Short School Years." Working Paper No. 9964, National Bureau for Economic Research.

Rouse, C. E., A. B. Krueger, and L. Markman. (2004). "Putting Computerized Instruction to the Test: A Randomized Evaluation of a 'Scientifically Based' Reading Program." Economics of Education Review 23: 323–338.

Schunk, D. H. (1987). "Peer Models and Children's Behavioural Change." Review of Educational Research 57: 149–174.

Vieira, J. A. C. (1999). "Returns to Education in Portugal." Labour Economics 6: 535–542.

Woessmann, L., and M. West. (2006). "Class-Size Effects in School Systems around the World: Evidence from Between-Grade Variation in TIMSS." European Economic Review 50: 695–736.

9

Equalizing Opportunity for Racial and Socioeconomic Groups in the United States through Educational-Finance Reform

Julian R. Betts and John E. Roemer

9.1 Introduction

Education is perhaps the main tool that democracies use to attempt to equalize economic opportunities among citizens. It is commonly thought that opportunity equalization, in that dimension, is implemented by the provision of equal educational resources to all students. We argue here that that is not so, and we attempt to compute the distribution of educational spending in public schools in the United States that would equalize opportunities for a measure of economic welfare—namely, earning capacity.

In the United States, lawsuits over the last 35 years have challenged the constitutionality of public education-finance systems in most states. Subsequent court orders have typically acted to reduce gaps in spending per pupil between have- and have-not districts, while increasing the power of state governments to control spending.[1] Further, these court cases have tended to shift in focus over time from the simpler view of equal opportunity described above (namely, equalizing resources) toward an alternative that instead espouses equalizing *outcomes*, such as test scores and graduation rates.

This approach is much closer but still not identical to the definition of equal opportunity presented in this chapter. This shift away from equal resources to equal outcomes has been embraced by the "school adequacy" movement, which through court cases has argued that all schools should be held to a set of minimum-outcome standards. In many cases, adequacy proponents have successfully argued that holding all schools to equal absolute standards means that society must spend *more* on schools that serve less affluent students. Hoff (2004) writes that "Plaintiffs' success in adequacy-based school finance suits began with the 1989 Kentucky Supreme Court decision that declared the state's school system unconstitutional and ordered the legislature to appropriate enough money 'to provide each child in Kentucky an adequate education.' The decision shifted the legal debate away from 'equitable' funding, or money spread fairly among districts to 'adequate' funding, or whether the state spends enough."

In one well-known adequacy case, *Campaign for Fiscal Equity v. State of New York*, the plaintiff sued on the grounds that the status quo did not offer New York City students the "sound, basic education" promised by the state constitution. In late 2004, a court referee panel recommended an increase in spending for New York City schools by $5.6 billion, or 45 percent (Hoff 2004).

Over the last 30 years and throughout the last century, public school systems have also radically increased real spending per pupil (see, e.g., Hanushek and Rivkin 1997 or Betts 1996). Significant bodies of empirical work examine the impact of school spending on adults' earnings. This literature has yielded mixed results, but most papers indicate that increased school spending is associated with, at best, rather small gains in adult earnings.[2] Relatively little work has used this literature to estimate the magnitude of educational reform required to equalize opportunities across workers from different backgrounds. An analysis requires estimates of the impact of finance reform on earnings for each type of worker and an analysis of the required reallocation, or increase, in education dollars needed to level the playing field. This chapter seeks to provide estimates of the extent to which increasing spending per pupil contributes to creating equality of opportunity.

We intend our work as a positive analysis of what is possible rather than as a normative analysis of what should be done. Indeed, both proponents and opponents of equal opportunity should share a desire for a better understanding of what retargeting of educational dollars might achieve and what the attendant costs might be.

Using the National Longitudinal Survey of Young Men (NLSYM) dataset, we find that implementing an equal opportunity policy across men of different races—using educational finance as the instrument and ensuring that no race received less than the average observed nationally—would require spending nine times as much on black students, per capita, as on white students. Even the lower bound of bootstrapped confidence intervals for the policy estimates suggests large reallocations between races. An equal opportunity policy across men from different socioeconomic backgrounds that ignores race does almost nothing to equalize wages across races. Similarly, an alternative definition of equal opportunity—which holds that all students should receive identically funded schools and wage results should be let to fall as they may—does almost nothing to reduce the wage gaps between racial groups. The main reason for this is that a policy of "equally funded schools" takes no account of the large gaps in human and social capital that exist among very young, even preschool children.[3]

For interracial allocations, we find evidence of a trade-off between equity and total product, with reallocation lowering the wage bill by about 5 percent. In contrast, for reallocations based on parental education, equalization increases the wage bill by about 2 percent because the impact of school spending appears to be slightly higher for those with less highly educated parents.

The next section outlines the theory of equal opportunity and discusses the evolution of equality of opportunity in the United States over the last 30 years. Section 9.3 describes the data and discusses estimates of the impact of school spending. Section 9.4 summarizes the algorithm used to compute the equal opportunity policy and the optimal spending per pupil by group. It also examines the implications of a "race-blind" equal-opportunity policy for the black-white wage gap. Section 9.5 compares the costs and benefits of reallocating educational expenditures. Section 9.6 provides a summary of the chapter's policy implications.

9.2   The Theory of Equality of Opportunity

Our goal is to calculate the reallocation of educational spending needed to equalize opportunities among students for future earning capacity. To do so first requires a short review of a theory of equal opportunity that one of us has recently elaborated (Roemer 1998), a theory that attempts to formalize the "level the playing field" metaphor. The troughs of the playing field, in that metaphor, are the disadvantages that individuals suffer, with regard to attaining some goal (here, the capacity to earn income), owing to *circumstances* for which society believes they should not be held accountable—such as their race or the socioeconomic status of their parents. In contrast to circumstances, an equal opportunity ethic maintains that differences in the degree to which individuals achieve the goal in question that arise from their differential expenditure of *effort* are, morally speaking, perfectly all right. It is crucial to understand that by *effort* we mean not only the extent to which a person exerts himself or herself but all the other background traits of the individual that might affect his or her success but that we exclude from the list of *circumstances*. The partition of causes into circumstances and effort is the central move that distinguishes an equal opportunity ethic from an equal-outcome ethic. Although an equal-outcome ethic implicitly holds the individual responsible for nothing, an equal opportunity ethic emphasizes that an individual has a claim against society for a low outcome only if he or she expended sufficiently high effort.[4]

Five words constitute the relevant vocabulary: circumstances, type, effort, objective, and instrument. A *type* is the set of individuals with the same circumstances. The *objective* is the condition for which opportunities are to be equalized, and the *instrument* is the policy intervention (in our case, educational finance) used to effect that equalization. Roughly speaking, the equal opportunity policy is the value of the instrument that ensures that an agent's expected value of the objective is a function only of his effort and not of his circumstances. Thus, educational finance, if it is to equalize opportunities for future earning capacity, should ensure that a young person's expected wage will be a function only of his effort and not of his circumstances.

Suppose that a list of circumstances has been specified as has a scalar measure of effort e. First, we partition the relevant population into T types. Let the expected value of the objective for individuals in type t be a function $u^t(x, e)$, where x is the "resource" that the individual is allocated by the policy instrument. Suppose for the moment that all those in type t are allocated an amount x^t of the resource—in our case, educational finance. The ensuing distribution of effort in that type will be denoted by a probability distribution $\mathbf{F}^t(\cdot, x^t)$ (x^t is a parameter of the distribution). These distributions will differ across types, even if different types receive the same amount of the resource. Note that the distribution functional $\mathbf{F}^t$ is a *characteristic of the type* and not of any individual. This apparently trivial remark is important.

Equality of opportunity holds that individuals should not be held responsible for their circumstances—that is, their type. In constructing an intertype-comparable measure of effort, we must recognize that some individuals come from types that have "good" distributions of effort and that some from types with "poor" distributions—for coming from a type with a poor distribution of effort should not count against a person. We therefore take the intertype comparable measure of effort to be the *quantile* of the effort distribution in his type at which an individual sits. We say that all individuals at the πth quantile of their effort distributions, across types, have tried equally hard.[5]

To restate this important point, it would be wrong to pass judgments on the quality of effort expended by individuals in different types by looking at their pure expenditure of effort, for those raw effort levels are polluted (as far as our theory is concerned) by being drawn from distributions for which we do not wish to hold the individuals responsible. The *distribution* of effort of a type is a characteristic of the type and not of any individual, and as such, it is a circumstance as far as the individual is concerned. To the extent that an individual's effort is low in absolute terms because he or she belongs to a type with a low mean effort, the individual should not be held responsible. We therefore say that the best measure of an individual's effort is effort relative to effort of others in his or her type, as captured by rank or quantile on the effort distribution of type. We thus treat two individuals in different types, who sit at the same quantile of the effort distributions of their types, as having tried equally hard.

Our task is therefore to find that value of the policy that makes it the case that, *at each quantile*, the expected value of the objective *across types*, is "equal." Since equality will virtually never be possible, we really mean "maximin" where we just wrote "equal." Unfortunately, even this instruction is incoherent, for it amounts to maximizing many objectives simultaneously, and so some second-best approach must be taken. We make the compromise as follows.

Let $v^t(\pi, x^t)$ be the (average) value of the objective for individuals in type t, at quantile π of the effort distribution in type t, if the type is allocated x^t in resource. (In the application we study, $v^t(\pi, x^t)$ is the logarithm of the wage at the πth quantile of the wage distribution of individuals of type i if x^i was invested in their education.) For a given value of π in the interval $[0, 1]$, there will be a policy $x(\pi) = (x^1, x^2, \ldots, x^T)$ solving

$$\underset{x^1, x^2, \ldots, x^T}{Max} \underset{t}{Min} \; v^t(\pi, x^t)$$

subject to $(x^1, \ldots, x^T) \in X$,

where X is the feasible set of policies. $x(\pi)$ is the policy that maximizes the minimum value of the objective for all agents of all types at effort quantile π. If $x(\pi)$ were the same policy for all π, that would be, unambiguously, the equal opportunity policy. But that will almost never be the case in actual applications, and so our compromise will be to average these policies—that is, we declare the equal-opportunity policy to be

$$x^{EOp} = \int_0^1 \underset{(x^1,\ldots,x^T) \in X}{ArgMax} \underset{t}{Min}\ v^t(\pi, x^t)\, d\pi. \tag{9.1}$$

If X is a convex set, then x^{EOp} is feasible.

For example, suppose we look at 10 deciles of wages in each type. We would compute, for each decile, the investment policy that maximized the minimum wage in that decile, across the various types. This would, in general, give us 10 different investment policies. We declare the equal opportunity policy to be the average of these 10 policies.

Thus, given a specification of the circumstances, the effort measure, the objective, the instrument, and the data necessary to calculate the functions v^t, we can solve for the equal opportunity policy. Note that the equalization of opportunities according to this formulation is always *relative* to a given resource constraint, specified by the feasible set X. In what follows, we apply this theory—which the reader can find elaborated at more length, and philosophically justified, in Roemer (1998)—to educational policy in the United States.

9.2.1 Equality of Opportunity in Practice

As argued in Roemer (1998), one conception of equal opportunity is the principle of nondiscrimination. This approach says that employers should judge job applicants solely on their productivity rather than on traits such as race or nationality. This requirement lies at the heart of the Civil Rights Act of 1964. But a second definition of equal opportunity, and the one that we use in this chapter, argues that nondiscrimination is insufficient for equalizing opportunities. One must compensate for historical inequities to the extent that they adversely affect the circumstances of living individuals.

Donohue (1994) argues persuasively that American employment law has evolved from a "nondiscrimination" view toward an approach resembling our conception of equal opportunity. His prime example is the 1991 Americans with Disabilities Act (ADA). The ADA requires employers to supply extra resources to disabled workers so that their productivity better reflects their effort.

As a second example, in 1975 the Education for All Handicapped Children Act began to require schools to provide additional educational services to handicapped children. This provides a clear example of equal opportunity legislation, since it attempts to level the playing field by spending *more* than the average on students with learning or physical disabilities.[6]

A third example derives from federal subsidies for K through 12 education. Title I spending flows to schools serving disproportionate shares of disadvantaged students. More recently, the federal No Child Left Behind Act of 2001 directs districts to allocate funding for "supplemental services" (that is, tutoring) for students in schools that have failed to meet the individual state's definitions of adequate yearly progress for several years in a row.

The admission policies of American universities provide a fourth example of how equal opportunity, rather than nondiscrimination, has come into common use. Typically, universities have set lower admissions standards for minorities to compensate for precollegiate differences in human-capital acquisition among races. Recent court decisions and voter initiatives have led public universities in Texas and California to end their policy of using race when making admission decisions. In both states, universities now use alternative forms of affirmative action in admissions that, for instance, take into account whether either parent of a student has attended university. As we show, a switch from a race-based equal opportunity program to one that conditions on socioeconomic traits such as parental education leads to radically different recommendations.

9.3   Data and Regression Results for Spending per Pupil

9.3.1   Data
We choose as objective the logarithm of an individual's weekly wages as a young adult. We model log weekly earnings from the NLSYM, computed as the log of the product of hours per week and hourly wages and adjusted to 1990 prices using the Consumer Price Index. Spending per pupil in the student's district, gathered from a 1968 survey of high schools, is also included in the analysis as the policy instrument. Betts (1996) finds that existing estimates of the impact of spending per pupil on wages based on the NLSYM fall roughly in the middle of published empirical estimates.[7] Furthermore, the confidence intervals of the black-white estimates we obtain encompass most of the results in the published literature. The regression sample for each race consists of all wage observations between 1966 and 1981 for workers

who were 18 or older and who were not enrolled in school or college in the given year. We drop a wage observation if weekly earnings are below $50 or above $5,000 in 1990 prices. See the working paper mentioned in an earlier note for the underlying regression models.[8]

9.3.2 Outline of the Empirical Estimates on Spending per Pupil

We examine the reallocation of spending per pupil that would be necessary to equalize opportunities for weekly earnings. Such reallocations have been at the heart of court-mandated school reform over the last quarter century. We first focus on reallocations across types of student, given a fixed educational budget. However, since such reallocations are virtually certain to reduce spending per pupil for certain types, we also calculate equal opportunity solutions where the constraint is not a fixed budget but a requirement that no type receive less than a prespecified amount per pupil. Since no students become worse off in an absolute sense, this second approach is perhaps more politically realistic but potentially quite costly.

Recall that we partition each person's traits into two sets—those against which we wish to indemnify the person (circumstances) and those for which we hold the person accountable (effort). The former traits are used to partition people into types; the latter traits are treated as the person's choice variables. If we define many types (for instance, by distinguishing people not only by race but also by, for example, parental education), our equal opportunity policy will typically call for a more differentiated allocation of spending.

With this in mind, we begin with a relatively conservative approach in which we define only two types—black and white—thus holding each person in our sample accountable for all other traits, such as family background and geographic location (both region of the country and rural/urban/suburban residence). The use of two types also allows for an intuitive discussion of the optimal policy. We then consider outcomes using parental education as an additional or alternative factor in determining type.

The theory outlined earlier emphasizes that the impact of school spending on earnings for a given type of worker may vary with the person's ranking in the earnings distribution, conditional on school spending. Quantile regression provides a technique that almost perfectly fits with this theory. We estimate models of log weekly wages that condition on spending per pupil in the district in which the worker attended school. We estimate a series of quantile regressions for a given type of worker:

$$\log w_i^t = \alpha^{tq} + \beta^{tq} x_i^t + Z_i^t \theta^{tq} + \varepsilon_i^t, \quad q = 0.1, 0.2, \ldots, 0.9, \tag{9.2}$$

where t indexes the worker's type, i indexes the observation, q is the discrete quantile that corresponds with the continuous variable π in the theory developed earlier, w_i^t is weekly wages, x_i^t is spending per pupil for observation i and worker type t, Z_i^t is a row vector of other regressors, ε_i^t is an error term, and the other Greek symbols indicate coefficients. Here,

$$Quan_q(\log w_i^t \mid x_i^t, Z_i^t) = \alpha^{tq} + \beta^{tq} x_i^t + Z_i^t \theta^{tq} \tag{9.3}$$

is the conditional quantile for the given quantile q. We estimate this model nine times for each type of worker for quantiles $q = 0.1, 0.2, \ldots, 0.9$. What quantile regression allows us to do is to estimate the impact of spending per pupil on workers at different points in the conditional wage distribution. By *conditional wage distribution*, we mean the ranking of workers in terms of the outcome variable after conditioning, or taking account of, the individual worker's values for spending per pupil and the other regressors in Z_t^i.

The coefficient estimates are calculated by minimizing the following objective function for the qth quantile for type t:

$$\sum_i |\log w_i^t - \alpha^{tq} - \beta^{tq} x_i^t - Z_i^t \theta^{tq}| \lambda_i, \tag{9.4}$$

where λ_i are weights defined by

$$\lambda_i = \begin{cases} 2q, & \text{if } \log w_i^t - \alpha^{tq} - \beta^{tq} x_i^t - Z_i^t \theta^{tq} > 0; \\ 2(1-q), & \text{otherwise.} \end{cases} \tag{9.5}$$

A key feature of quantile regression is that by construction a proportion $1 - q$ of the observations will have positive residuals with the remaining observations having negative residuals. In this way, the weights will give proportionately more weight to workers whose log earnings, conditional on the regressors, are "close" to the quantile in question.[9]

We condition not only on spending x_i^t but also on a vector of other regressors Z_i^t. These other variables, while exogenous to the worker, might influence his earnings. Without taking account of family background, for instance, our estimates of the impact of school spending could suffer from omitted variable bias. Accordingly, we include in our vector Z_i^t the worker's age and its square, dummies for whether the person's mother and father were present in the home when the person was 14, and the number of siblings. In addition, in the black and white typology we also condition on the level of education of the more highly educated parent. Lacking experimental data, there is still a chance that additional omitted variables could bias our results in an unknown direction.

We do not condition on the worker's own level of education because this is a choice variable, and the impact of spending per pupil may work partly through its influence on students' subsequent years of education completed. If we had controlled for years of education but spending per pupil influenced this variable, then we would be understating the impact of spending per pupil on students' later wages. Betts (1996) finds weak evidence in the literature that spending per pupil is positively associated with years of education.

This method has two distinct advantages. It is entirely consistent with the theory in that π is defined conditional on x_i^t. Second, the pattern of coefficients obtained from the nine quantile regressions performed for each worker type allows for nonlinearities in the relation between wages and spending per pupil x_i^t and other regressors.

These quantiles conform closely to the quantiles of effort—that is, the person's percentile ranking by log wages, conditional on type and spending per pupil. Thus, roughly speaking, the coefficient estimates for $q = 0.9$ describe the determinants of wages for people ranked at the 90th percentile of log wages after conditioning on the regressors or, in terms of the theory, for people ranked at the 90th percentile of effort. Recall that *effort* is shorthand for what we more accurately called the *aspect of autonomous volition* in a person's behavior. In reality, effort is multidimensional and includes not only years of schooling but marital status, region, and other personal choices. Further, an individual who earns a high wage simply by virtue of inheriting his father's good job will be classified as one who expended high effort. It is important to bear in mind the *conservative* nature[10] of this assumption when considering the estimates presented below.

9.3.3 Regression Results

We obtained quantile regression estimates based on three different partitions of the sample of workers into types. First, we partition workers into blacks and whites. Second, we examine a race-blind typology that assumes that workers should be compensated not for their race but rather for the level of education of their parents. Finally, we discuss a hybrid typology that divides black and white workers separately into two approximately equally sized groups based on the years of schooling of the more highly educated parent.

Because of space constraints, we do not display the quantile regression results, although they are available on request from the authors. The empirical results generally conform to past results using this and similar datasets. Family socioeconomic status, especially number of siblings and parental education, are strongly related to log wages of workers later in life. Earnings rise with age but at a decreasing rate. Spending per pupil appears to be positively and significantly related to earnings, as past research with the NLS-YM has suggested (see Betts 1996 for a review). In the final typology, which divides workers based on both race and parental education, the estimated effect of school spending is estimated less precisely than for the other typologies.

While we found that the estimated effect of school spending varies among types at $q = 0.5$, there is no definitive relationship between the coefficient on school spending and the degree of a person's advantage.

The next step involves using these regression estimates to compute the equal opportunity policy. We need to boil down the individual predicted wages from these models to a simple summary consisting of the pair (a^{tq}, b^{tq}) that predicts average log wages for type t conditional on quantile q and spending per pupil x^t:

$$v^t(q, x^t) = a^{tq} + b^{tq}x^t, \tag{9.6}$$

where $v^t(q, x^t)$ is the log of weekly earnings predicted for workers of type t at quantile q who received spending per pupil of x^t. Our estimate of b^{tq} is simply β^{tq} from (9.2). To obtain our estimates of the part of predicted weekly log earnings that does not depend on school spending a^{tq}, we must first identify those workers in type t who belong to a given quantile q. Therefore, after each quantile regression we rank observations i in type t by the residuals and assign observation i in type t a ranking ρ_i^{tq} such that $\rho_i^{tq} \in [0, 1]$, and $\rho_i^{tq} = 1$ indicates the wage observation with the largest residual in the quantile regression for that type. We selected observations i in type t with ρ_i^{tq} within ± 0.05 of a given q and calculated the mean predicted log wage of those workers assuming that $x^t = 0$ and that all workers are aged 30—that is,

$$a^{tq} = \hat{\alpha}^{tq} + (Z_i^t \,|\, age = 30)\hat{\theta}^{tq}, \tag{9.7}$$

where circumflexes indicate estimated coefficients. We remove variations in predicted wages related to age because it is unlikely that policymakers would aim to remove all age-related variations in earnings among types. However, we leave in our estimate of a^{tq} variations related to other background variables such as the number of siblings. In sum, these intercept estimates are estimates of predicted earnings of workers who are close to the given quantile, after setting the workers' age to 30 and spending per pupil to zero.

The equal opportunity policy will not remove variations in predicted earnings *within* types, but the policy will attempt to compensate for variations *across* types at given quantiles.

9.4   Calculation of the Spending Allocations That Implement Equal Opportunity

9.4.1   Main Results
We solve a discrete version of program (9.1), where the effort quantile π takes on nine values, which we denote $q = 1, \ldots, 9$. For each quantile q and type t, we have an estimated relationship, as described in section 9.3:

$$v^t(q, x^t) = a^{tq} + b^{tq} x^t, \tag{9.8}$$

where v is logarithm of the future wage and x^t is the amount invested in the education of the student. The set X is defined by the budget constraint

$$\sum_t p^t x^t = R, \tag{9.9}$$

where p^t is the fraction of individuals of type t, and R is spending per student. Thus, for each q we solve

$$x(q) = \text{ArgMax}_x \ \text{Min}_t (a^{tq} + b^{tq} x^t)$$

$$\text{subject to } \sum_t p^t x^t = R. \tag{9.10}$$

We then define the equal opportunity policy as

$$x^{EOp} = \frac{1}{9} \sum_{q=1}^{9} x(q). \tag{9.11}$$

Program (9.10) is solved by solving a series of linear programs. Typically, at the solution of (9.10), the most disadvantaged type will be the worst off at the solution, and so the solution of (9.10) is the solution of the following linear program, where type one is the most disadvantaged type, and in our example there are four types:

$$\underset{x}{Max}(a^{1q} + b^{1q}x^1)$$

subject to $a^{tq} + b^{tq}x^t \geq a^{1q} + b^{1q}x^1, \quad t = 2,3,4$ \hfill (9.12)

and $\sum_t p^t x^t = R.$

To solve (9.10), we solve four linear programs, where, in turn, each of the four types is assumed to be the worst-off type at the solution, and we then take the solution to be the one of these four, which maximizes the value of (9.10).

We report on various aspects of the equal opportunity policies. To generate confidence intervals for these policies, we bootstrapped the equal opportunity policy using a bootstrap sample of 1,500. One remark is in order. For a small proportion of the bootstrap estimates, the coefficient $b^{1q} < 0$. The solution to (9.12) in these cases would entail $x^{1q} = 0$. Instead of taking this to be the solution, we set $x^{tq} = R$ for all (t, q) for which $b^{tq} < 0$.

Beginning with the simple black and white typology, we first calculated the optimal allocation of educational funding under the assumption that average spending per pupil (R) is $2,500 in 1990 prices, which is approximately the average in the NLSYM sample.[11]

Egalitarian policies are criticized for being "inefficient"—that is, for decreasing output. It is possible but not certain that reallocation of educational spending between types will cause the overall wage bill to shrink if the marginal product of educational resources is higher for the type from which funding is being removed. Therefore, we also calculate the ratio of the wage bill that is predicted to result from the equal opportunity policy to the wage bill under the *equal resource* policy, in which all students receive the same amount of the financial resource. Our calculations based on the black-white typology assume that 12.0 percent of the population is black and that 88.0 percent is white, which matches the population frequencies in 1966 in the NLSYM (table 9.1).[12]

We also calculate the required aggregate budget, which assures that, under the equal opportunity policy, all types would receive at least

Table 9.1
Sample sizes, population shares, mean earnings, and mean spending per pupil by worker type, for two typologies

Panel A

	Type	
	Black	White
Observations	2,737	14,475
Estimated share of population, 1966	12.0%	88.0%
Estimated mean earnings of workers in this type, 1966–1981	385.34	533.96
Mean spending per pupil (000s)	2.091	2.243

Panel B

	Type			
	Parental education < 9 yrs.	Parental education 9–11 yrs.	Parental education = 12 yrs.	Parental education > 12 yrs.
Observations	3,907	3,201	6,860	3,244
Estimated share of population, 1966	21.1	17.0	39.0	23.0
Estimated mean earnings of workers in this type, 1966–1981	493.54	523.45	586.40	631.72
Mean spending per pupil (000s)	2.138	2.202	2.179	2.261

(approximately) $2,500 per capita. Such a no-lose option might be politically necessary to implement an equal opportunity policy in reality.

For each of our 1,500 bootstrap estimates under the no-lose scenario, we calculated the value of R at which the most advantaged type would receive an investment in the interval ($2,450, $2,550). These results are reported in the bottom three lines of tables 9.2 and 9.3.

We report the results for two partitions of the sample into typologies: a two-type typology for black (B) and white (W) and a four-type typology where the circumstance is the educational level of the more highly educated parent. We also briefly discuss results from a third typology obtained by crossing race and parental education.

9.4.1.1 Type Partition: Black and White The results are reported in table 9.2. At the equal opportunity solution, in our point estimate, blacks receive approximately 18 times what whites receive when $R = 2.5$. The .025 and .975 values of this ratio from the bootstrap samples are 7.76 and 79.17. We can thus assert, conservatively, that equal-

Table 9.2
Point and bootstrap estimates, educational spending (x) and wages (w), black or white (B or W) typology, average spending per pupil $R = \$2,500$, and minimum spending per pupil $x_{min} = \$2,500$ with no limit on average spending R

	Average spending per pupil R	Spending per pupil, blacks x^B	Spending per pupil, whites x^W	Ratio x^B/x^W	Weekly wages, blacks w^B	Weekly wages, whites w^W	Average wages under equal resources w^{ER}	Average wages under equal opportunity w^{EOp}	Efficiency ratio v
Average spending $R = 2.5$:									
Point estimate	2.50	14.76	0.828	17.82	0.584	0.604	0.631	0.602	.953
.025 estimate	2.50	10.71	0.241	7.76	0.462	0.586	0.625	0.571	.905
.975 estimate	2.50	19.07	1.381	79.17	0.688	0.622	0.636	0.628	.944
Minimum spending per type $X_{min} = 2.5$:									
Point estimate	4.85	22.18	2.49	8.92	0.709	0.653	0.701	0.660	.942
.025 estimate	3.85	13.58	2.45	5.39	0.642	0.647	0.668	0.651	0.807
.975 estimate	8.55	53.12	2.55	21.49	1.039	0.659	0.832	0.699	1.000

Note: All dollar amounts are expressed in thousands of 1990 dollars.

Table 9.3
Point estimates and bootstrap estimates, educational spending x and wages u, four-type parental education typology, average spending per pupil $R = \$2,500$ and minimum spending per pupil $x_{min} = \$2,500$ with no limit on average spending R

	Average spending per pupil R	Spending per pupil (1 = lowest parental education)				Weekly wages (1 = lowest parental education)				Average wages		
		x_{E1}	x_{E2}	x_{E3}	x_{E4}	w_{E1}	w_{E2}	w_{E3}	w_{E4}	Equal resources w^{ER}	Equal opportunity w^{EOp}	Efficiency ratio v
Average spending per pupil $R = 2.5$:												
Point estimate	2.50	5.36	3.62	1.88	1.10	0.656	0.653	0.638	0.659	0.633	0.649	1.026
.025 estimate	2.50	4.47	2.87	1.34	0.22	0.605	0.616	0.620	0.641	0.627	0.635	1.007
.975 estimate	2.50	6.28	4.20	2.21	1.14	0.670	0.674	0.647	0.692	0.638	0.655	1.034
Minimum spending per type $x_{min} = 2.5$:												
Point estimate	4.33	7.31	4.75	3.61	2.51	0.749	0.714	0.698	0.694	0.695	0.710	1.023
.025 estimate	3.58	5.44	3.69	2.60	2.45	0.657	0.663	0.662	0.682	0.665	0.675	1.004
.975 estimate	4.93	9.69	6.34	4.53	2.55	0.821	0.790	0.716	0.706	0.714	0.730	1.031

Note: All dollar amounts are expressed in thousands of 1990 dollars. E_1 = parental education less than or equal to eight years. E_2 = 8 < parental education < 12. E_3 = parental education = 12. E_4 = parental education > 12.

izing opportunities for this typology and, at this budget, requires an investment in black students of *at least seven or eight times* the investment in whites.

If R is increased to the point where whites receive approximately $2,500 per capita, then this ratio falls, so that blacks receive approximately nine times as much per capita, and the confidence interval on this ratio from the bootstrap samples is (5.39, 21.49).

The columns labeled w^B and w^W show estimated average weekly earnings of black and white workers under the two scenarios in thousands of dollars and corresponding confidence intervals. The predicted wages after an equal opportunity policy is implemented in table 9.2 are much higher for blacks than is the raw earnings of blacks reported in table 9.1. The average wages of the two types are not equalized exactly. The lack of perfect equalization follows directly from the stipulation that all students of a given race receive the same x^t. (Policymakers under an equal opportunity policy would aim to equalize outcomes on average across types while not attempting to remove variations in the outcome within types that are attributed to variations in "effort.")

The second and third columns from the right-hand side of table 9.2 report the average weekly wage at the equal-resource and equal opportunity solutions, respectively (in thousands of dollars), and the last column is the ratio of these two numbers—our measure of "efficiency." We see there would be a substantial decrease in the average wage if we implemented the equal opportunity policy for this typology, in comparison to implementing the equal-resource policy. Under both the fixed-budget and the no-lose equal opportunity policies, the total wage bill drops by roughly 5 percent.

The reallocation of school resources needed to equalize opportunity between black and white men is substantial. Note, though, that our wage sample covers the years 1966 to 1981. To check whether it is possible that today smaller reallocations would be required, we examined data on usual weekly earnings of full-time male workers by race, as reported for the year 1996 in the Current Population Survey. The ratio of blacks' earnings to those of whites in 1996 was 71.0 percent, compared to 72.2 percent in our sample over the period 1966 to 1981. In absolute terms, the black-white wage gap in the NLSYM data was $149 per week in 1990 prices (table 9.1). In 1996, the same gap was $140.[13] Some readers may be surprised that the ratio and absolute gap in wages between black and white males changed so little between 1966 to 1981 and 1996. However, several papers, including Bound and

Freeman (1992), have documented the slowing of the convergence in wages between blacks and whites during the 1980s.

Thus, although our wage observations are centered in the 1970s, the black-white wage gap has changed so little over the last two decades that our results would be virtually unchanged if we used recent wage distributions.

9.4.1.2 Type Partition Based on Parental Education

Table 9.3 reports the results for the partition of the sample into four socioeconomic types, based on the educational attainment of the more highly educated parent.

The inequality in educational spending needed to equalize opportunity is strikingly less, in this typology, than in the black-white typology. The ratio of spending for the groups with the highest and lowest spending are 4.9 and 2.9 for the fixed-budget and no-lose scenarios, less than a third of the spending disparities required in the black and white typology. We also note that the size of the average wage at the equal opportunity policy is consistently larger than in the equal-resource policy. Thus, both equity and efficiency are improved here under the equal opportunity policy. This reflects the generally larger wage responses to increased spending among the two lower parental-education types relative to the two more advantaged types.

9.4.1.3 Type Partition: Low Black (LB), High Black (HB), Low White (LW), High White (HW)

This typology yields four types in total. It is an appropriate partition if society takes into account that more than race influences a young person's chances in life. We chose cutpoints in parental education that would divide the black and white samples into approximately equal halves.

Because of space constraints we do not present the results, although they are available from the authors. As expected, when we divide the white and black populations into higher and lower socioeconomic groups, the ratio of spending between the highest and lowest groups under the equal opportunity policy becomes larger. The spending ratio is higher because we have shifted parental education from the list of many factors determining "effort" and have labeled it a circumstance against which we seek to indemnify workers. Here the ratio of maximum spending per pupil to lowest spending among types is 23.9 and 9.2 for the $R = 2.5$ and the X_{min} scenarios, respectively, compared to 17.8 and 8.9 for the black and white typology.

9.4.2 Do Race-Blind Equal Opportunity Policies Do Much to Reduce Black-White Inequality?

As we wrote earlier, the emerging view in the United States seems to be that affirmative action, at least with regard to university admissions, is desirable when it favors students of low socioeconomic status but not when it is used to favor students of color.[14] In our language, this view holds that the type partition into types based on socioeconomic circumstances is ethically acceptable but not for the types that predicate on race. The natural question is, to what extent will opportunities be equalized by recognizing differential socioeconomic, but not differential racial, circumstances?

Our results suggest a pessimistic conclusion. Far less would be invested in black students under the equal opportunity policy associated with the socioeconomic typology of table 9.3 than under the equal opportunity policies that predicate on race. It is important to note, however, that the large investments in blacks of table 9.2 (contrasted with the relatively small investment in the most disadvantaged socioeconomic type of table 9.3) happen because blacks have an extra disadvantage and because blacks are a small share of the population (low p values), it is relatively cheap to subsidize them in the equal opportunity policy. In other words, it would be wrong to infer that blacks are three times as disadvantaged as the most disadvantaged socioeconomic type $(E1)$ because approximately three times as much is invested in the former compared to the latter at the equal opportunity policies in their *respective* typologies.

To study more formally the impact on blacks if equal opportunity policies condition on socioeconomic status rather than education, we calculate the percentage of black men in the regression samples in each of the earnings quintiles before and after the various policies are put into place. We adjust each worker's earnings as follows. For a given typology, we assign each worker a level of spending x^t dependent on his type in that typology. To calculate the earnings that would result for that worker, we multiply the change in spending that he would receive by the coefficient on spending from the black and white typology and the worker's actual quantile. We then find the quantile q that for worker i solves

$$q_i^t = \underset{q \in \{0.1, 0.2, \ldots, 0.9\}}{ArgMin} |q - \rho_i^{tq}|, \quad \text{where } t = B, W \tag{9.13}$$

for each wage observation i in the black and white types. This is simply the quantile that most closely matches the given wage observation.

Table 9.4
The percentage of black workers in each earnings quintile in raw data and after various types of reallocation of educational expenditure

	Earnings quintile (5 = Bottom)				
Description of allocation	5	4	3	2	1
Raw data	46.73	20.5	15.67	11.66	5.44
Average spending $R = 2.5$ for all workers	46.44	21.59	16.77	10.38	4.82
Equal opportunity black and white ($EOp\ B$ or W), average spending $R = 2.5$	25.43	21.99	16.11	20.09	16.37
Equal opportunity black and white ($EOp\ B$ or W), minimum spending per type $x_{min} = 2.5$, average spending $R = 4.85$	34.27	14.91	8.95	13.85	28.02
Equal opportunity (4-type parental education), average spending $R = 2.5$	38.29	21.56	21.67	12.31	6.17
Equal opportunity (4-type parental education), minimum spending per type $x_{min} = 2.5$, average spending $R = 4.33$	37.96	27.37	24.19	7.38	3.11

Note: Earnings data are adjusted for variations in earnings by age using regression coefficients from the black and white typology. Quintile 5 refers to the fifth of the population with the lowest earnings. Calculations are based on spending under various equalization and equal opportunity policies and regression coefficients from the black and white typology.

In addition, to put workers of different ages on an equal footing, we adjusted the wages of each worker to the predicted value if he had been 30.

Table 9.4 shows the results. The top row shows that in the raw data, blacks predominantly occupy the bottom two earnings quintiles. We next examine the outcome under a conservative definition of equality of opportunity in which all that society needs to do is to ensure equal funding per pupil at all schools. The second row shows the result when all students receive spending of 2.5. The results are similar to the raw data. This suggests that the court struggles over the last three decades to *equalize* spending across schools, even when successful, will have done little to equalize earnings between blacks and whites.

We then estimate the wages each worker would earn if various reallocations were put into effect under Roemer's definition of equality of opportunity. The fixed-budget equal opportunity policy (B or W, $R = 2.5$) greatly improves the earnings of blacks relative to whites, so that the median black now occupies the middle earnings quintile, and the percentage of blacks in the top earnings quintile triples. The alternative policy, with $R = 4.85$, pushes blacks away from the middle three quintiles and toward the top and bottom quintiles, where they are now overrepresented. Again, however, the median black belongs to the middle earnings quintile, suggesting a dramatic interracial equalization compared to the raw data or the school spending equalization shown in the first two rows.

A quite remarkable result is shown in the next two rows: when type is defined independently of race, by using only parental education, the equal opportunity reallocations leave the distribution of black workers across earnings quintiles little changed from the status quo in row 1. Even though 42 percent of blacks in the sample are in the type with low parental education and so receive spending of 5.36, this is a small reallocation relative to the more advantaged type, which receives 1.10. Moreover, 19 percent of whites also fall into the bottom socioeconomic group, while representing 70 percent of workers in this group. Together, these facts explain why the race-blind equal opportunity policy does so little to narrow the black-white gap in earnings.

Note that this striking result obtains because of the large numbers of whites in the lower categories of various measures of socioeconomic status in the United States. We believe that our finding therefore will apply to attempts to equalize opportunity in realms apart from K through 12 education: using proxies for race, such as parental education, will lead to equality-of-opportunity policies that only very partially equalize opportunity across races.

9.5   Comparing Costs and Benefits of Alternative Means of Equalizing Opportunity

We now compare the costs and the benefits of various equal opportunity policies. We work with the typology $\{B, W\}$. We measure benefits as the value of the objective function—that is, the mean of the lower envelope of the earnings:q functions for blacks and whites. (The lower envelope is the function whose value is the value of the objective, at each quantile, of the worst-off type.) To be precise, we define the *weekly* benefits from a policy φ as

$$\frac{1}{9} \sum_{q=0.1}^{0.9} \underset{t}{Min} \, \exp(v^t(q, \varphi)),$$

where $\exp(v^t(q, \varphi))$ is the average of the wage (the exponential of the dependent variable, the logarithm of the weekly wage) of individuals

Table 9.5
Estimated gains in the objective function and costs per student of various interventions using the black-white typology

Policy Description	Value of objective function ($)	Change relative to base case	P.D.V of estimated cost per student
Base case, unequal resources, mean spending = 2.5	$464.58	N/A	N/A
Equal resources, mean spending = 2.5	$465.68	$1.10	0
Equal opportunity, mean spending = 2.5	$510.91	$46.33	0
Equal opportunity, minimum spending per type = 2.5	$530.37	$65.79	$34,597.83

Note: Estimated cost per person is calculated as total program cost divided by the number of persons in the sample, where costs are calculated as a present value in the year in which the person reaches age 18. The "value of objective function" is derived from the average value of the lower envelope in log weekly wage: q space, reexpressed in average earnings per week for workers on the envelope. N/A: Not applicable.

at the qth quantile of the effort distribution of type t when the policy is φ.

Table 9.5 shows the value of the equal opportunity objective function for various scenarios. The table presents this mean in dollar terms to aid understanding. The base-case scenario is one in which mean x is $2,500 $(R = 2.5)$.[15] The value of the mean along the lower envelope, which in the base case consists of blacks at every quantile is $464.58 per week. The second row (equal resources) shows the gains that would result if all schools spent exactly $2,500 per pupil. As shown, the average gain in earnings for workers on the lower envelope is $1.10 per week or about 0.25 percent. Again, we see evidence that a more conservative definition of equal opportunity, which calls merely for equalization of school resources, is quite ineffective. The next two rows show the mean of wages on the lower envelope for the two equal opportunity solutions—first where average spending is held constant at $2,500 per week and then the cost-increasing intervention in which both types receive at least $2,500 per week. The gains in average earnings along the lower envelope are very large in both cases, between $46 and $66 per week with increases in the average wage well over 10 percent above the base case.

We now ask a related question: what are the relative sizes of the costs of implementing the various programs? Starting from a base of

$2,500 per pupil, neither equalizing spending at that level nor imple-
menting the equal opportunity plan with mean spending $R = 2.5$
has any impact on costs. Even equalization of spending across schools,
let alone the radical reallocation suggested by equal opportunity
with $R = 2.5$, may not be politically feasible, since some types (whites,
in the present analysis) face lower spending per pupil after the
reallocation.

Consider next the cost of the equal opportunity program with minimum spending of $2,500 per person of either type. To evaluate its cost
per pupil, we assume that any change in spending occurs from kindergarten through the year in which the pupil leaves school, which is appropriate since our measure of spending per pupil is measured for the
school district in which the student attended school. Using the empirical distribution of years of schooling, we then calculate the cumulative
change in spending per pupil from kindergarten up to the year in
which the student left school (or grade 12 in the case of high-school
graduates). We convert all expenditures to their value in the year in
which the student would have been in grade 12, using a discount rate
of 2.67 percent, which is the mean real interest rate between 1953 and
1997.[16]

The equal opportunity plan increases the mean earnings along the
lower envelope by $65.79 per week. But the costs of achieving equal
opportunity in this way are extremely large: in terms of present value
of spending in the year in which the person turns 18, the cost is over
$34,500 per person. This figure is obtained by dividing total program
cost by the number of people in the entire population. All of this
additional spending is directed toward blacks, who on average would
receive an extra $293,000 while in school. This is spread out over
the entire population, bringing the cost down to roughly $34,500 per
person.

Note that in table 9.4 it is inappropriate to compare the costs and
benefits directly since the costs are the present value of accumulated
spending for all students in all grade levels, while our measure of
benefit focuses on workers who are on the lower envelope only and
represents the gains during a typical week rather than over the entire
working lifetime. Both the benefits and the costs are sizeable. The predicted earnings gain works out to about $3,400 per year for each black
worker assuming 52 weeks of work or paid vacation annually. If we
think of this as an investment project, the upfront cost of $293,000 per
black would yield an annual payback of about 1.2 percent.

There are two reasons why the rate of return on increasing school expenditures through the equal opportunity algorithm is relatively small. The first reason is that spending per pupil has a modest impact on students' subsequent earnings. The second reason is that under the no-lose equal opportunity plan average spending rises dramatically. Furthermore, the value of the objective at its optimum, viewed as a function of R (the per capita resource endowment), is a concave increasing function, and the ratio of this "value function" (our "benefit") to R is a convex, decreasing function. Therefore, the benefit-cost ratio of an equal opportunity program that increases spending dramatically will be small.[17]

9.6 Concluding Comments

We conclude by summarizing the most important policy implications of our analysis.

First, even though court battles on educational finance have typically centered on the goal of equalizing spending across schools, our analysis suggests that this alone will do little to equalize opportunity, especially across races. The reason is that the impact of school spending on students' subsequent wages is rather modest compared to the racial gap in earnings. We estimate that full equalization of spending per pupil would increase the weekly earnings of workers along the lower envelope by only $1.10 or about 0.2 percent. Notably, some of the more recent court cases have moved beyond a conservative equal-spending credo to the notion of adequacy, which calls for spending more on the students most in need.

Second, to equalize opportunity across races, government would have to reallocate spending radically. Our results vary depending on whether overall spending is held constant or whether spending is increased such that no type experiences a decrease in school funding. In the first case, equalizing opportunity between races entails spending 18 times as much on blacks as on whites. In the second case, nine times as much must be spent on blacks. These estimates are uncertain. However, we have directly controlled for statistical uncertainty by bootstrapping our estimates of optimal policy. We note that even the lower bound of our 95 percent confidence interval yields black and white spending ratios of eight and five, which similarly suggest that mere equalization of spending can accomplish little.

A key issue difficult to overcome is that we extrapolate well beyond the range of spending per pupil observed in our data. Our estimates may be too high because, in extrapolating so far, we are missing increasing returns to school expenditures. However, we note that Betts and Johnson (1997) use the large range of spending per pupil observed at the state level over the period 1920 to 1959, do not find strong evidence of increasing returns to school resources, and, in fact, find some evidence of the opposite. Similarly, spending per pupil has risen dramatically since an average of about $2,500 per pupil in 1968, our survey year, to about $5,600 per pupil in 1999–2000 nationally and to as high as $9,060 in the District of Columbia.[18] In spite of more than a doubling in spending nationally and almost a quadrupling in D.C. relative to the national average in 1968, we know of no evidence of an "education miracle" over this period either nationally or in high-spending areas such as the District of Columbia and New Jersey. In other words, if there were strongly increasing returns in the education production function, we should have seen these begin to emerge over time. Our central point remains: mere equalization in spending achieves little.

Third, we compared the costs of the equal opportunity reforms with the annual payback measured by the increase in weekly earnings along our objective function. Under the equal opportunity policy that holds spending constant, the cost is by definition zero, but the benefits to workers along the lower envelope are substantial—an increase in earnings of 10 percent. The political drawbacks of this zero-cost reallocation are clear: it is financed by reducing spending for whites. Such a reform is likely to be much less politically feasible than a more expensive one that guarantees that no student sees a reduction in school spending. Our second equal opportunity policy sets a floor on spending per pupil for both races and is predicted to achieve more, increasing weekly earnings of workers along the lower envelope by just over 14 percent. But the cost is about $293,000 per black student or about $34,500 per student when distributed across all students.

Fourth, it matters enormously whether a program to equalize opportunity takes race into consideration. This insight is important given recent moves in California and Texas to eliminate race as a factor that is considered in university admissions. We found that a color-blind equal opportunity program that equalizes opportunities between types of student differentiated only by parental education does almost nothing to change the distribution of blacks across earnings quintiles. In the language of our model, given such a race-neutral policy, any variations in earnings that are correlated with race would be attributed to variations in effort rather than circumstance. Thus, a color-blind equal opportunity program based on socioeconomic traits other than race costs relatively little but achieves relatively little as well. We believe that this finding, because it merely reflects the demographics of the U.S. population, has similar implications for equal opportunity reforms well beyond the K through 12 sector.

Both opponents and proponents of equal opportunity should want information about the costs of implementing equal opportunity through educational-finance reform. This chapter has offered a positive analysis of the benefits and costs of such policies. But it is necessary to discuss the practical implementation of the educational financial reforms analyzed here. Implementing such reforms, which allocate more money to disadvantaged types than to advantaged ones, is a remote possibility in a society that has not yet fully implemented the more moderate equal-resource policy. The positive analysis needs to be separated from a discussion of what reforms are politically feasible or even desirable. (One might believe, for example, that the cost in average income associated with equalizing opportunities subject to the dual-type black and white typology is too great.) Knowing what theory and the data imply, the public will be better prepared to reform educational finance subject to political reality and to their own values.

Finally, our findings suggest that money alone will not suffice to equalize educational opportunity. This realization suggests the urgent need for finding complementary means of improving educational and life outcomes for the disadvantaged.

Notes

An extended version of this chapter, which contains regression results, can be obtained from the University of California at San Diego Department of Economics. Discussion Paper 2005-14 is available at ⟨http://econ.ucsd.edu/publications/papers2005.shtml⟩. The research for this project has been partially funded by the John D. and Catherine T. MacArthur Foundation and the Public Policy Institute of California. For many helpful suggestions, we thank two anonymous referees, Paul Peterson and Ludger Woessmann, audiences at numerous conferences (including the CESifo/PEPG conference in Munich, the Association for Public Policy Analysis and Management (APPAM), the North American Winter Meetings of the Econometric Society, and the annual meetings of the Canadian Economic Association), and audiences at departmental seminars (including the University of Texas, Austin, the Massachusetts Institute of Technology, Stanford University, Claremont Graduate University, and the University of California, Santa Cruz). We also would like to thank Ron White for valuable research assistance.

1. See Evans, Murray, and Schwab (1997) for a review of court-ordered spending equalization in the United States.

2. See, for instance, the review by Betts (1996).

3. See Coley (2002) for evidence of large achievement gaps in reading and mathematics skills among U.S. kindergarten students. These gaps are strongly related to socioeconomic status.

4. It is possible that the disadvantage that children from less educated parents face is not only social and cultural but genetic. In either case, the disadvantage has a source beyond the control of the individual and hence should be rectified at the bar of equal opportunity.

5. We admit this is arbitrary, yet it would be worse to attempt to make no correction for the fact that absolute levels of effort are not the right measures to compare across types. Discovering the right way to compare effort across types is a problem intrinsically as complex as comparing the subjective welfares of very different individuals.

6. For a description of this legislation and its impact on overall educational spending between 1980 and 1990, see Hanushek and Rivkin (1997, section IV).

7. For reviews of this literature, see Betts (1996), Heckman, Layne-Farrar and Todd (1996), and Card and Krueger (1996).

8. One issue in the past literature has been whether there is measurement error in district reports of spending per pupil. This dataset does not contain repeat measures of spending per pupil, but other papers point to, at best, a modest effect of measurement error. Betts (1995), in a model of log wages as a function of school-level resources using the National Longitudinal Survey of Youth 1979, instruments school-level measures of resources with state-level averages and does not find an increase in the level of significance, even though the state-level measures by themselves are significant if placed in the log wage equation. One interpretation is that the state-level aggregates are measuring something orthogonal to resources at the high school level. Grogger (1996) performs a similar analysis with High School and Beyond, modeling log wages as a function of spending per pupil. Uniquely, his paper also has two measures of spending per pupil at the district level for two different years. When he instruments one measure with the other measure, coefficients do rise, suggesting some measurement error in the data. However, his preferred estimates suggest an elasticity of wages with respect to spending per pupil that is quite close to our own estimates. For instance, in our black and white typology we find an elasticity of 0.116 and 0.119 for blacks and whites, respectively. Grogger, using OLS, obtains an elasticity of 0.068, but when he instruments one measure of district spending per pupil with the other district measure, his average elasticity rises to 0.097, which is still slightly below our estimate.

9. For more details on quantile regression, see, for instance, Koenker and Bassett (1982).

10. *Conservative* in the sense that Robert Nozick (1974) says that a person is morally entitled to benefit by virtue of luck—for instance, by being born into a wealthy family.

11. Taking all observations in 1966, the weighted mean spending per pupil in 1990 prices was $2,233. Spending per pupil has grown steadily since then. Current expenditures per pupil in American public schools during the 1990–1991 school year were $4,847 (National Center for Education Statistics, 1991, 155).

12. Table 9.1 shows estimates of the share of the population of men in 1966 by type and mean spending per pupil by type. These were calculated using sampling weights from 1966 on all available 1966 observations. This table also shows weekly earnings by type

averaged over all wage observations in all years, using sample weights. The frequencies of worker types do not exactly add up due to a slightly smaller sample once observations missing covariates such as parental background are removed.

13. Data for 1996 earnings by race and data for the Consumer Price Index required to deflate to 1990 prices were taken from U.S. Bureau of the Census (1997, 431, 497).

14. Indeed, Ward Connerly, who spearheaded the initiative to persuade the University of California Board of Regents to abolish race-based affirmative action admissions, holds this view. He said, "UC should use economic status and other genuine hardships when making special admissions, not race" (*Sacramento Bee*, "UC Regents Find Answers Elusive in Affirmative Action Debate," 1995, B1).

15. We use $2,500 to provide comparability with the simulations based on the equal opportunity solutions presented in the previous section. Because the actual mean spending per pupil was slightly below $2,500 in the sample, we increased spending per pupil proportionately across workers and calculated the predicted gain in earnings using the quantile regression results.

16. This real interest rate was calculated as the yield on 10-year federal bonds minus the percentage change in the Consumer Price Index (for all urban consumers) for the period 1953 to 1997. Sources are the *Economic Report of the President 1998* (Council of Economic Advisers 1998) and the U.S. Bureau of the Census (1997), respectively.

17. In an early draft of this chapter, we also calculated the impact and cost of increasing the school-leaving age by one year, based on OLS regressions of log earnings on years of schooling. This is only a rough estimate of what increasing the school-leaving age might do. Still, the results are illuminating. Along the lower earnings envelope in our black and white typology, average weekly earnings are predicted to increase by $2.38, at a cost in present-value terms of $142.25. Both the predicted impact and the costs are extremely small compared to the impact and cost of the no-lose equal opportunity scenario. When compared to the program that increases total spending per pupil, increasing the school-leaving age is predicted to have a proportionately bigger impact on the objective function than on cost. But this is to be expected given our earlier argument that the ratio of the benefit of equal opportunity to spending increase is a decreasing function, which reduces the effectiveness of large increases in spending per pupil.

18. All figures in 1990 prices. Authors' calculations based on U.S. Department of Education (2003, 196).

References

Betts, Julian R. (1995). "Does School Quality Matter? Evidence from the National Longitudinal Survey of Youth." *Review of Economics and Statistics* 77(2): 231–250.

Betts, Julian. (1996). "Is There a Link between School Inputs and Earnings? Fresh Scrutiny of an Old Literature." In G. Burtless (ed.), *Does Money Matter? The Effect of School Resources on Student Achievement and Adult Success*. Washington, DC: Brookings Institution.

Betts, Julian R., and Eric Johnson. (1997). "A Test for Diminishing Returns to School Spending." Manuscript, Department of Economics, University of California, San Diego.

Bound, John, and Richard Freeman. (1992). "What Went Wrong? The Erosion of Relative Earnings and Employment among Young Black Men in the 1980s." *Quarterly Journal of Economics* 107(1): 201–232.

Card, David, and Alan Krueger. (1996). "Labor Market Effects of School Quality: Theory and Evidence." In G. Burtless (ed.), *Does Money Matter? The Effect of School Resources on Student Achievement and Adult Success*. Washington, DC: Brookings Institution.

Coley, Richard J. (2002). *An Uneven Start: Indicators of Inequality in School Readiness*. Princeton, NJ: Educational Testing Service, Policy Information Center.

Council of Economic Advisers. (1998). *Economic Report of the President 1998*. Washington, DC: U.S. Government Printing Office.

Donohue III, John J. (1994). "Employment Discrimination Law in Perspective: Three Concepts of Equality." *Michigan Law Review* 92: 2583–2612.

Evans, William N., Murray, Sheila E., and Robert M. Schwab. (1997). "Schoolhouses, Courthouses and Statehouses after *Serrano*." *Journal of Policy Analysis and Management* 16(1): 10–31.

Grogger, Jeff. (1996). "School Expenditures and Post-Schooling Earnings: Evidence from High School and Beyond." *Review of Economics and Statistics* 78(4): 628–637.

Hanushek, Eric A., and Steven G. Rivkin. (1997). "Understanding the Twentieth-Century Growth in U.S. School Spending." *Journal of Human Resources* 32(1): 35–68.

Heckman, James, Anne Layne-Farrar, and Petra Todd. (1996). "Does Measured School Quality Really Matter? An Examination of the Earnings-Quality Relationship." In Gary Burtless (ed.), *Does Money Matter? The Effect of School Resources on Student Achievement and Adult Success*. Washington, DC: Brookings Institution.

Hoff, David J. (2004). "States on Ropes in Finance Lawsuits." *Education Week* 24(15): 1, 23.

Koenker, Roger, and Gilbert Bassett, Jr. (1978). "Regression Quantiles." *Econometrica* 46(1): 33–50.

National Center for Education Statistics. (1991). *Digest of Education Statistics*. Washington, DC: U.S. Government Printing Office.

Nozick, Robert. (1974). *Anarchy, State, and Utopia*. New York: Basic Books.

Roemer, John E. (1998). *Equality of Opportunity*. Cambridge, MA: Harvard University Press.

Sacramento Bee (1995). "UC Regents Find Answers Elusive in Affirmative-Action Debate," B1, May 20.

U.S. Bureau of the Census. (1997). *Statistical Abstract of the United States: 1997* (117th ed.). Washington, DC: U.S. Government Printing Office.

U.S. Department of Education, National Center for Education Statistics. (2003). *Digest of Education Statistics, 2002*. NCES 2003-060. Edited by Thomas D. Snyder. Washington, DC: U.S. Government Printing Office.

IV

**Solutions or Aggravations?
Standards and Choice**

Educational Reform and Disadvantaged Students in the United States

John H. Bishop and Ferran Mane

10.1 Introduction

The growing concern that many students who leave high school are unprepared for college or for work has made educational reform a top priority in every state in the United States. Many states have decided to raise minimum standards for obtaining a high-school diploma and to make students and schools accountable for achieving these higher standards. Advocates for these reforms claim that they will cause teachers to set higher standards and induce students to try harder. Equality of opportunity will be enhanced because the incentive effects are focused on lower-performing students and schools will be forced to shift resources toward helping these students catch up. Opponents of increasing state-mandated minimum standards for getting a high-school diploma claim that the performance gap between students from poor and wealthy backgrounds will grow because the dropout rates of at-risk students will rise, particularly in the absence of other systemic reforms. They argue that smaller class sizes and higher teacher salaries are a preferable means of increasing student achievement and closing achievement gaps.

This chapter subjects this controversy to empirical analysis using U.S. longitudinal data following a cohort of eighth graders in 1988 through young adulthood until the year 2000. We start the chapter by briefly describing the mechanisms by which state governments have been trying to make schools accountable. The empirical work that follows assesses the effects on test-score gains, high-school completion, college attendance and completion, and labor-market success of four state policies: (1) state-defined minimums for the total number of courses students must take and pass to get a high-school diploma, (2) state-defined minimums for the number of academic courses necessary to get a diploma, (3) state minimum-competency graduation tests, and (4) a voluntary curriculum-based external exit exam system (the New York State Regents Examinations). We also compare these four policies to the more traditional spending-oriented policies of reducing pupil-teacher ratios and increasing teacher salaries. The models we estimate include an interaction of a parental socioeconomic status (SES) composite with each of the policy variables. This allows us to calculate separate impact estimates for low SES, medium SES, and high SES students. In the final section, we present a summary of results and propose an agenda for future research.

This chapter attempts to bring together in one short article the many strands of a research program that began seven years ago with a narrow focus on minimum-competency exams (MCEs) and short-run labor-market outcomes. The availability of the year 2000 follow-up to the National Educational Longitudinal Study (NELS-88) allows us, for the first time, to study whether high-school graduation standards have effects that last for at least eight years after graduation. We will present models predicting earnings, employment, and wage rates in 2000 and receipt of an associate's degree or better by 2000, receipt of a bachelor's degree or better by 2000, and completion of a high-school degree or graduate equivalency diploma (GED) by 2000. As our theorizing and data analysis have proceeded, we discovered that simple representations of policy options were often misleading. For example, end-of-course examination systems like New York's Regents Exams are very different from minimum-competency tests. When these two types of graduation exams are pooled into one variable, graduation exams have no effect on learning. When separate estimates are calculated for each type of exam system, we conclude that students in New York learn during their four years in high school about half a grade-level equivalent (GLE) more than students in other MCE states.

In a similar vein, we have also come to the conclusion that increases in the number of academic courses required to graduate is likely to have different effects than increases in the total number of courses required to graduate. This chapter is the first to present estimates of the separate effects of these two policies. We find, for example, that increases in the number of elective courses required to graduate lowered college-attendance rates and earnings. By contrast, a four-credit increase in academic-course graduation requirements increased academic achievement by .37 GLEs, reduced SES differentials by a similar amount, and raised wages eight years after graduation.

10.2   Policies for Raising Student Achievement and Improving Labor-Market Success

10.2.1   Smaller Class Sizes and Higher Salaries to Attract Better Teachers

The extensive literature on the effects of class size and teacher salaries on student learning was recently reviewed by Hedges, Laine, and Greenwald (1994), Hanushek (1997), Ballou and Podgursky (1999), and Krueger (2000). These policies are costly, and there is controversy about their cost effectiveness, so state policymakers have also looked for less expensive ways of increasing student achievement. They believed that learning could be increased by getting teachers to set higher standards and by inducing students to study more diligently. Consequently, many of the education reforms introduced during the 1980s and 1990s have focused on increasing the academic focus of schools, raising the standards and expectations of teachers, and inducing students to study harder. Four different policy instruments will be examined.

10.2.2   State-Set Minimums for the Number of Courses Required to Obtain a High-School Diploma

The National Commission on Excellence in Education recommended in 1983 that all high-school students take at least three credits (full-year courses with 120 to 150 hours of instruction) each in mathematics, science, and social studies and four credits of English. This recommendation represented a major departure from customary course taking patterns at that time. Only 14 percent of high-school graduates in 1982 had completed the package recommended by the Commission. No state made it a requirement.

10.2.2.1   Increased Academic Course Graduation Requirements   Responding to the Commission, many states increased the number of mathematics, science, and social studies courses required to graduate. Seventeen states now require students to take the 13 core academic courses recommended by the Commission. The increase in the payoff to college during the 1980s and toughened graduation requirements appear to be having the desired effect (Bishop and Mane 2005). Low-level math courses are losing popularity, and credits earned in algebra, geometry, and higher-level math courses have increased 57 percent. The number of science courses taken has increased 42 percent.

Fifty-five percent of the class of 1998 completed the 13-credit academic program recommended by the National Commission. The total number of full-year courses completed during high school has risen from 21.6 in 1982 to 25.9 for the class of 2000 (NCES 2004).

10.2.2.2 *Increased Total Course Graduation Requirements* Increases in state academic-course graduation requirements typically resulted in increases in total number of courses required to graduate as well. In 1980, only seven states required 20 or more Carnegie units to graduate (school districts were able to set higher requirements if they wanted). In 2002, entering students faced a 24-course state-mandated minimum in five states, a 22- or 23-course minimum in 13 states, a 21-course minimum in nine states, and a 20-course minimum in another eight states.

Critics have pointed out, however, that increased course graduation requirements may cause a decline in high-school graduation rates. Consider a student who has failed a few courses and has therefore accumulated only eight Carnegie units by the end of his second year in high school. In states that require only 16 Carnegie units to graduate (as Illinois does), getting a high-school diploma still looks feasible. If, by contrast, the state requires 23 Carnegie units to graduate (as Louisiana and the District of Columbia did in 1992), getting a diploma looks very difficult. Economic theory predicts that increases in the total number of courses required to graduate will induce some students to give up on getting a regular high-school diploma and choose instead to get a graduate equivalency diploma (GED) or drop out of high school.[1]

As a different path, the total number of Carnegie units required to graduate could have been held fixed and the number of required electives reduced as academic requirements were increased. This would possibly avoid stimulating an increase in dropout rates. But it is also possible that required academic courses are a bigger barrier to graduation than required electives. At-risk students may find compulsory academic courses more difficult than the electives they would otherwise choose. Insufficient enrollment can result in the cancellation of an elective course, so teachers may be under greater pressure to be entertaining and pass all students. On the other hand, almost all students have the option of choosing lower-track academic classes where regular attendance and civility is all that is required to pass. These classes are often less demanding than the heterogeneously grouped elective classes. The class cutting and poor study habits that are the primary cause of failing grades generate problems in nonacademic courses as well as academic courses. We predict, therefore, that dropout rates and graduation rates will respond to the total number of courses required, not to how they are distributed between electives and academic courses. This, however, is an empirical question that will be tested below by including both the number of required academic courses and the total number of courses required to graduate in our models predicting educational outcomes.

10.2.2.3 Minimum-Competency Exam Graduation Requirements

In 1996, 17 states were awarding high-school diplomas only to students who had passed a minimum-competency exam. MCE graduation requirements were often established in response to a popular perception that the state's K through 12 education system had failed. Generally speaking, it has been southern states and states with large urban populations that have established MCEs.

MCEs raise standards but not for everyone.[2] The standards set by the teachers of honors classes and advanced college-prep classes are not changed by an MCE. Students in these classes pass the MCE on the first try without special preparation. Typically, high-school transcripts report only who has passed the MCE, not how far above the passing standard the student scored. The higher standards are experienced by the students who are in the school's least challenging courses.

School administrators will not want to be embarrassed by high failure rates, so it seems reasonable to expect they will try to raise standards in the early grades and improve the instruction received by struggling students. In most states, science, history, and civics/ government are not covered by the MCE, so their impact on achievement in these subjects is indirect. Presumably, they raise achievement in reading, writing, and mathematics, and this then helps students do better in history and science classes and on tests covering these subjects.

MCEs typically set a relatively low minimum standard. In 1996, only four of the 17 states with MCEs targeted their graduation exams at a tenth-grade proficiency level or higher. Failure rates for students taking the test for the first time varied a great deal: from a high of 46 percent in Texas, 34 percent in Virginia, 30 percent in Tennessee, and 27 percent in New Jersey to a low of 7 percent for Mississippi. However, since students can take the tests multiple times, eventual pass rates for the class of 1995 were much higher: 98 percent in Louisiana, Maryland, New York, North Carolina, and Ohio; 96 percent in Nevada and New Jersey; 91 percent in Texas; and 83 percent in Georgia (American Federation of Teachers 1996). Since the tests are designed to determine who falls below a relatively low standard, they typically do not assess material that college-bound students study in tenth and eleventh grades (e.g., algebra 2 and geometry proofs). As a result, MCEs should not be expected to influence learning during high school of students who did well in the first eight years of school. Since SES correlates with achievement in eighth grade, we hypothesize the MCEs will also have smaller effects on high SES students than low SES students.

10.2.2.4 Voluntary End-of-Course Examinations: New York State Regents Examinations in the Early 1990s
End-of-course exams (EOCEs) are different from MCEs in that they typically assess more difficult material and are taken by students nearing the end of a specific course or sequence of courses—such as biology, French, American history, or calculus.[3] Teachers are inevitably viewed as responsible (at least in part) for how well their class does on the exam. EOCEs signal the student's achievement level in the subject, not just whether the student exceeds or falls below a specific cut point that all high-school graduates are required to surpass. All students in the class, not just those at the bottom of the class, have an incentive to study hard to do well on the exam, so an EOCE is more likely to improve classroom culture than an MCE (Costrell 1994). The stakes tend to be different, as well. For EOCEs, the stakes are typically getting an A rather than a B in a course or getting college credit for a high-school course. For MCEs, the stakes are getting a high-school diploma.

At the time our data were being collected, there was only one system of EOCEs in the United States: the New York State's curriculum-based Regents Examinations system.[4] In fact, it should be called voluntary EOCE because Regents courses and their associated exams were not compulsory. However, many students did take them. In 1992, the most popular exam, course I mathematics, was taken by 62 percent of students, the global studies exam was taken by 57 percent of students, and the English and biology exams were taken by 50 percent of students. Overall, 38 percent of 1992–1993 graduates earned Regents diplomas, signifying completion of a sequence of Regents courses and passing the associated exams.

10.3 Empirical Evidence on the Effects of Tougher Graduation Requirements: An Analysis of NELS-88 Data

10.3.1 Description of the Data and Econometric Model
Our analysis makes use of micro data from the National Educational Longitudinal Study (NELS-88), a longitudinal dataset that followed a nationally representative sample of eighth graders in 1988 through the year 1992. In addition, two post–high-school follow-ups were conducted in 1994 (two years after scheduled graduation) and in 2000 (eight years after graduation). Information used in this chapter comes from the student, school, and family questionnaires. We study the full sample of NELS-88 high-school graduates, which comprises both graduates and dropouts and also students from public and private high schools.

We use the restricted dataset that identifies the state in which the student's high school was located. This allows us to merge information on state policies and characteristics into the dataset. Four policy variables were defined characterizing graduation requirements. The first variable measures the state-government-defined minimum number of academic courses (English, math, science, and social studies) required to get a regular high-school diploma. The second variable is the total number of credits the state required to get a high-school diploma.[5] We include separate measures of academic and total course requirements because they correlate only .22 with each other and are likely to have different effects on learning, dropout rates, and post–high-school outcomes.

The third variable takes on a value of 1 for states with minimum-competency exam graduation requirements in 1992 (Alabama, Florida, Georgia, Hawaii, Louisiana, Maryland, Mississippi, Nevada, New Mexico, New Jersey, North Carolina, South Carolina, Tennessee, and Texas) and zero elsewhere.[6] Thirty-two percent of our sample lived in states that mandate the MCE and set the graduation standard on the exam. Finally, we capture the unique effect of New York's package of graduation requirements (including voluntary Regents Exams) by defining a variable that has a value of 1 if the student's high school was in New York State and 0 elsewhere. The final two policy variables are teacher-salary level (using the salary paid to first-year full-time teachers in thousands of dollars) and the pupil-teacher ratio at the school.[7]

Since the outcomes studied are primarily determined by the student's background and environment, we control for as many characteristics of the community and the student as possible to increase efficiency and reduce omitted-variable bias. Our estimations include controls for grade-point average in eighth grade; an average of eighth-grade test scores in English, mathematics, science, and social studies; family socioeconomic status; and other characteristics of the student in eighth grade. These included whether the student took remedial courses in eighth grade or earlier, has taken advanced courses, or has a computer at home; TV and homework hours; reading for pleasure; an indicator for being handicapped; socioeconomic status of the student's family; logarithm of the number of books in the home; parent-involvement index; family size; marital and parental status in eighth grade; locus of control index; self-esteem index; hours working for pay during eighth grade (and its square); an index for smoking in eighth grade; dummies for race, ethnicity, and religion; dummies for rural, suburban, and urban residence; and 10 indicators describing the character and quality of the high school. From the principal's questionnaire, we take the following indicators of quality of the student's secondary school: average teacher salary, the pupil-teacher ratio, percent free lunch, percent students that were white, school is a vocational high school, percentage of the school's full-time faculty who are vocational educators, and average enrollment per high-school grade (and its square). Two other measures of the quality of the school attended in tenth grade—the average socioeconomic status and eighth-grade test scores of students at the school—were calculated by averaging student responses for each high school in the NELS-88 database.

Controls for characteristics of the regional labor market (SMSA or state) included the unemployment rate, mean weekly wage in retailing and in manufacturing, ratio of the high-school graduate earnings to the high-school dropout earnings in 1989, ratio of college graduate earnings to high-school graduate earnings in 1989, ratio of tuition at four-year public colleges to the weekly earnings in retailing, and dummies for four census regions.

The basic specification used for regression models is

$$Y_i = \alpha_i + \beta_1 X_i + \beta_2 SES_i + \beta_3 MCE_i + \beta_4 ACAD_i + \beta_5 TOTAL_i + \beta_6 NY_i$$

$$+ \beta_7 TCHWAGE_i + \beta_8 PupTchR + \beta_9 (SES \times MCE)_i$$

$$+ \beta_{10}(SES \times ACAD)_i + \beta_{11}(SES \times TOTAL)_i + \beta_{12}(SES \times NY)_i$$

$$+ \beta_{13}(SES \times TCHWAGE)_i + \beta_{14}(SES \times PupTchR)_i + \mu_i,$$

where Y_i is a battery of dependent variables for individual i, X_i is a vector of control variables, and *MCE, ACAD, TOTAL, NY, TCHWAGE,* and *PupTchR* are the policy variables.

SES is a continuous variable measuring the student's family socio-economic status. We are particularly interested in the effects of these policies on equality of opportunity, so interactions were formed between each policy indicator and the socioeconomic status of the student's parents.[8] Interactions were defined by deviating SES and the continuous policy variables from zero and then forming their product. This ensures that the main-effect coefficients on the policy variables (β_3 to β_8) represent both the average effect of the policy and its impact on students at the midpoint of the SES distribution. We also include inter-action and main-effect terms for each policy to get separate estimates of the effects of policies on low SES students and high SES students. We then conduct three hypothesis tests about the impacts of each policy on students at the midpoint of the SES distribution, at one SES stan-dard deviation (SD) above the midpoint, and at one SD below the mid-point. These tests will allow us to comment on whether a policy helps one group more than another. Other than these specified interactions with SES, we have no reason to expect the effects of policy variables to be systematically different in the special subsamples of blacks and Hispanics included in the NELS-88 dataset. We therefore do not weight the data when we estimate regressions (giving these special subsamples equal weight with the main body of students respond-ents). This reduces heteroscedasticity and improves the efficiency of our estimates.

We are aware that states may set standards endogenously. A posi-tive selection bias is unlikely, however. By 1992, MCEs had been adopted by every southern state except Arkansas and Oklahoma. With the exception of New Mexico, none of the Mountain, Plains, or Mid-western states had established an MCE prior to 1992 (NCES 1993). Bond and King (1995) and Amrein and Berliner (2002) interpret this South and Southwest concentration as a sign that policymakers were more pressured by a perception that the state's schools were failing to teach basic skills.

A final issue that must be taken into account is the clustered nature of the data. We follow the empirical strategy employed in Warren and Edwards (2005) and use the SVY family of commands in Stata to esti-mate models clustering by state.

10.3.2   Dropout Rates and Completion of High School

Critics of higher graduation standards contend that they will increase dropout rates, postpone the graduation of some, induce others to instead pursue a graduate equivalency diploma (GED), and prevent the graduation of still others. Critics also argue that these effects will be larger for low SES students. Advocates argue that tougher standards will induce teachers to set higher standards for at-risk students and that these students will end up learning more. They also predict that employers will become more willing to hire recent high-school graduates and that this will increase the payoff to getting a diploma. As the payoff to the diploma increases, students, teachers, parents, and principals may respond in ways that overcome the initial negative effects.

Empirical evidence is mixed. Well-controlled cross-section studies of aggregate state-level data have found no tendency for aggregate completion rates to be significantly lower in states with MCEs (Bishop and Mane 2001a; Lillard and DeCicca 2001; Jacobs 2001; Dee 2003). However, when subgroups are studied, students in low-income neighborhoods (Reardon 1996) and disadvantaged students (Reardon and Galindo 2002) appear to have lower graduation rates when the high-school principal reports they must pass an MCE to graduate. Warren and Edwards (2005, 57) point out, however, that the principal reports of state exit exams are often inaccurate, so they dispute Reardon's conclusions. When Warren and Edwards use restricted data with state IDs to create the MCE variable, they conclude that chances of obtaining a GED or of leaving school without a GED or a diploma were not higher in MCE states, even among low-SES and low-achieving students. Bishop, Mane, Bishop, and Moriarty (2001) also use state IDs to identify who was subject to an MCE. We concluded that students with low or average GPAs in eighth grade were significantly more likely to get their diploma late or to get a GED when they were from a state with an MCE. In addition, low GPA students (but not students with average or above average GPAs) were significantly more likely to fail to get a diploma or a GED when they lived in MCE states.

Studies of the effects of course-taking standards have generally found that they lower the number of students who graduate from high school. Lillard and DeCicca (2001), Bishop and Mane (2001a), and Bishop, Mane, Bishop, and Moriarty (2001) found that states with a higher than average total number of courses required for graduation have lower high-school enrollment and graduation rates and higher numbers of GEDs awarded when other characteristics of the state are controlled. Dee (2003) also concluded that this reform led to reductions in educational attainment that were particularly large for black students. Only Hoffer (1997) found no effect on the probability of completing high school.

Models were estimated predicting whether a student drops out at any time during high school, whether the student gets her diploma late, and whether the student fails to get either a GED or a high-school diploma by February 1994 and also by June 2000. Results are presented in table 10.1.[9]

Students living in MCE states were *not* more likely to drop out and *not* more likely to fail to get a diploma or a GED by 1994 or by 2000. SES interactions were not statistically significant for these completion outcomes. Students living in MCE states were, however, more likely to experience delays in getting a regular diploma and also more likely to get a GED rather than the standard diploma. Contrary to our hypothesis, these two effects became larger as the student's SES increased. Indeed, effects were so small for low SES students that we are not able to reject the hypothesis that MCEs had no effect on GED and delayed graduations of low SES students.

Students living in New York State were significantly more likely to drop out, more likely to take extra time to get the diploma, and a lot more likely to get a GED rather than a regular high-school diploma by year 2000. Low SES students were significantly less likely to get a diploma or GED by 1994 but not by 2000. The graduation rates of medium and high SES students, by contrast, were not significantly changed.

Students living in states with higher elective and nonacademic-course graduation requirements were not more likely to drop out of high school. On the other hand, low SES students (but not middle and high SES students) were significantly more likely to get their diploma late and to get a GED. We find some weak support for the hypothesis that academic-course graduation requirements have bigger effects on dropout and noncompletion rates than increased elective requirements. Academic-course requirements had positive coefficients in all five models, and the effect was significant for "No diploma or GED by 1994" and significant for the dropout rates of high SES students.

The school-resources variables—teacher salaries and pupil teacher ratios—had no effect on dropout rates or overall completion rates. Teacher salaries were, however, significantly related to lower probabilities of getting a GED diploma and for high SES students to lower

Table 10.1
Effects on dropping out and getting the diploma or GED

	Ever drop out of high school	Diploma obtained late	No HS diploma or GED by 1994	No HS diploma or GED by 2000	Obtained a GED by 2000
Mean standard deviation	.121	.082	.081	.050	.064
	(.326)	(.274)	(.273)	(.219)	(.245)
Socioeconomic status	−.571***	−.492***	−.657***	−.647***	−.407***
	(.068)	(.091)	(.081)	(.168)	(.096)
State minimum-	.070	.446***	.192	−.255	.385*
competency exam	(.113)	(.140)	(.187)	(.208)	(.235)
State MCE*SES	.059	.311**	−.021	−.347	.260*
	(.116)	(.133)	(.151)	(.273)	(.156)
New York	.421***	1.08***	.181	−.022	.859***
	(.136)	(.208)	(.194)	(.164)	(.201)
New York*SES	−.134	.284***	−.235**	−.276	−.024
	(.093)	(.112)	(.119)	(.261)	(.127)
Academic courses	.024	.015	.066*	.036	.011
	(.030)	(.036)	(.039)	(.041)	(.062)
Academic courses*SES	.068**	−.014	.066*	.049	.019
	(.030)	(.043)	(.036)	(.069)	(.039)
State minimum credits	.021	.012	−.033	.004	.016
to graduate	(.016)	(.018)	(.031)	(.030)	(.030)
State minimum*SES	−.018	−.046**	−.039	−.0002	−.046
	(.021)	(.023)	(.025)	(.044)	(.029)
Teacher salary	−.010	−.024	−.007	−.007	−.040**
	(.016)	(.018)	(.019)	(.030)	(.020)
Teacher salary*SES	.019	−.015	.024	−.017	−.010
	(.017)	(.016)	(.020)	(.025)	(.020)
Pupil teacher ratio	−.010	−.028**	−.003	.008	.006
	(.012)	(.014)	(.017)	(.026)	(.010)
Pupil teacher ratio*SES	.004	.013	.011	.004	.022*
	(.009)	(.013)	(.016)	(.024)	(.013)
Number of observations	15867	10590	11922	9873	9873

Source: Authors' analysis of National Education Longitudinal Study of 88 data.
Note: Estimations using SVY commands in stata with states as the primary sampling units. Sample includes dropouts and high school graduates from private schools.
Control variables: The MCE variable is a 1 for AL, FL, GA, HI, LA, MD, MS, NV, NM, NJ, NC, SC, TN, and TX. Models also contain a full set of student background variables measured in the eighth grade: family SES, books in the home, single parent, parents divorced, number of siblings, ethnicity, religion, gender, handicapping condition, test scores, GPA in eighth grade, hours watching TV, hours doing homework, read for fun index, smoking, dummy for in advanced courses, dummy for in remedial courses, dummies for central city and rural, locus of control index, self-esteem index, and hours working for pay (plus its square).

Table 10.1
(continued)

The following characteristics of the school the student attended during tenth grade were also controlled: Catholic school, secular private school, private school controlled by a church other than the Catholic church, percent student body white, percent free lunch, mean eighth-grade test score, mean family SES, enrollment per grade (plus its square), and the share of vocational education teachers on the total number of full-time teachers.

Apart from dummies for four Census regions, the following characteristics of the state were controlled for in the short-term results (using values for 1992): dropout unemployment rate, weekly wages for dropouts, ratio of dropout earnings to high school graduate earnings, ratio of college graduate earnings to high school graduate earnings, ratio of tuition at four-year public colleges to the weekly earnings in retailing. In the medium-term models, the state controls were mean unemployment rate, mean weekly wages, and mean weekly wages in manufacturing.

*Statistically significant at 10% level on a two-tail test, **5% level, ***1% level.

---

probabilities of delays in getting a diploma. Higher pupil-teacher ratios were associated with fewer students graduating late.

10.3.3 Learning in High School

The Web sites of most of the state education departments implementing tougher graduation standards report that scores are rising on state accountability tests. One cannot conclude from this, however, that the tougher standards caused student achievement to rise. The rising scores on state tests might reflect teaching to the test (that is, improved alignment of instruction with the topics and question formats found on the state's high-stakes test) and not real gains in true learning (Linn 2000; Koretz, McCaffrey, and Hamilton 2001). Consequently, studies evaluating the effects of tougher standards on achievement must track their effects by studying scores on a zero-stakes audit tests (such as the NELS-88 tests) that represent a broader domain of knowledge than the content standards that informed the construction of the state's high-stakes tests.[10]

An even more serious problem with drawing inferences from trends in one state is the lack of a counterfactual. Test scores may be rising everywhere, not just in the states that have recently toughened graduation standards.[11] An inference that a policy causes a change in learning requires either (1) a study of the effects of changes in policy by contrasting test-score trends in states that recently raised graduation standards to those that did not or (2) a study of rates of learning during high school as a function of state graduation standards while controlling for a comprehensive set of student, school, and state characteristics.

The difficulty with the first approach is that data on trends in test scores are generally not available. Announcements of policy changes precede actual implementation by many years, and it is not clear how long it takes for responses to cumulate before a new equilibrium is reached. Other state policies are also changing, so inferring the effects of a specific policy is difficult. Fredricksen (1994) found that states introducing high-stakes testing systems (minimum-competency tests for graduation, for the most part) achieved larger gains on National Assessment of Educational Progress (NAEP) mathematics questions between 1978 and 1986. Studies of eighth-grade NAEP trends during the 1990s also conclude that scores rose more rapidly in states introducing high-stakes school-accountability systems (Carnoy and Loeb 2002; Rosenshine 2003; Braun 2004; Hanushek and Raymond 2003).[12] The indexes of new high-stakes testing programs used by these studies primarily reflect the growth of school-accountability systems and not minimum-competency tests, so they provide no real evidence on the unique impact of high-school graduation tests. The only study (Bishop 2005) to estimate separately the effects of new minimum-competency tests, the Curriculum-Based External Exit Exam Systems (CBEEES), and school-accountability systems on NAEP trends for 1992 to 2003 found that all three policies had significant positive effects, with the CBEEES having the biggest effects.

Cross-section studies attempt to estimate the long-run effects of exit exams and so have fewer problems specifying the dynamics of adjustment to policy changes. Studies employing this approach have not found that residence in MCE states was significantly associated with the level of eighth-grade test scores or with gains in scores from eighth to twelfth grades (Bishop, Mane, Bishop, and Moriarty 2001; Jacob 2001). These studies also failed to find that minimum-competency exams had larger effects on students with below-average grades and test scores. It has been previously shown that higher academic-course graduation requirements increase the number of academic courses taken and passed by students (Bishop and Mane 2005), but we have not found any previous studies measuring the effects of course graduation requirements on learning.

In the second column of table 10.2, we present the results of predicting test score gains between eighth and twelfth grades using a specification that interacts socioeconomic status with six policy instruments. Our previous work (Bishop et al. 2001) specified grade-point-average interactions with two policy variables: minimum-competency exams and voluntary curriculum-based external exit-exam systems. Students who dropped out of high school were given the tests along with those who remained in school, so the reduced learning that results from some students dropping out of school is taken into account. The control variables used in this model are with one exception the same as those used in predicting dropping out. To prevent the error in measuring true eighth-grade achievement from biasing the results, the lagged value of the composite test did not appear on the right-hand side of the regression predicting the gain on the composite from eighth to twelfth grades.

Our most important finding is that academic-course requirements have significant positive effects on learning. Students in states requiring four extra academic courses to graduate learned .37 grade-level equivalents more in the four core academic subjects $[(4 * .18)/(.25 * 7.86)]$ than comparable students in other states. Increased elective and nonacademic course requirements, by contrast, had no effect on learning core academic subjects. MCEs also had no effect on learning.

Our third finding is that combining end-of-course exams with MCEs—or something else in the New York State policy mix—appears to have had large significant effects on learning for students of all SES levels. The New York effect was slightly more than one-half a grade-level equivalent and somewhat larger for high SES students. This occurred despite the fact that students who dropped out of school were included in the sample. Since dropouts learn considerably less than students who stay in school, one would expect New York's high dropout rates to drag down overall learning gains for New York. Quite the reverse happened, so those who stayed in school must have learned enough extra to counterbalance the negative effects of New York's higher dropout rate.

Reductions in the pupil-teacher ratio are associated with a statistically significant increase in learning during high school. The regression predicts that reducing the number of pupils per teacher by four (a one standard deviation change in the variable) will increase learning over the four-year period by about 12 percent of a GLE. This 3 percent increase in the rate of learning seems to be rather modest when one considers that the policy requires a 25 percent increase in the number of teachers at the school (probably implying a 10+ percent increase in costs per student).

Table 10.2
Effects on college attendance and completion

	Total test score gains	Enrolled in Fall 1992	Enrolled in Spring 1994	Obtained an asso- ciate or higher	Obtained a bachelor or higher
Mean standard deviation	7.86	.592	.558	.420	.346
	(4.75)	(.491)	(.496)	(.493)	(.475)
Socioeconomic status	.484***	.740***	.683***	.657***	.818***
	(.081)	(.050)	(.046)	(.042)	(.050)
State minimum- competency exam	.098	.018	.164*	.040	−.014
	(.279)	(.108)	(.099)	(.111)	(.147)
State MCE*SES	−.048	.002	.198**	.109	.077
	(.148)	(.076)	(.096)	(.080)	(.095)
New York	1.09***	.053	.084	−.068	−.332***
	(.230)	(.101)	(.108)	(.126)	(.102)
New York*SES	.237**	−.271***	−.016	−.121***	−.160***
	(.098)	(.064)	(.050)	(.042)	(.060)
Academic courses	.180***	.032	−.015	−.019	−.025
	(.048)	(.020)	(.018)	(.028)	(.028)
Academic courses*SES	−.111***	.014	−.046*	−.007	−.015
	(.031)	(.030)	(.026)	(.016)	(.020)
State minimum credits to graduate	.011	−.016	−.019	−.003	−.002
	(.020)	(.015)	(.012)	(.014)	(.013)
State minimum*SES	−.002	.018	.027**	.012	.020
	(.022)	(.016)	(.012)	(.013)	(.015)
Teacher salary	.016	.024***	.024***	.038***	.037***
	(.018)	(.008)	(.009)	(.010)	(.010)
Teacher salary*SES	−.002	−.030***	−.003	−.011	−.016
	(.021)	(.010)	(.009)	(.010)	(.012)
Pupil teacher ratio	−.059***	.002	−.011	−.022**	−.015*
	(.016)	(.008)	(.007)	(.010)	(.009)
Pupil teacher ratio*SES	−.011	−.016*	−.028***	−.007	−.011
	(.011)	(.009)	(.008)	(.012)	(.010)
Number of observations	11369	11828	11829	9902	9902

Source: Authors' analysis of National Education Longitudinal Study of 88 data.

Note: Estimations using SVY commands in stata with states as the primary sampling units. Sample includes dropouts and high school graduates from private schools.

Control variables: The MCE variable is a 1 for AL, FL, GA, HI, LA, MD, MS, NV, NM, NJ, NC, SC, TN, and TX. Models also contain a full set of student background variables measured in the eighth grade: family SES, books in the home, single parent, parents divorced, number of siblings, ethnicity, religion, gender, handicapping condition, test scores, GPA in eighth grade, hours watching TV, hours doing homework, read for fun in- dex, smoking, dummy for in advanced courses, dummy for in remedial courses, dum- mies for central city and rural, locus of control index, self-esteem index, and hours working for pay (plus its square).

Table 10.2
(continued)

The following characteristics of the school the student attended during tenth grade were also controlled: Catholic school, secular private school, private school controlled by a church other than the Catholic church, teacher salary, percent student body white, percent free lunch, mean eighth-grade test score, mean family SES, and enrollment per grade (plus its square).

Apart from dummies for four Census regions, the following characteristics of the state were controlled for: mean unemployment rate, mean weekly wages in retailing (in log), ratio of college graduate earnings to high school graduate earnings, and ratio of tuition at four year public colleges to the weekly earnings in retailing.

*Statistically significant at 10% level on a two-tail test, **5% level, ***1% level.

10.3.4 College Attendance and Completion

Opponents of high-stakes graduation tests argue that "preparation for high stakes tests often emphasizes rote memorization and cramming of students and drill and practice teaching methods" (Madaus 1991, 7) and that test preparation will displace the teaching of other skills and knowledge that are more important to success in college and jobs. The same issue arises with respect to mandated increases in the number of academic courses that must be taken to graduate. Consequently, an examination of the impacts of tougher graduation standards on college attendance, college completion, and labor-market success is called for.

Our dataset is particularly good for addressing this question because we are following eighth graders for as much as 12 years. By studying the proportion of eighth graders (rather than the share of high-school graduates) who subsequently go to college, we capture any negative effects on college attendance of reductions in the number of graduates that might have been caused by tougher graduation standards. Second, having data from the year 2000, eight years after scheduled high-school graduation, allows us to examine degree completion and to study the long-term effects of graduation standards. We can test whether the high stakes attached to the graduation test actually produced an increase in the number of high-school graduates who have the skills and knowledge necessary to succeed and thrive in college.

Specifically, logistic regressions were estimated predicting college enrollment in the fall of 1992 and the spring of 1994 and completion with an associate's or bachelor's degree or better by the year 2000. The model specifications were the same as those used in the dropout and high-school-completion models.[13] The results are presented in columns three to six in table 10.2.

Academic-course requirements had no significant effects on college attendance or college completion. Increases in the total number of courses required to graduate (holding academic-course requirements constant) significantly lowered college-attendance rates in spring of 1994. This negative effect was significantly larger for low SES students. A four-credit increase in elective and nonacademic-course graduation requirements is predicted to reduce college enrollment of low SES students by 3.4 percentage points in fall 1992 and by 4.6 percentage points in spring 1994. These enrollment effects seem to be transitory because neither policy had significant impacts on the probability of getting college degrees by the year 2000.

MCEs had significant positive effects on college attendance, but only in the sixth year after eighth grade and not the fifth year. Students in MCE states had rates of college attendance that were about 4 percentage points higher in 1994. The positive effect was larger for students from high SES backgrounds. MCEs had no effect on 1994 college attendance rates of low SES students. Again, these enrollment effects seem to be temporary because attending high school in an MCE state has no effect on the likelihood of getting college degrees. Attending school in New York had positive effects on college attendance rates of low SES students in fall 1992. Four-year college completion rates, on the other hand, are lower in New York, particularly for high SES students.

Of the six policies reviewed, teacher salary had the most consistent and statistically significant impact on college attendance and completion. A 15 percent (one standard deviation) increase in teacher salary raises college-attendance rates by 1.8 percentage points and college-completion rates by 2.8 percentage points. The 1992 enrollment effect is 3.6 percentage points for low SES students. No other SES interactions were significant. The pupil-teacher ratio has significant effects on college completion but not on freshman-year enrollment rates. A 20 percent decrease in the pupil-teacher ratio is associated with a 1.4 percentage point increase in the proportion getting a bachelor's degree and a 2.1 point increase in the probability of getting an associate's degree or better.

10.3.5   Labor-Market Outcomes

Policymakers have justified increased graduation requirements as necessary to prepare young people to compete in the world economy. MCEs and tougher course graduation requirements are hypothesized to improve job opportunities in two ways. First, if they improve student achievement, they raise worker productivity (Bishop 1992). Even when this does not immediately raise workers' earnings, the effect of academic achievement on wages grows with time and eventually becomes very large (Altonji and Pierret 2001).

The second way that MCEs and higher course graduation requirements could improve job opportunities is by sending a signal to employers that graduates meet or exceed their minimum hiring standards. In most communities, competencies developed in the local high school are poorly signaled to employers. As a result, employers with the best jobs are reluctant to risk hiring recent high-school graduates. Raising course graduation requirements and instituting graduation tests, therefore, are strategies some states have pursued to attract high-wage employers and help recent graduates compete for good jobs. When tougher standards are instituted, diplomas now signal that the student took a core academic curriculum and met or exceeded certain minimum standards in core subjects. High-wage employers are hypothesized to become more willing to hire recent high-school graduates. Students previously stigmatized by race or social background are hypothesized to benefit most of all.

Previous studies have found that MCEs raise earnings immediately after high school, particularly for students with low eighth-grade GPAs.[14] Do MCEs continue to have a positive effect on wages seven years later? How do students from low-income backgrounds fare? To answer this question, we estimate models predicting labor-market outcomes in both 1993–1994 and 2000 and interacted our policy variables with family SES. The early indicators were total number of months worked during the 21-month period from July 1992 to March 1994, hourly wage rate (logged), and earnings in calendar year 1993. The three indicators of medium-term labor-market success were annual earnings of the job occupied during the first quarter of the year 2000, the hours worked per week in that job, and the hourly wage rate of that job. Wage rates are not defined for respondents who did not report a job sometime during 1993–1994 or 2000. The other variables treated those who reported no work during the reference period as a zero (the variable was missing if the individual reported work but did not report earnings or hours worked).

Since attending college reduces the time available for work, we include an extensive set of controls for current and past college attendance: the number of semesters of full-time college attendance during the period from fall 1992 to spring 1994, the number of semesters of part-time college attendance during that same period, the number of semesters attending a two-year institution full-time, and the number of semesters of part-time attendance at a two-year institution. We also include controls for "Attending college full time in the first quarter of 2000," "Attending college part time in the first quarter of 2000," "Ever dropped out of high school," "Obtained a GED," "Graduated early," and for late graduates, "Length of the delay in graduation." In the models predicting medium-term outcomes, we include dummy variables for some college, for "Ever attended a four-year college," and for earning a vocational certificate, an associate degree, a bachelor's degree, a master's degree, and graduate or professional degrees. Family structure in 2000 was controlled by four indicator variables: married male, married female, male with children, and female with children.

Our analyses of the effects of graduation requirements on early labor-market outcomes are presented in table 10.3.

Increases in the number of elective courses required to graduate did not have positive effects on any labor-market indicator. In fact, increased elective-course requirements significantly lowered wage rates and earnings in both 1993 and 2000. The negative effects for year 2000 are larger for high SES students and essentially zero for low SES students. Academic-course requirements were significantly related to higher wage rates in 1994 and 2000 and to higher earnings in 2000. This effect did not vary significantly by SES. Being required to take extra academic courses had a significantly more positive effect on wage rates than elective-course requirements. This implies that if total graduation requirements are fixed, increasing academic requirements will increase wage rates by roughly one percentage point for each one credit increase in academic-course requirements. However, when an increase in academic-course requirements is associated with an equal increase in total course requirements, wages and earnings remain essentially unchanged.

Minimum-competency exams had large and significant effects on many of the labor-market indicators. Those who attended high school in MCE states earned 11 percent ($548) more in 1993 and 4.2 percent ($1,114) more in 2000. Wage rates were also a significant 2.6 percent higher in 2000. Consistent with our hypothesis, the SES interactions show that MCE effects were significantly more positive for low SES students in 1993. Contrary to our hypothesis, this pattern reversed six years later. In 2000, our estimates of the MCE effect are $2,330 for high SES graduates and essentially zero for low SES graduates. Attending school in New York appears to reduce the hours worked in 2000 of low SES youth but increase their wage rates. New York also appears to increase the earnings of high SES students.

Pupil-teacher ratios did not have significant effects on wage rates or earnings. Teacher salary was negatively related to time spent working in both 1993 and 2000. It was also positively related to year 2000 wage rates of middle SES and high SES students but not for low SES students.

10.4 Summary and Policy Implications

The purpose of this chapter has been to measure the effects of increased academic standards both on average achievement levels and on equality of opportunity. The four policies evaluated were (1) voluntary curriculum-based external exit-exam systems with partial coverage (such as New York State Regents Exams in 1992), (2) state minimum-competency graduation tests, (3) state-defined minimums for the total number of courses students must take and pass to get a high-school diploma, and (4) state-defined minimums for the number of academic courses necessary to get a diploma. We also measure the effects of school-to-school variations in teacher salaries and student-teacher ratios for comparison purposes.

In table 10.4, we summarize our main findings for test scores, high-school attendance and completion, college attendance and completion, and success in the labor market. Each outcome considered has two columns. The first one presents the estimate of the mean percentage change that the regressions predict would be generated by introducing a discrete reform (such as an MCE) or by a large (four-credit) increase in the number of courses (academic or total) required to get a regular diploma. For comparison purposes, we also calculate and present the predicted effects of increasing teacher wages by 30 percent (or two standard deviations) and decreasing student teacher ratios by 40 percent (eight fewer students per teacher).

The second column within each outcome presents estimates of the effect of each policy on the size of the *gap* between the outcomes of high SES and low SES students. High status is defined as a SES index that is one standard deviation (.8 units) above the mean. Low status is one s.d. below the mean, so the change from low to high is 1.6 units on the SES scale. Thus, a four-credit increase in academic requirements reduces the size of the test score gap between high and low SES

Table 10.3
Labor-market effects

	Short-term results		
	Employment (months)	Wages (log hourly wage)	Earnings (yearly)
Mean standard deviation	13.51 (7.64)	1.272 (.563)	5152 (5453)
Socioeconomic status	−.445*** (.154)	−.019 (.012)	−105 (106)
State minimum-competency exam	.069 (.201)	−.002 (.018)	548*** (173)
State MCE*SES	−.409* (.226)	.007 (.018)	−415*** (141)
New York	−.090 (.281)	−.005 (.024)	−314 (242)
New York*SES	−.557*** (.207)	−.006 (.013)	10 (131)
Academic courses	.064 (.083)	.011** (.005)	−5 (61)
Academic courses*SES	−.022 (.062)	−.005 (.007)	1 (47)
State minimum credits to graduate	−.028 (.034)	−.006*** (.002)	−44 (30)
State minimum*SES	−.008 (.042)	−.002 (.003)	18 (29)
Teacher salary	−.090*** (.030)	−.002 (.002)	−14 (22)
Teacher salary*SES	−.016 (.033)	.001 (.002)	31** (17)
Pupil teacher ratio	−.015 (.024)	.002 (.002)	8 (15)
Pupil teacher ratio*SES	.050** (.024)	.002 (.002)	28* (15)
Number of observations	11656	11594	9885
R^2	.147	.092	.238

Source: Authors' analysis of National Education Longitudinal Study of 88 data.
Note: Estimations using SVY commands in Stata with states as the primary sampling units. Sample includes dropouts and high school graduates from private schools.
Control variables: The MCE variable is a 1 for AL, FL, GA, HI, LA, MD, MS, NV, NM, NJ, NC, SC, TN, and TX. Models also contain a full set of student background variables measured in the eighth grade: family SES, books in the home, single parent, parents divorced, number of siblings, ethnicity, religion, gender, handicapping condition, test scores, GPA in eighth grade, hours watching TV, hours doing homework, read for fun index, smoking, dummy for in advanced courses, dummy for in remedial courses, dummies for central city and rural, locus of control index, self-esteem index, and hours working for pay (plus its square).

| | Medium-term results | | |
	Employment (hours per week)	Wages (log hourly wage)	Earnings (yearly)
Mean standard deviation	36.19 (16.07)	2.53 (.447)	26137 (19426)
Socioeconomic status	−.044 (.312)	.011 (.010)	59 (404)
State minimum-competency exam	.030 (.460)	.026* (.015)	1114** (557)
State MCE*SES	.498 (.459)	.036*** (.014)	1520*** (573)
New York	−.913** (.400)	.037** (.017)	760 (569)
New York*SES	1.90*** (.346)	−.025*** (.010)	1422*** (437)
Academic courses	.007 (.118)	.007** (.003)	239** (114)
Academic courses*SES	−.084 (.115)	.003 (.003)	20 (142)
State minimum credits to graduate	.034 (.039)	−.007*** (.001)	−196*** (61)
State minimum*SES	.028 (.070)	−.005*** (.002)	−201** (87)
Teacher salary	−.099** (.050)	.003* (.002)	−13 (57)
Teacher salary*SES	−.033 (.070)	.004** (.002)	33 (65)
Pupil teacher ratio	−.015 (.040)	.002 (.002)	2 (63)
Pupil teacher ratio*SES	−.106** (.047)	−.001 (.002)	−123** (56)
Number of observations	9810	8108	9378
R^2	.330	.220	.285

The following characteristics of the school the student attended during tenth grade were also controlled: Catholic school, secular private school, private school controlled by a church other than the Catholic church, teacher salary, percent student body white, percent free lunch, mean eighth-grade test score, mean family SES and enrollment per grade (plus its square).

The following characteristics of the state were controlled for: mean unemployment rate, mean weekly wages in retailing and manufacturing and dummies for four Census regions. We also included college experience and status in 1993 and in the models predicting outcomes for the year 2000 there also were included marital status, number of dependents, higher degree obtained by 2000, college status, and date of degree.

*Statistically significant at 10% level on a two tail test, **5% level, ***1% level.

Table 10.4
Effects of school policies (% effect relative to the mean of a two standard deviation change in policy)

Policies	Outcomes							
	Average test scores (% of a GLE)		Attend high school		Get GED or H.S. diploma by 1994		Attend college or university in 1994	
	Mean	Gap	Mean	Gap	Mean	Gap	Mean	Gap
Voluntary end-of-course exams	55***	19**	−5.0*	2.6	−1.5	3.0**	3.7	0
Minimum-competency exam	5	−4	−0.7	−1	−1.5	0	7.2**	14**
4 more academic credits required	37***	−36***	−1.1	−5**	−2.0*	−3.2*	−2.6	−13**
4 extra total credits required	2	0	−1.0	1.4	1.0	2.0	−3.3	7.6**
40% decrease in student-teacher ratio	24***	7	1.0	0	0	1.1	3.9	16***
30% increase in teacher salary	5	0	0.7	−2	0	−1.8	6.3**	0
Mean dependent variable for NELS-88	1 GLE		88%		92%		56%	

Note: Statistically significant effects are in larger bold type and are starred. The effect estimates are calculated using coefficients presented in tables 10.1, 10.2, and 10.3. It reports impacts as a percent of the mean in the bottom row of the table. Test score results are from predictions of test score gains over a four-year period, so divide by 4 to get effects on the rate of learning. Effects of policies on the GAP between high SES and low SES students are for a two standard deviation increase in student SES. Negative numbers in these columns imply the gap is being closed. High school completion is by 1994. College attendance models are for the second year after high school graduation.

*Statistically significant at 10% level on a two-tail test, ** 5% level, *** 1% level.

	Outcomes							
	Get 2- or 4-year degree by 2000		Earnings first year after H.S. graduation		Earnings eighth year after H.S. graduation		Wage rate eighth year after H.S. graduation	
Policies	Mean	Gap	Mean	Gap	Mean	Gap	Mean	Gap
Voluntary end-of-course exams	−4	−11***	−6	0	2.9	8.7	3.7	−4.0
Minimum-competency exam	2	10	11***	−13***	4.2*	9.3***	2.6*	5.8***
4 more academic credits required	−4	−2.6	0	0	3.7	0	2.8	1.9
4 extra total credits required	0	4	−3**	2	−3.0***	−4.9**	−2.8***	−3.2***
40% decrease in student-teacher ratio	10***	5	−2	6**	0	6.0	−1	1
30% increase in teacher salary	13***	−6	0	7*	0	1	1.8*	3.8**
Mean dependent variable for NELS-88	42%		$5152		$26137		$12.5	

students by $[4 * (-.113) * 1.6/(1.965)]$ or $-.37$ GLE. Since all outcome variables are scaled so that more is better, a negative number implies that differentials between the achievements of high and low SES students are diminished by the policy or alternatively that equality of opportunity is improved. A positive number implies the policy has a more positive effect on high SES students than on low SES students.

Earlier in the chapter, we hypothesized that higher minimum-course graduation requirements and MCEs would increase resources and standards in schools serving low SES neighborhoods and induce low SES students to devote more time to learning core academic subjects. Political leaders pressing for higher standards and better funding often claim their proposal will not only increase everyone's achievement but reduce achievement gaps as well. Only one of the policies examined delivers on this compound promise: higher academic-course graduation requirements. A four-credit increase in academic-course graduation requirements is predicted to increase average achievement by .37 GLEs and to reduce the achievement gap by a similar amount. It also appears to have boosted wages and earnings in 2000 and reduced SES differentials in college attendance (but not in college completion).

Other policies were less successful in raising achievement and enhancing equality of opportunity. Increases in state minimum total-course graduation requirements did not have positive effects on any of the outcomes studied. Students from states that required an additional four courses to graduate did not learn more, were 3 percent less likely to attend college, and earned 3 percent less both immediately after high school and seven years later. This suggests that states should reduce elective-course requirements even while they increase academic-course requirements.

State minimum-competency exam graduation requirements had no significant relationship with mean rates of learning or achievement gaps but were associated with higher rates of college attendance and larger college-attendance differentials by SES. All types of students in MCE states earned more. Middle SES students in MCE states earned 11 percent more in 1993 and 4.2 percent more in 2000. The short-term earnings benefits of MCEs were significantly larger for low SES students. The medium-term benefits of MCEs, however, were significantly smaller for low SES students.

New York's hybrid voluntary end-of-course exam/compulsory minimum-competency exam system had a large (.55 GLE) impact on test score gains during high school. Since eighth-grade achievement levels were also higher (Bishop et al. 2001), New York students were about one GLE ahead of students in other states by the end of high school. None of the SES interactions was statistically significant. Because of the small size of the sample of students from New York in NELS-88, statistical tests for a New York State effect lack power. Point estimates suggest that while high-school- and college-graduation rates are not changed much, wages and earnings were higher eight years after high-school graduation. Socioeconomic status had significantly larger effects on high-school graduation in New York than in other states but substantially smaller effects on college completion rates.

Traditional spending-oriented policy recommendations (like smaller class sizes and higher teacher salaries) had statistically significant effects on college attendance and completion rates but no effect on high-school attendance or completion or on earnings after high school (holding educational attainment constant). The spending-oriented policies did not improve outcomes for low SES students more than they improved outcomes for high SES students. Indeed, general reductions in class size were associated with larger learning and college-attendance gaps between high and low SES students. This suggests that spending-oriented policies must be redistributive if they are to reduce the correlation between social background and student achievement.

A 40 percent reduction in the student-teacher ratio increased learning during high school by roughly a quarter of a GLE and four-year college completion by 10 percent. A 30 percent increase in teacher salary was associated with a 13 percent increase in two- or four-year college completion and a 10 percent increase in BAs awarded. The earnings and productivity benefits of a four-year college education have a present discounted value exceeding $600,000 at a 4 percent real discount rate. Thus the social benefits of the stimulus to college completion resulting from these traditional spending-oriented policy instruments would be about $24,000 per high-school student (assuming our estimates reflect causal effects). Spending per student would need to rise by about 20 percent, so costs are also high and similar in magnitude to the benefits. Standards-oriented policy proposals are much less costly and seem to produce even larger benefits. Consequently, it seems inevitable that politicians will focus their energies on refining and adding to their accountability-oriented policy initiatives.

Notes

1. In models developed by Kang (1985) and Costrell (1994), some of the students faced with higher graduation standards conclude that the effort necessary to get a diploma is too great and give up on the idea of getting a diploma. While these theoretical models associate giving up with dropping out of school, this is not necessarily the case. Students who believe they cannot graduate might nevertheless continue to attend high school because they enjoy socializing and playing sports or because they are learning a trade.

2. Minimum-competency exams are additions to, not a replacement for, teacher-imposed standards. In an MCE regime, teachers continue to control the standards and assign grades in their own courses. Students must still get passing grades from their teachers to graduate. The MCE regime imposes an additional graduation requirement and thus cannot lower standards (Costrell 1997). The graduate equivalency diploma (GED), by contrast, offers students the opportunity to shop around for an easier (for them) way to a high-school graduation certificate. As a result, the GED option lowers overall standards. This is reflected in the lower wages that GED recipients command.

3. End-of-course examinations (EOCEs) are similar to MCEs in the following ways. Both are set by and graded to rubrics devised by a state government or a national organization (such as The College Board), and both carry consequences for students, teachers, and school administrators.

4. See Bishop and Mane (2001b) for a detailed description of the characteristics of the New York State Regents Examinations system.

5. Many school districts choose to set higher requirements than the state minimum. States without statewide minimum-course graduation requirements were assigned a value of 13—the lowest minimum total Carnegie unit requirement for the states with a requirement. A control variable was included in the models.

6. When a student moved to another state between tenth and twelfth grades, an average of the MCE variables for tenth and twelfth grades was used. Then the MCE variable can have three values: 1, 0, or 0.5. The last represents moving out from or into an MCE state. When information on the state was not available for tenth grade, residence in twelfth grade was used. If that was missing as well, eighth-grade residence was used.

7. Both variables come directly from the high school principal questionnaire.

8. We used a composite created by NELS staff from family income and parent's education and occupation.

9. The approximate effect of Xi (at the mean of the dependent variable) on the probability of the event considered can be obtained by multiplying βi times $P(1 - P)$.

10. For a more extensive discussion of methodological issues surrounding estimating the effects of external examination systems, see Bishop (1996), Linn (2000), Koretz, McCaffrey, and Hamilton (2001), Hanushek and Raymond (2003), and Jacobs (2001).

11. Neill and Gayler's study (2001) suffers from this problem.

12. Amerein and Berliner's (2002) interrupted time-series approach to measuring the effects of high-stakes tests suffers from multiple flaws: errors in dating the introduction of high-stakes tests, the use of national average scores as a comparison rather than states

that did not implement high-stakes testing, and an arbitrary way of handling changing rates of exclusion. For a detailed critique, see Hanushek and Raymond (2003).

13. There were two exceptions to the generalization of identical sets of control variables. The state unemployment rates and weekly earnings in retailing were updated to 1992 and 1993. The payoff to completing high school was not included in the model.

14. Analyzing high school and beyond data and controlling for college attendance and a host of other variables, Bishop, Moriarty, and Mane (2000) found that females graduating from high schools with a minimum-competency exam graduation requirement (student report) earned more than women graduating from schools without an MCE. Concern about the accuracy of student reports of the existence of an MCE at their high school led Bishop and Mane (2001a) to reanalyze HSB data using principal reports of the existence of an MCE graduation requirement. They found even larger effects. Principal reports of an MCE graduation requirement had positive effects (significant in some but not all years) on wage rates of male and female graduates and on the earnings of graduates four and five years after graduation. The wage-rate effects of MCEs appeared to be larger for students in the bottom three-quarters of the test-score distribution.

References

Altonji, J., and C. R. Pierret. (2001). "Employer Learning and Statistical Discrimination." *Quarterly Journal of Economics* 116(1): 313–350.

Amerein, A. L., and D. C. Berliner. (2002). "The Impact of High-Stakes Tests on Student Academic Performance." Educational Policy Studies Laboratory, Arizona State University, ⟨http://asu.edu/educ/epsl/EPRU/documents/EPSL-0211-125-EPRU.pdf⟩.

American Federation of Teachers. (1996). *Making Standards Matter 1996*: An Annual Fifty-State Report on Efforts to Raise Academic Standards, Matthew Gandal (author).

Ballou, D., and M. Podgursky. (1999). "Teacher Training and Licensure: A Layman's Guide." *Better Teachers, Better Schools*. Washington, DC: Fordham Foundation.

Bishop, J. H. (1992). "Impact of Academic Competencies on Wages, Unemployment and Job Performance." *Carnegie-Rochester Conference Series on Public Policy* 37: 127–194.

Bishop, J. H. (1996). "The Impact of Curriculum-Based External Examinations on School Priorities and Student Learning." *International Journal of Education Research* 23(8): 653–752.

Bishop, J. H. (2005). "High School Exit Examinations: When Do Learning Effects Generalize?" In Joan Herman and Ed Haertel (eds.), *Uses and Misuses of Data in Accountability Testing*. Chicago: University of Chicago Press.

Bishop, J. H., and F. Mane. (2001a). "The Effect of Minimum Competency Exam Graduation Requirements on College Attendance and Early Labor Market Success of Disadvantaged Students." Gary Orfield and Mindy Kornhaber (eds.), *Raising Standards or Raising Barriers*. New York: Century Foundation Press.

Bishop, J. H., and F. Mane. (2001b). "Incentive Effects of New York's Minimum Competency Exams." In Margaret Wong and Herbert Walberg (eds.), *School Choice vs. Best Systems: What Improves Education*. New Jersey: Lawrence Erlbaum.

Bishop, J. H., and F. Mane. (2005). "Raising Academic Standards and Vocational Concentrators: Are They Better Off or Worse Off?" *Education Economics* 13(2): 173–189.

Bishop, J. H., F. Mane, M. Bishop, and J. Moriarty. (2001). "The Role of End-of-Course Exams and Minimum Competency Exams in Standards-Based Reforms." In Diane Ravitch (ed.), *Brookings Papers on Education Policy*. Washington, DC: Brookings Institution.

Bishop, J. H., J. Moriarty, and F. Mane. (2000). "Diplomas for Learning: Not Seat Time." *Economics of Education Review* 19(3): 333–349.

Bond, L. A., and D. King. (1995). *State High School Graduation Testing: Status and Recommendations*. Oak Brook, IL: North Central Regional Educational Laboratory.

Braun, H. (2004). "Reconsidering the Impact of High Stakes Testing." *Educational Policy Analysis Archives* 12(1), retrieved from ⟨http://epaa.asu.edu/epaa/v12n1/⟩.

Carnoy, M., and S. Loeb. (2002). "Does External Accountability Affect Student Outcomes?" *Educational Evaluation and Policy Analysis* 24(4): 305–331.

Costrell, R. (1994). "A Simple Model of Educational Standards." *American Economic Review* 84(4): 956–971.

Costrell, R. M. (1997). "Can Centralized Educational Standards Raise Welfare?" *Journal of Public Economics* 65(3): 271–293.

Dee, T. S. (2003). "The 'First Wave' of Accountability." In Paul E. Peterson and Martin West (eds.), *No Child Left Behind? The Politics and Practice of Accountability*. Washington, DC: Brookings Institution.

Frederickson, Norman. (1994). "The Influence of Minimum Competency Tests on Teaching and Learning." Princeton, NJ: Educational Testing Service.

Hanushek, E. A. (1997). "Assessing the Effects of School Resources on Student Performance: An Update." *Educational Evaluation and Policy Analysis* 19(2): 141–164.

Hanushek, E. A., and M. Raymond. (2003). "Improving Educational Quality: How Best to Evaluate Our Schools?" Yolanda Kodrzycki (ed.), *Education in the Twenty-first Century: Meeting the Challenge of a Changing World*. Boston: Federal Reserve Bank of Boston.

Hedges, L. V., R. Laine, and R. Greenwald. (1994). "Does Money Matter? A Meta-Analysis of Studies of Differential School Inputs on Student Outcomes." *Education Researcher* 23(3): 5–14.

Hoffer, T. B. (1997). "High School Graduation Requirements: Effects on Dropping Out and Student Achievement." *Teachers College Record* 98(4): 584–607.

Jacobs, B. A. (2001). "Getting Tough? The Impact of High School Graduation Exams." *Educational Evaluation and Policy Analysis* 23(2): 99–122.

Kang, S. (1985). "A Formal Model of School Reward Systems." In J. Bishop (ed.), *Incentives, Learning and Employability*. Columbus, OH: National Center for Research in Vocational Education.

Koretz, D., D. McCaffrey, and L. Hamilton. (2001). "Toward a Framework for Validating Gains under High-Stakes Conditions." CSE Technical Report 551, National Center for Research on Evaluation, Standards and Student Testing.

Krueger, A. (2000). "Economic Considerations and Class Size." Working Paper No. 447, Industrial Relations Section, Princeton University.

Lillard, D., and P. DeCicca. (2001). "Higher Standards, More Dropouts? Evidence within and across Time." *Economics of Education Review* 8(2): 133–148.

Linn, R. (2000). "Assessments and Accountability." *Educational Researcher* 29(2): 4–16.

Madaus, G. (1991, June). "The Effects of Important Tests on Students: Implications for a National Examination or System of Examinations." American Educational Research Association Invitational Conference on Accountability as a State Reform Instrument, Washington, DC.

National Center for Educational Statistics. (1993). *The Condition of Education: 1993* (vol. 1). Washington, DC: U.S. Department of Education.

National Center for Educational Statistics. (2004). *The Condition of Education: 2004* (vol. 1). Washington, DC: U.S. Department of Education.

Neill, M., and G. Keith. (2001). "The Effect of Minimum Competency Exam Graduation Requirements on College Attendance and Early Labor Market Success of Disadvantaged Students." Gary Orfield and Mindy Kornhaber (eds.), *Raising Standards or Raising Barriers*. New York: Century Foundation Press.

Reardon, S. F. (1996). "Eighth-Grade Minimum Competency Testing and Early High School Drop Out Patterns." Paper presented at the annual meeting of the American Educational Research Association, New York.

Reardon, S. F., and C. Galindo. (2002). "Do High-Stakes Tests Affect Students' Decisions to Drop Out of School? Evidence from NELS." Working Paper 03-01, Population Research Institute, Pennsylvania State University.

Rosenshine, B. (2003). "High Stakes Testing: Another Analysis." *Educational Policy Analysis Archives* 11(4), retrieved from ⟨http://epaa.asu.edu/epaa/v11n24⟩.

Warren, J. R., and M. R. Edwards. (2005). "High School Exit Examinations and High School Completion: Evidence from the Early 1990s." *Educational Evaluation and Policy Analysis* 27(1): 53–74.

11

The Impact of School Choice on Sorting by Ability and Socioeconomic Factors in English Secondary Education

Simon Burgess, Brendon McConnell, Carol Propper, and Deborah Wilson

11.1 Introduction

The analysis of choice in education markets is currently enjoying a boom. As both Howell and Peterson (2002) and Hoxby (2003b) make clear, one of the important questions in this field is the potential impact of choice on the sorting or stratification of pupils across schools. Sorting may arise through decisions of families on where to live, through the differential use of vouchers, or through the operation of parental choice given residence and school selection. Because of the interlocking decisions on choice of residence and school, this issue is complex. Hoxby (2003b, 6) notes that the "most complicated effects of school choice are on student sorting—how students will allocate themselves among schools when allowed to choose schools more freely."

In this chapter, we exploit a large administrative dataset of pupils in England to address a component of the choice and sorting issue. We examine the differential degree of sorting of students across schools relative to their sorting across neighborhoods. This *postresidential* sorting varies considerably across the country, and we relate it to variation in the feasibility of school choice. This is measured simply as the number of schools that could be reached instead of the school actually attended. This therefore refers to the postresidential component of choice, taking a family's home location as given. We show that measured in this way, choice and sorting are positively related. The more alternative schools that are reachable from a given school—the more postresidential choice there is—the greater the degree of sorting across schools relative to sorting across neighborhoods. This relationship is statistically and quantitatively significant.

Such information is timely in the context of UK education policy. The legislative program announced in the summer of 2005 includes proposals to reform and strengthen school choice. This may include measures to support transport to alternative schools and to reform school-admissions policies. The findings presented in this chapter are the first contribution to the choice literature for England using the new, universal Pupil Level Annual School Census (PLASC) dataset (described below).

The rest of the chapter is structured as follows. Section 11.2 relates our analysis to the relevant literature, and section 11.3 briefly discusses the nature of choice in the English education market. Section 11.4 details our dataset, section 11.5 presents our results, and section 11.6 provides a brief conclusion.

11.2   Previous Evidence

In this chapter, we contribute to the literature on school choice with an analysis of ability sorting of students in England and the role of choice given a place of residence. Recent contributions surveying the field include Howell and Peterson (2002), Hoxby (2003a), Ladd (2002), and Neal (2002). Howell and Peterson (2002) set the school-choice debate in an historical and political context. They chart the discussion from choice as a tool to remedy market inefficiencies (Friedman 1955), through choice to empower the disadvantaged (Jencks 1970), to choice as a governance issue (Chubb and Moe 1990). Chubb and Moe argue that schools subjected to competitive pressure will raise their game and perform better.

One of the central questions in this field is the impact of choice on stratification or sorting of pupils. This is acknowledged by Howell and Peterson (2002) in one of their five key questions about the operation of school choice. Hoxby (2003b) also focuses on this: the two main forces operating to determine the outcome of increased choice are (1) the competitive force working to increase effectiveness and productivity in schools and (2) the impact of any consequential differences in the allocation of students to schools. It is this latter issue that we focus on in this chapter.

In a voucher setting, evidence on stratification is provided by Howell (2004), Campbell, West, and Peterson (2004), and Petersen, Howell, Wolf, and Campbell (2003). Howell uses data from a voucher scheme in New York to study selection at different stages of the process—who applies for vouchers, who uses them once awarded, and who stays in the private school. He shows differential use at each stage, with differences by ethnicity, income, religious identity, and the child's mother's education. These findings are echoed in Campbell et al. (2004) and Peterson et al. (2003).

Voucher schemes are only one choice mechanism, however. As Howell and Peterson (2002) point out, choice of school through choice of residence is an established part of the system in the United States. This is also one key part of choice in the English educational system, as we explain in the next section. We can think of choice of residence and choice of school given residence as two components of the process, though they are obviously linked. Both of these influence the degree of sorting of pupils across schools.

The complex problem of choice and sorting has been studied in the context of computable general equilibrium models by Nechyba (1999, 2003a, 2003b, 2004) and Epple and Romano (2003). Nechyba (2004) discusses three different channels of sorting—decentralized sorting based on choice of residence, sorting out of the state system altogether into private schools, and centralized sorting (tracking) within the public school system. Much of the work focuses on the first two of these, exploring the relationship between school finance, the degree and nature of choice, and spatial residential segregation by income and ability. Nechyba (2003b) establishes that a pure public schooling system leads to more spatial segregation than a private system. In Nechyba (2003a), the role of private schools is examined further through simulations of different voucher systems within the model. In the presence of private schools, "residential segregation patterns within heterogeneous public school systems are then predicted to be quite different from school segregation patterns, with private school markets fostering *reduced* residential segregation by income and peer quality but *increased* school segregation along these same dimensions" (Nechyba, 2004, 24, italics in original).

Similarly, Epple and coauthors (Epple and Romano 1998, 2003; Epple, Figlio, and Romano 2004) have a set of papers looking at Tiebout sorting, formation of jurisdictions, and sorting. Epple and Romano (2003) model three different student-assignment regimes— neighborhood schooling (a strict residence requirement for admission), school choice with no choice costs, and multijurisdictions Tiebout sorting. They show that different public-policy regimes have dramatic impacts on the nature of sorting. Neighborhood schooling leads to strong income stratification across neighborhoods, with differences in school quality arising from peer-group differences. Costless, frictionless choice equalizes peer groups across schools. Epple and Romano argue that it is the residence requirement that is fundamental to sorting rather than the single or multijurisdictions. Again, the differential sorting between schools and neighborhoods is apparent.

Evidence from the United States on sorting typically uses school- and district-level data. One important issue is that in the United States, any dimension of school segregation is closely tied up with racial and ethnic segregation and the pure effects of choice on sorting are difficult to disentangle. Clotfelter (1998) argues that (district) choice influences sorting, but Hoxby (2000) disagrees. Her focus is chiefly on controlling for the potentially confounding effect of sorting when trying to isolate the competitive effect of the degree of choice on productivity. She shows that the effect of the degree of choice on outcomes is largely un-affected by the inclusion or exclusion of measures of student heterogeneity across districts. On the other hand, the more schools that there are in a metro area, the greater the ethnic segregation. She concludes that student sorting is more relevant across schools within districts than across districts.

Bradley, Crouchley, Millington, and Taylor (2000) use school-level average data to look at sorting by disadvantage in England. They show evidence of an increase in the concentration of free-school-meal (FSM) pupils in schools doing poorly in the published school-performance tables.

Close in spirit to our chapter is the work of Söderström and Uusitalo (2004), using student-level data from Sweden. They compare student sorting along a number of dimensions before and after a significant reform to the school-admission process in Stockholm. This reform switched from a predominantly residence-based admissions system to an explicitly ability-based system. Comparison of Stockholm and a neighboring area without the reform enables them to run a difference-in-difference analysis on the impact of the reform on sorting. They find a significant increase in ability sorting in schools but no change in residential sorting. They find the same result for ethnic and income sorting.

11.3   The Secondary-School System and the Nature of Choice in England

The nature of choice in the English school system has different layers. First, parents can choose where to live, constrained by their incomes and job locations. Since residence matters, this has implications for choice of school. Second, given a place of residence, there will be different school options: the system is set up to respond to parents' choices. Third, if the chosen school is oversubscribed, then selection or choice by the school or local education authority (LEA) is required.[1] We have no data tracking families' choice of residence, so we focus here on the outcome of the second and third elements. We discuss how these mechanisms work in turn. By convention, *school choice* refers to choice by parents, not choice by schools. We also briefly discuss a small minority of LEAs in which pupils are assigned to schools by a different mechanism entirely—by ability. In these selective LEAs, pupils are assigned to grammar schools if they do well in tests and to secondary modern schools if they do badly. This assignment mechanism is very different than choice.

The Education Reform Act of 1988 introduced significant changes to the education system in England. Previously, children were assigned to schools primarily by residence, and LEAs allocated funding from the central government to schools. The new system had the following key features. First, open enrollment: parents were given the right to choose the school they wanted their child to go to. Second, funding and management of schools was devolved to a more local level, and schools were funded on the basis of the number of pupils enrolled. Funding was still provided and raised by central government out of general taxation. The intention was that parental choice and per capita funding would induce competition between schools, raising educational outcomes (Glennerster 1991).[2]

Parental choice of school is informed by two types of formal performance measure and through more informal networks. First, a government agency (Ofsted 2003) makes in-depth site visits to each school at least once every six years and produces reports that are generally available. Second, annual summary statistics on each school's performance are published annually and report a range of test-score outcomes for all schools.

If a pupil's chosen school has empty places, then that choice is fulfilled. If it is oversubscribed, then the school or LEA has to select pupils: the power of choice moves to the school. West, Hind, and Pennell (2004) document in detail the admissions criteria governing these choices. Around 30 percent of schools—predominantly foundation and voluntary-aided schools (mostly religious schools)—determine their own admissions. For the rest, the LEA sets the criteria. For all bodies, however, the admissions criteria are governed by a Code of Practice (DfES 2003) and are required to be clear, fair, and objective. West et al. (2004) show that most schools used the presence of siblings already in the school in their admissions criteria. They also show that 86 percent used distance as a criterion, and 73 percent mentioned the school's catchment area. Comprehensive schools were more likely to use distance and catchment area and more likely to take note of being a pupil's first-choice school. The authors also discuss a number of ways in which schools can use their selection criteria to engage in covert selection, particularly by ability.[3]

Thus, residence matters, and the school-assignment mechanism is appropriately described as a mixture of neighborhood-based schooling and choice-based schooling: it is not a pure choice system. Below we present results showing that only around half of all children attend the school that is nearest their residence. For those who do not, this outcome arises from a series of decisions by parents and by schools.

Our data yield the assignment of pupils to schools. This therefore captures the outcome of the process of choice by parents together with selection by schools and LEAs, though we cannot straightforwardly distinguish the two. This familiar problem was noted by Howell in his study of vouchers: "it is difficult to distinguish the free choices of parents from the selective admissions of private schools" (2004, 226).

Finally, we return briefly to the 19 LEAs that we define as selective. In these areas, at least 10 percent of pupils go to grammar schools. This is very different from choice: pupils are assigned to schools on the basis of their performance in tests. For most of the analysis below, we use data on nonselective LEAs only.

11.4   Data

For this analysis, we use the Pupil Level Annual School Census (PLASC) dataset, which forms part of the National Pupil Database (NPD). PLASC covers all pupils in both primary and secondary schools in England, with approximately half a million pupils in each cohort. We analyze the cohort that transferred to secondary school in 1997 and took their final exams in 2002. At the pupil level, the dataset provides linked histories of test scores, school attended, plus some individual characteristics: gender and within-year age, ethnicity, disadvantage (measured by eligibility for free school meals, an indicator of low household income). We also have access to the home postcode of every pupil in the dataset, enabling us to locate each pupil in relation to schools.[4]

Pupils take Key Stage 2 (KS2) tests at age 11 at the end of their primary-school education. The pupils then move on to secondary schools to complete their education. We analyze the sorting of pupils into secondary schools on the basis of their KS2 scores.

We analyze state secondary schools, which pupils attend between the ages of 11 and 16 or 18, and omit private (fee-paying) schools. The main reason for this is that these schools are not required to take the Key Stage exams, and so only some report these data. In fact, we have KS2 data for only around half of our cohort who are in private schools. It seems unlikely that this will be a random sample of private schools, so the clearest strategy is to leave them all out. Also, it is not a big quantitative issue: around 7 percent of pupils in our cohort attend private schools.

We use the coordinates for each school to construct our measure of choice. Overlaying school locations with a complete road network, we construct drive-time zones (DTZs) around schools. In this chapter, we choose a 10-minute DTZ around every secondary school in England and count the number of schools within this area: this number of nearby schools is our measure of the feasibility of choice in a local market.

We characterize student sorting across three different dimensions—ability, ethnicity, and disadvantage. Sorting is a characteristic of an aggregate of units, and we take the LEA as the aggregate, measuring sorting across both schools and electoral wards (neighborhoods) within an LEA.[5] We take the neighborhood basis for sorting as approximating where people want to live and compare that with the outcome of their school choice conditional on where they live.

We use the dissimilarity index D as our measure of segregation. This is the most widely used segregation index, following the foundational work of Duncan and Duncan (1955). Massey and Denton (1988) provide an extensive discussion and evaluation of different measures of segregation. The dissimilarity index is based on the idea of segregation as unevenness of the distribution of different types of students across units within the aggregate area. The more uneven the spread, the higher the degree of segregation. D ranges from 0 to 1 and can be interpreted as the fraction of students in the aggregate area that would need to move for there to be an even distribution of groups across units (schools or wards) in the area. Cutler, Glaeser, and Vidgor (1999) quote

Massey and Denton (1993) suggesting that values of 0 to 0.3 are considered to be low, 0.3 to 0.6 moderate, and 0.6 and above high.

11.5   Results

We first establish the facts on the feasibility of school choice, defined simply as the number of schools close to the focus school. Then we characterize pupil sorting. The main point of the chapter is made by bringing these together to link the feasibility of choice with the degree of pupil sorting.

11.5.1   The Feasibility of Choice

Choice can be exercised in two ways—(1) in the dual choice of residential location and school and (2) in the choice of school given residence (though these are clearly linked). The former will depend on the nature and location of jobs (among other things). Here we take the labor and housing markets as given and focus on the second.

Using the 10-minute drive-time zone (DTZ), table 11.1 shows the distribution of the number of nearby schools for the whole country and split by area type—London, non-London urban, and rural areas. The results show that, on average, secondary schools in England have more than six schools within 10 minutes' drive. The modal category is between one and five schools, and 14 percent have no close alternatives. The pattern across the three area types is as expected: in the densest area, London, the mean is 17, falling to seven in non-London

Table 11.1
Number of nearby schools and school assignment

	Number of nearby schools			School assignment	
	Mean number of nearby schools	Percent of schools with no other nearby schools	Total schools	Percent of students attending nearest school	Number of students
All	6.69	14.52	3127	44.59	524,609
London	17.19	0.48	414	24.09	66,348
Non-London Urban	6.74	3.63	1873	43.43	319,128
Rural	1.41	45.71	840	57.01	139,133

Note: Nearby = within a 10-minute drive.

urban, and just over one in rural areas. Note that nearly half of schools in rural areas have no alternatives within 10 minutes.[6]

As we have noted, the assignment of a pupil to a school depends on the combination of parental choice and school/LEA choice. We can use the geographic information in the dataset to address this directly. For each student, we determine the school nearest to their home address[7] and thus define whether they attend their nearest school. We present the mean proportion attending their nearest school and by different subareas. Table 11.1 shows that overall some 45 percent of children attend their nearest school. As we have emphasized, this may be because the parents have chosen a farther-away school, or it may be because the local school was oversubscribed and could not admit them. The general equilibrium implications of school choice are complex in such an environment, and it is not possible to identify the actions of the different parties straightforwardly.

Nevertheless, it is a striking finding that fewer than half of secondary-school pupils in England attend their nearest school. This suggests that postresidential school choice may be an important component of the overall schooling decision. The breakdown by area types is as expected: the proportion attending the nearest school is lowest in denser environments. Splitting the sample into selective and nonselective LEAs (not shown in the table), in the latter more pupils go to their closest school. Since location is not a key part of the student-assignment mechanism in selective LEAs, this is not surprising.

It is worth reiterating that the initial choice of residence is unlikely to be exogenous. Indeed, the feasibility of postresidential school choice may well be a factor in choosing location, so an overall assessment of choice needs to model both together.

11.5.2   Characterization of Sorting

We measure sorting by ability, student disadvantage, and ethnic group. As discussed above, ability is measured by the score in the test that students complete at the end of primary schooling, and we consider how students are resorted into secondary schools. We create two dichotomous measures of ability[8]—high ability (a student having a KS2 score above the 80th percentile) and low ability (a KS2 score below the 20th percentile). We calculate the dissimilarity indices for each LEA separately and then look at the distribution across LEAs, weighting by the LEA student population. Each measure is calculated for each LEA, and the distribution refers to the distribution over LEAs, so the 75th

Table 11.2
Segregation indices (dissimilarity index)

	Mean	p10	p25	p50	p75	p90
Basis of segregation:						
High ability	0.293	0.175	0.205	0.253	0.321	0.469
Low ability	0.252	0.18	0.205	0.245	0.283	0.336
Disadvantage	0.29	0.2	0.246	0.293	0.327	0.369
Ethnic group:						
Black Caribbean	0.623	0.233	0.419	0.684	0.883	0.936
Black African	0.683	0.277	0.548	0.772	0.887	0.933
Black, other	0.654	0.344	0.532	0.689	0.847	0.916
Indian	0.585	0.345	0.462	0.601	0.726	0.831
Pakistani	0.684	0.426	0.582	0.72	0.837	0.917
Bangladeshi	0.707	0.427	0.615	0.748	0.861	0.932
Chinese	0.624	0.418	0.546	0.637	0.733	0.788
Other	0.504	0.323	0.386	0.503	0.625	0.707
Black	0.534	0.273	0.394	0.526	0.668	0.806
South Asian	0.554	0.369	0.458	0.585	0.662	0.175

percentile is to be interpreted as giving the value of the dissimilarity index, above which 25 percent of LEAs are to be found. Table 11.2 shows the means and some details of the distribution of the segregation measures.

The levels of ability and disadvantage segregation are generally not high. Three-quarters of LEAs have ability and poverty segregation measures of 0.32 or below. Even at the extremes, segregation is not very high. The situation is very different for ethnic segregation, with high average values and very high values in some LEAs (see Burgess and Wilson 2005 for a more detailed analysis of ethnic segregation in England's schools).

11.5.3   Postresidential Choice and Sorting
In this section, we address our main concern—the relationship between the feasibility of postresidential choice and the degree of ability sorting. We do this by comparing the degree of sorting in schools with the degree of sorting of the same students in terms of where they live and relating the ratio of these to the feasibility of choice.

One of the powerful aspects of our dataset is the ability to place students in their neighborhood context. We can use the postcode data to assign each student to a ward (an electoral unit of around 5,000 people on average, including approximately 600 10- to 17-year-olds) within an LEA. This means that we can compare the spatial patterns of students in two different but related domains—their home and their school. Having located students in wards, we can analyze the distribution of ability (and other characteristics) across space. As far as we know, this is only possible using our dataset and has not been examined before. This allows us to compute measures of sorting of students in the neighborhoods where they live as well as the schools they attend.

Figure 11.1 graphs the school-based segregation measure (vertical axis) against the neighborhood-based measure (horizontal axis). This gives us a picture of the impact of postresidential choice on the degree of sorting. These are for nonselective LEAs only. The first two panels examine high- and low-ability segregation, and the third income (free school meals) segregation.[9] Focusing on the ability segregation results, it is striking that there is not a close relationship between segregation in schools and segregation in neighborhoods. Levels of school segregation vary considerably for any level of neighborhood segregation. This suggests that other factors—such as the feasibility of choice—may influence the former given the latter.

The 45 degree line shows that these nonselective LEAs split about evenly into those in which the student-school assignment process increases the segregation of high-ability students and those in which it attenuates it. The same pattern is observed for low-ability student segregation and for disadvantage (free school meals) segregation. For the latter, there is a wider range of sorting levels by residence than by school.

This leads to an analysis of the feasibility of choice and the concentration or dilution of residential segregation by the pupil-school assignment process. It is clear that one cannot take residence as exogenous and think about school choice conditional on that. Choice of residence depends on the nature of the pupil-school assignment rule, with school and residence choice determined jointly. But it is also clear from our results above that postresidence school choice is an important part of the process. It is worthwhile characterizing the (partial equilibrium) nature of this process while being aware that the degree of school and neighborhood segregation may be a factor in initial housing choice.

We take the ratio of the school-based segregation index to the neighborhood-based segregation index as an indicator of this process. In table 11.3, we regress this on our measure of the feasibility of school choice—the average number of schools that are reachable in a

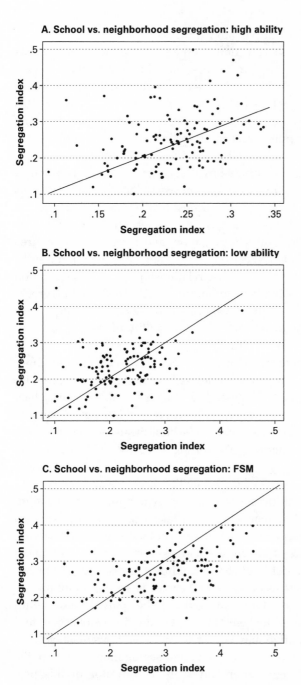

Figure 11.1
School and neighborhood segregation along different dimensions

Table 11.3
Relationship between school/neighborhood ratio and school choice
Dependent variable: Ratio of school-based to neighborhood-based segregation on the basis of the indicated variable:

	(1) High ability	(2) Low ability	(3) Disadvan-tage	(4) Black students	(5) South-Asian students
All LEAs:					
Number of nearby schools	0.020	0.026	0.034	0.024	0.020
(LEA average)	(2.14)*	(4.59)**	(9.58)**	(7.13)**	(7.11)**
Constant	1.155	0.962	0.743	0.725	0.768
	(12.01)**	(16.30)**	(19.82)**	(20.24)**	(26.25)**
Observations	144	144	144	142	143
R-squared	0.03	0.13	0.39	0.27	0.26
Nonselective LEAs only:					
Number of nearby schools	0.021	0.027	0.036	0.025	0.019
(LEA average)	(5.27)**	(6.20)**	(10.08)**	(7.15)**	(7.02)**
Constant	0.905	0.864	0.710	0.720	0.761
	(20.62)**	(18.17)**	(18.64)**	(19.19)**	(26.51)**
Observations	125	125	125	123	124
R-squared	0.18	0.24	0.45	0.30	0.29

Note: Absolute value of *t* statistics in parentheses.
*Significant at 5%, **significant at 1%.

10-minute drive from a school in the LEA, averaged over the LEA. We repeat this for all the dimensions of segregation considered and separately for all LEAs and nonselective LEAs. The degree of pupil sorting may depend on a variety of factors, and we are reporting only a bivariate relationship here. But the fact that we are looking at school sorting relative to neighborhood sorting will take out a lot of the influence of other factors. The use of this ratio focuses the analysis on differences in school sorting on top of neighborhood sorting.

We find a strong positive correlation between the feasibility of choice and the extent of school segregation, controlling for residential segregation. We find this for all dimensions of segregation. The correlation is statistically significant in all the analyses and stronger among nonselective LEAs. In other words, in areas in which there are a more schools to choose between, school segregation is higher relative to neighborhood segregation. Quantitatively the effect is significant as well: a one standard-deviation difference in the choice measure adds

0.13 to the high-ability segregation measure, 0.17 to low-ability segregation, and 0.23 to disadvantage segregation, relative to standard deviations of 0.175, 0.18, and 0.20, respectively. This can be described in two ways: more feasible choice means greater school sorting conditional on where parents live, or more feasible choice means less segregated neighborhoods conditional on school assignment.

We turn briefly to another issue and bring the selective LEAs into the analysis. We compare the impact of ability selection in the selective LEAs, with the choice-based system in the nonselective LEAs that we have studied above. As in figure 11.1, we graph school-based high-ability sorting against neighborhood-based high-ability sorting. In figure 11.2, the first panel shows all LEAs, the second panel selective LEAs, and the third panel nonselective LEAs. As expected, it is clear that the selective LEAs exhibit very high levels of high-ability segregation in schools. But it is also clear that they do not, in general, have very high levels of neighborhood segregation of ability. This illustrates the divorce of residence choice from school choice that arises in elite schooling areas. This confirms the findings of Nechyba (2003a) on the impact of the availability of such schools on residential sorting.

Finally, we illustrate a thought experiment with the data. We determine which school is a pupil's nearest school and assign them to that school. We can then compare the degree of ability sorting that would occur with that hypothetical assignment to the sorting that occurs with pupils in their actual schools. This is in figure 11.3, plotted for nonselective LEAs only. The figure strikingly illustrates the higher sorting that occurs through the two-sided choice system: for almost all LEAs, sorting is higher than it would be if all went to their nearest school, and in some cases it is considerably so. It is clear that this is just a hypothetical case: if a policy were announced that all pupils would be assigned to their nearest school, then clearly some parents would change residence to ensure access to their chosen school. Nevertheless, for our purposes here, it demonstrates the role of postresidential choice in producing ability sorting of pupils.

11.6 Conclusion

It is clear that the potential impact of choice on the sorting of pupils is one of the major questions in the discussion of the merits of school choice (Howell and Peterson 2002; Hoxby 2003a). In this chapter, we address a component of this issue using a large administrative dataset

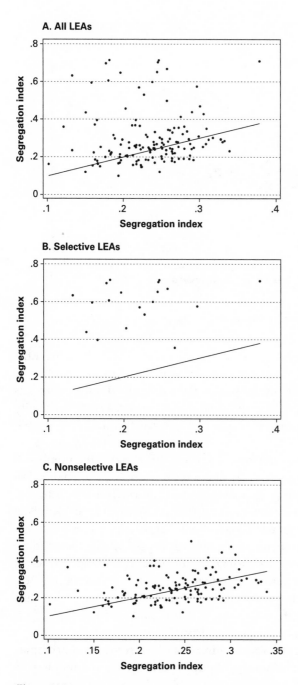

Figure 11.2
School versus neighborhood segregation: high ability

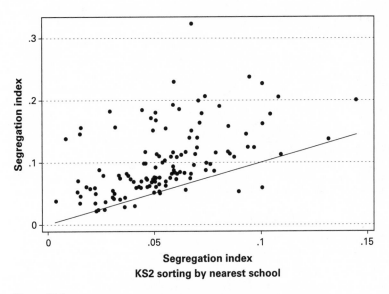

Figure 11.3
Comparing school sorting and nearest school sorting: nonselective LEAs

for England. England has a system of generalized but differential choice. All parents have some choice of school, but this choice is constrained by the availability of places. So the observed outcome results from the interaction of demand- and supply-side selection, feasibility of choice, and the assignment rule that governs the allocation of children to school.

We consider the feasibility of postresidential choice—the number of schools easily reachable as an alternative to the one attended. We examine the relationship of postresidential choice with the sorting of pupils across secondary schools. Our data allow us to locate pupils in their neighborhoods as well as in schools, so we can also measure the degree of ability sorting in terms of where people live. It is then natural to think of postresidential sorting as being the differential degree of sorting in schools relative to the degree of sorting in neighborhoods. We take the ratio of these two and relate it to our measure of the feasibility of choice. The results show that this postresidential sorting is greater where there is more postresidential choice.

These data hold great promise in unraveling some of the complex patterns involved in the sorting of pupils between schools and, in particular, the roles of the feasibility of school choice and the nature of the pupil-assignment rule.

Notes

1. About 30 percent of schools act as their own admissions authority (West et al. 2004).

2. This system differs from Tiebout choice in that it is not a system of local taxation and so not one of local determination of school funding or quality. Funding is raised by central government taxation and allocated to LEAs on the basis of pupil numbers.

3. The structure of the market gives incentives for schools to attract more able pupils. While the simple financial gain from attracting more able pupils is no different to that from attracting less able pupils, there are indirect gains. First, if peer-group effects are important, schools with a high proportion of able children will achieve higher outcomes. Second, career concerns of head teachers mean that they may want to be associated with "successful" schools. Third, more able children may be easier to teach for a given level of teacher input.

4. Note that the data on postcode, free school meals and school attended are recorded only once, in 2002. This is not perfect, since it postdates the transfer date. There may well be biases in either direction—people moving closer to school to ease the journey or moving further away. In any case, the net bias is likely to be small as in practice few families move in the United Kingdom.

5. We have replicated some of this analysis at the drive-time-zone level. Results are available from the authors.

6. The use of a single time may underestimate the amount of choice in rural areas. Longer drive times for everything are the norm in rural areas, and the utility equivalent of a 10-minute drive time in an urban area may be a longer distance in rural areas.

7. This is using straight-line distances. We convert the postcode information to latitude and longitude and then use Pythagoras's theorem to determine distances to each school. For three subsets, we have checked this against road distances and found a correspondence of 85 percent in the two methods' designation of nearest school. We are pursuing this analysis in more depth in a companion paper.

8. In a longer version of this paper, we treat the test score as a continuous variable and exploit the whole ability distribution to provide a rich graphical characterization of ability sorting (Burgess, McConnell, Propper, and Wilson 2004) using quantile profiles.

9. Ethnic segregation is discussed in more detail in Burgess, Wilson, and Lupton (2005).

References

Bradley, S., R. Crouchley, J. Millington, and J. Taylor. (2000). "Testing for Quasi-Market Forces in Secondary Education." *Oxford Bulletin of Economics and Statistics* 62(3): 357–390.

Burgess, S., B. McConnell, C. Propper, and D. Wilson. (2004). "Sorting and Choice in English Secondary Schools." CMPO Discussion Paper 04/111, CMPO, University of Bristol.

Burgess, S., and D. Wilson. (2005). "Ethnic Segregation in England's Schools." *Transactions in British Geography* 30: 20–36.

Burgess, S., D. Wilson, and R. Lupton. (2005). "Parallel Lives? Ethnic Segregation in the Playground and the Neighbourhood." *Urban Studies* 42(7): 1027–1056.

Campbell, D. E., M. R. West, and P. E. Peterson. (2004). "Participation in a National Means-Tested School Voucher Program." Mimeo.

Chubb, J., and T. Moe. (1990). *Politics, Markets and America's Schools*. Washington, DC: Brookings Institution.

Clotfelter, C. (1998). "Public School Segregation in Metropolitan Areas." Working Paper No. 6779, National Bureau for Economic Research.

Cutler, D. M., E. L. Glaeser, and J. L. Vidgor. (1999). "The Rise and Decline of the American Ghetto." *Journal of Political Economy* 107(3): 455–506.

Department for Education and Skills. (2003). *Code of Practice on Schools Admissions*. London: DfES.

Duncan, O. D., and B. Duncan. (1955). "A Methodological Analysis of Segregation Indexes." *American Sociological Review* 20: 210–217.

Epple, D., D. Figlio, and R. Romano. (2004). "Competition between Private and Public Schools: Testing Stratification and Pricing Predictions." *Journal of Public Economics* 88: 1215–1245.

Epple, D., and R. Romano. (1998). "Competition between Private and Public Schools, Vouchers and Peer Group Effects." *American Economic Review* 88(1): 33–62.

Epple, D., and R. Romano. (2003). "Neighborhood Schools, Choice, and the Distribution of Educational Benefits." In C. Hoxby (ed.), *The Economics of School Choice*. Chicago: University of Chicago Press.

Glennerster, H. (1991). "Quasi-Markets for Education?" *Economic Journal* 101(408): 1268–1276.

Howell, W. G. (2004). "Dynamic Selection Effects in Means-Tested, Urban School Voucher Programs." *Journal of Policy Analysis and Management* 23(2): 225–250.

Howell, W. G., and P. E. Peterson. (2002). *The Education Gap: Vouchers and Urban Schools*. Washington, DC: Brookings Institution.

Hoxby, C. (2000). "Does Competition among Schools Benefit Students and Taxpayers?" *American Economic Review* 90(5): 1209–1238.

Hoxby, C. (ed.). (2003a). *The Economics of School Choice*. Chicago: University of Chicago Press.

Hoxby, C. (2003b). Introduction. In C. Hoxby (ed.), *The Economics of School Choice*. Chicago: University of Chicago Press.

Ladd, H. (2002). "School Vouchers: A Critical View." *Journal of Economic Perspectives* 16(4): 3–24.

Massey, D. S., and N. A. Denton. (1988). "The Dimensions of Residential Segregation." *Social Forces* 67: 281–315.

Massey, D. S., and N. A. Denton. (1993). *American Apartheid: Segregation and the Making of the Underclass*. Cambridge, MA: Harvard University Press.

Neal, D. (2002). "How Vouchers Could Change the Market for Education." *Journal of Economic Perspectives* 16(4): 25–44.

Nechyba, T. (1999). "School Finance-Induced Migration Patterns: The Impact of Private School Vouchers." *Journal of Public Economic Theory* 1(1): 5–50.

Nechyba, T. (2003a). "Introducing School Choice into Multidistrict Public School Systems." In C. Hoxby (ed.), *The Economics of School Choice*. Chicago: University of Chicago Press.

Nechyba, T. (2003b). "School Finance, Spatial Income Segregation and the Nature of Communities." *Journal of Urban Economics* 54(1): 61–88.

Nechyba, T. (2004). "Income and Peer Quality Sorting in Public and Private Schools." In E. Hanushek and F. Welch (eds.), *Handbook of Economics of Education*. North Holland: Elsevier.

OFSTED. (2003). "Inspecting Schools: Framework for Inspecting Schools." Retrieved from ⟨http://www.ofsted.gov.uk/publications/index.cfm?fuseaction=pubs.displayfile& id=3266&type=pdf⟩, accessed November 8, 2004.

Peterson, P., W. Howell, P. Wolf, and D. Campbell. (2003). "School Vouchers: Results from Randomized Experiments." In C. Hoxby (ed.), *The Economics of School Choice*. Chicago: University of Chicago Press.

Söderström, M., and R. Uusitalo. (2004). "School Choice and Segregation." Preliminary draft.

West, A., A. Hind, and H. Pennell. (2004). "School Admissions and "Selection" in Comprehensive Schools: Policy and Practice." *Oxford Review of Education* 30(3): 347–369.

12

The Impact of Perceived Public-School Quality on Private-School Choice in Italy

Daniele Checchi and Tullio Jappelli

12.1 Introduction

The presence of a private sector in school provision affects the equality of opportunities in accessing education, widening school choice and alleviating the constraints imposed by the uniform provision of public-education standards. But private schools often require greater financial involvement of families, discriminating against students from poorer backgrounds (Stiglitz 1974). When students differ in family income and abilities, some of these problems can be overcome if students self-sort according to these characteristics. In this context, school vouchers targeted at liquidity-constrained households and talented children may increase equality of opportunity (De Fraja 2002).

In this chapter, we provide evidence of the determinants of school choice in a sample of Italian households. Italy constitutes an interesting case: it has a highly centralized educational system and in principle grants equality of opportunity to all citizens. However, the actual working of the public-school system features significant differences in resource endowments across regions. Therefore, Italian households do not obtain equal treatment from the public sector in terms of education provision, and when possible they tend to escape from situations that they perceive as low quality.

Throughout the chapter, we focus on the choice between public and private schools in elementary (grades one to five) and lower secondary schools (grades six to eight), which represented compulsory education at the time of the survey (1993).[1] The empirical analysis relates school choice to child demographic characteristics, household socioeconomic variables, objective indicators of public-school quality (proxied by resources available), and subjective indicators reported by survey participants. Our analysis is subject to important qualifiers, as previous research shows that resource indicators, such as class size, may not be associated with the true quality of schools (Woessmann 2005). On the other hand, subjective indicators might be correlated with individual preferences, ideology, or religious attitudes but may also capture immaterial elements (like school discipline, teachers' moral, quality of supervision) that are perceived by households as important ingredients of school quality.

We find that the choice of a private school is associated with household resources (rich households are more likely to use private schools) but not with parental education. There is also a negative association between the choice of a private school and both resource-based and subjective quality indicators. The association between the self-reported quality indicator and school choice exists even if we control for provincial fixed effects, possible reporting bias, and interactions with household incomes or parental education. An important caveat of the analysis is that the sample size is limited and that some of the quality indicators we use are potentially endogenous.

Our analysis stresses the potential contribution of private schools to the equality of educational opportunities expressed in terms of available school quality. As long as household opinions capture true differences in school quality and to the extent that they are informed about educational options, the availability of private schools might attenuate the risk that students are trapped in low-quality schools. However, owing to differences in economic resources, the option of private schools is not available to all students. In this case, school vouchers might represent a possible policy instrument to restore a more equitable situation.

This chapter is organized as follows. Section 12.2 reviews the economics of school choice and provides background information on the Italian educational system. Section 12.3 describes the measures of school quality and the sample. Section 12.4 presents probit estimates for the choice between private and public schools and various robustness results. Section 12.5 concludes.

12.2 Background

12.2.1 The Effect of School Quality on School Choice

The relationship between school choice and quality of education can go in both directions. Increased opportunities raise competition among schools and may have beneficial effects on the quality of education. On the other hand, variation in school quality might affect parents' choice between different schools, which is the link we explore in this chapter.

Private schools widen households' opportunity sets. Human-capital investment models often assume that private schools are desirable because they allow parents to choose the amount and the quality of education that they believe appropriate, given their degree of altruism and the expected talent of their offspring (Stiglitz 1974; Glomm and Ravikumar 1992). When peer effects play a role, private schools have an incentive to attract the best students to increase the quality of education provided and therefore charge higher tuition (De Fraja 2002).

With perfect capital markets, parents' choice is unconstrained, and students' selection through tests or tuition yields similar outcomes: more talented students choose private schools, which therefore cream-skim the market (Fernandez and Gali 1999). But when households have limited borrowing capacity and parental choice is constrained, school vouchers conditional on family resources and students' ability increase the equality of opportunity among students of different backgrounds (De Fraja 2002). There are also other reasons for choosing private schools. Some parents elect to send their children to private schools because they explicitly support certain values, such as religion (Sander 2001).[2] Others because private schools have better sport facilities or lower transportation costs. Sometimes the quality of education or facilities is not the main issue. Some people consider private education a status symbol (Fershtman, Murphy, and Weiss 1996) or a way of improving their own and their children's social networks, of shielding their children from social problems, and of avoiding contact with immigrants and children with handicaps. Some simply do not approve of the open and more heterogeneous public-school environment (Gradstein and Justman 2001). Empirically, it is not easy to determine the factors that drive parents' choices and, in particular, the effects of the perceived quality of education on school choice.[3]

Most available empirical evidence refers to the United States and points out that the decision to enroll in private schools depends on household income and parents' education, the racial composition of public schools, and the juvenile crime rate in the area of residence (see Lankford, Lee, and Wyckoff 1995; Long and Toma 1988; Buddin, Cordes, and Kirby 1998; Figlio and Stone 2001). Our reading of the empirical literature is that there is no compelling empirical evidence for the hypothesis that parents choose private schools because they provide higher-quality education.

The estimated low price elasticity of the demand for private education indicates that the perceived opportunity costs of ignoring quality
are also relatively low. And the lack of strong evidence of substantial
benefits from attending private schools weakens the hypothesis that
parents should invest in private education from a purely monetary
point of view. These studies are based mostly on aggregate data (for
example, at the state or Standard Metropolitan Statistical Area [SMSA]
level), where variables are likely to be correlated with unobserved
determinants of school choice, such as family background, preferences,
and social networks. Our contribution extends this line of research using individual-level data.

12.2.2   Choice in the Italian School System

Italy features a centralized school system that sets national standards
for both public and private schools. Italian laws specify not only the
length of compulsory education (ages 6 to 14 until 1999, when it was
raised to 16) but also the types of private and public schools that can
operate, the maximum number of students in each class, and the minimum number of teachers per class. For each type of school, the law
provides guidelines on the subjects that must be taught, course outlines, evaluation and grading methods, vacation periods, and even
school entry and exit times. Most of the funding comes from the
general government, as all teachers are employees of the ministry of
education.

Despite centralization, given the considerable geographical variation
in population density and fertility rates and the different financial
involvement of local governments in the provision of buildings and
facilities, there is ample heterogeneity of schools, resulting in different
quality indicators among regions, among provinces within the same
region, and even within provinces. The Programme for International
Student Assessment (PISA) survey, conducted by the Organization for
Economic Cooperation and Development to assess reading ability of
15-year-old students, confirms wide school heterogeneity within Italy.
In 2000, the country average score in a sample of 4,946 students was
491. But there were large differences across five macroregions, even
conditioning by school types: the average score in high schools in
northwestern regions was 572 against 503 in the south; the corresponding values for vocational schools were 473 and 398, respectively. In
the same survey, the average score of students in private schools was
slightly higher than the corresponding value in public schools (502

against 490). Unfortunately, the PISA survey does not allow further geographical disaggregation within Italy.

While the private enrollment rate in elementary and secondary schools for the OECD countries totals just 2.9 percent on average, reflecting the massive role of government in providing education, Italy's 6.4 percent rate is considerably above the OECD average.[4] At the primary and secondary levels, about half of private schools are religious. Private enrollment is higher for young children (because private schools admit children below regular school age) and for older students (because Italian private schools are sometimes a remedial resource for less talented students from rich families) (see Bertola and Checchi 2002).[5] Given the constitutional mandate that privately managed schools cannot receive direct government support, parents who choose private schools must also pay tuition out-of-pocket.

12.3 Measures of School Quality

One could measure school quality with outcome indicators, resource indicators, or subjective questions. Arguably, outcome indicators—assessment of academic quality with standardized tests or success in students' achievement in the labor market—are the best measures of quality. However, in Italy they are not always available or accessible. Furthermore, aggregate resource indicators do not allow one to distinguish geographical effects from genuine quality differences. In cross-sectional studies, objective indicators do not vary across individuals in the same geographical unit and might be correlated with unobserved heterogeneity. On the other hand, subjective measures are contaminated by measurement error but have the advantage that they refer to local public schools where parents expect to enroll their children. By combining the two types of variables, we can therefore relate private-school choice not only to aggregate resources but also to quality indicators that vary at the individual level.

12.3.1 The Quality Score in the Survey of Household Income and Wealth

The Survey on Household Income and Wealth (SHIW) provides a good opportunity to estimate the effect of school quality on the choice between public and private education. Conducted biannually by the Bank of Italy, in 1993 the survey collected data on a representative sample of 8,089 households (24,013 individuals). Respondents provide

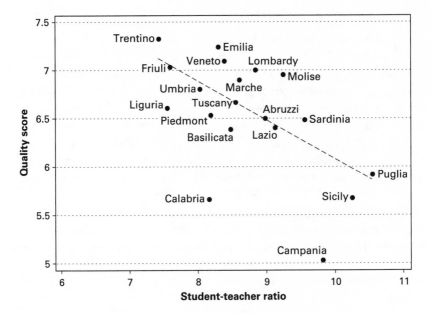

Figure 12.1
The self-reported quality score and the student-teacher ratio (regional averages)

information on parent's income, educational attainment, and other demographic variables.[6] The 1993 survey contains a section on the perceived quality of public services (schools, hospital, transportation, waste disposal) and the use of alternative private services. Survey respondents (the household head or the person responsible for the financial matters of the household) rate the quality of public schools in their area of residence. Unfortunately, the question is asked only in 1993, and a similar question for private schools is not asked.[7]

Descriptive analysis reveals that the self-reported quality score of public schools is correlated with resource indicators. Figure 12.1 plots the student-teacher ratio against the self-reported quality score in each region.[8] On average, quality is considerably lower in the south (the minimum is in Campania) and peaks in two northern regions, Trentino and Emilia. The relation between the quality score and the student-teacher ratio is negative and statistically different from zero, suggesting that subjective evaluations tend to conform to objective data.[9] The quality score is also correlated with other aggregate indicators of school resources, such as the proportion of students in rotating shifts (some students have classes in the morning and others in the after-

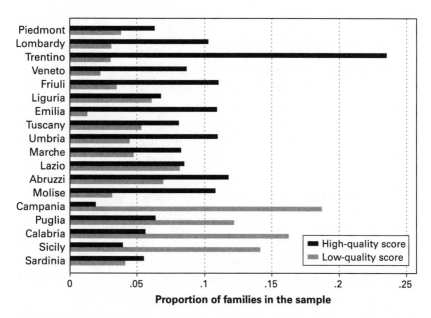

Figure 12.2
Sample proportion reporting low or high quality of local public schools (regional averages)

noon), the proportion of students in buildings that are unfit as a school, and the proportion of full-day students whose schedule extends beyond lunchtime (the standard schedule calls for six mornings per week).[10] Since these indicators are collinear, in the empirical analysis we focus mainly on the student-teacher ratio as a summary measure of school resources available to students. Quality scores vary substantially even within regions or provinces. Figure 12.2 reports, by region, the proportion of respondents whose rating is poor (3 or less) or excellent (above 7). Even in top-quality regions, such as Trentino, where 20 percent give excellent scores, about 5 percent of the sample assigns very poor scores. On the other hand, even in Campania, the lowest-quality region, where almost a third give very low scores, some people rate locally available public schools as excellent. As we shall see, it is this intraprovince variability that allows us to identify the quality effect when we introduce in the estimation a full set of geographical dummies.

Subjective quality indicators based on survey questions vary across individuals, allowing identification of the impact of quality on school choice even when controlling for provincial fixed effects. Furthermore, individual choice is based on perceived quality, which does not necessarily correspond to objectively measured quality. On the other hand, survey measures are contaminated by individual characteristics, tend to be correlated with individual preferences for public schools, and suffer from cognitive dissonance, the *ex post* rationalization that confirms the choice. Although we try to address some of these problems in the estimation, they prevent us from giving a causal interpretation to the empirical correlations.

12.3.2   The Sample

We select 2,015 children (ages 6 to 13) enrolled in primary and lower secondary schools. We then match each child with household information, including disposable income, parents' education, province of residence, and city size. Our analysis is conducted at the child rather than parent level. This allows us to retain siblings (45 percent of the sample) as separate observations.[11] The survey tends to underestimate considerably the private-school attendance rate at compulsory age (grades one to eight), which in our data is estimated at 4.7 percent, against 6.4 percent resulting from official statistics. We do not have a good explanation of this underestimate, which does not disappear if we use sample weights.[12]

In table 12.1 we report sample means for selected variables distinguishing between public and private schools. Children in private schools are almost one year younger because private schools allow earlier enrollment. They come from parents with more education (among private-school users, the fraction of parents with education beyond compulsory is 20 percentage points higher than the corresponding fraction among public-school users) and higher income. Single parents, large households, and residents in the south tend to be overrepresented among public-school users. Two-thirds of private enrollment is in medium-sized or large cities.

On average, parents who send their children to private schools do not rate the public-school system as of lower quality than parents with children in public schools do (6.36 against 6.30), and the provincial average of the student-teacher ratio does not differ between the two groups (8.97 against 8.93). But comparison of sample means does not take account of the correlation of quality with income and other geographical characteristics. For this we must turn to regression analysis.

Table 12.1
Sample statistics: Children attending compulsory education (grades 1–8)

	Public school	Private school
Age of child	9.59 (2.25)	8.61 (2.18)
Female child	0.46 (0.50)	0.39 (0.49)
Enrolled in primary school	0.61 (0.48)	0.77 (0.42)
Enrolled in lower secondary school	0.39 (0.48)	0.23 (0.41)
Age of father	38.2 (12.5)	40.3 (7.4)
Age of mother	37.2 (7.9)	36.6 (6.8)
Father's education (lower secondary diploma or higher)	0.40 (0.49)	0.56 (0.49)
Mother's education (lower secondary diploma or higher)	0.37 (0.48)	0.62 (0.48)
Disposable income (thousand euro)	39.3 (27.5)	62.0 (31.6)
Single parent	0.08 (0.27)	0.03 (0.17)
Number of children	2.31 (0.92)	1.76 (0.69)
Housewife (at least one person at home)	0.50 (0.50)	0.38 (0.48)
Resident in the north	0.38 (0.48)	0.44 (0.50)
Resident in the center	0.17 (0.38)	0.24 (0.43)
Resident in the south	0.45 (0.49)	0.31 (0.46)
City size less than 20,000	0.50 (0.50)	0.15 (0.36)
City size 20,000 to 39,999	0.14 (0.35)	0.11 (0.32)
City size 40,000 to 499,999	0.26 (0.44)	0.41 (0.49)
City size 500,000 or more	0.10 (0.30)	0.32 (0.47)
Quality score, subjective indicator (1 to 10 scale)	6.36 (2.05)	6.30 (2.28)
Student-teacher ratio	8.97 (1.03)	8.93 (0.99)
Observations	1921	94

Note: Standard deviations are in parentheses. Sample means are computed using population weights.

12.4 Regression Results

12.4.1 Basic Specification

Table 12.2 relates the probability of private-school attendance to various potential determinants of school choice: child's sex and age, dummies for parents' education, single parents, siblings, income quartiles, and two indicators of the quality of public schools (the self-reported quality, averaged by province, and the provincial student-teacher ratio).[13]

The results suggest that the decision to enroll in private schools is positively associated with income. The probability that a child with parents in the fourth income quartile attends private school is 6

Table 12.2
Probit regressions for enrollment in private schools

	(1)	(2)	(3)
Quality score (provincial average)	−0.019	−0.02	−0.015
	(2.51)*	(2.85)**	(1.86)
Student-teacher ratio (provincial average)	0.009	0.008	0.007
	(2.33)*	(2.13)*	(1.82)
State primary full-time share (provincial average)		−0.025	
		(1.2)	
State primary shift share (provincial average)			0.223
			(1.05)
Age of child	−0.005	−0.005	−0.005
	(1.99)*	(1.94)	(2.00)*
Female child	−0.005	−0.005	−0.005
	(0.78)	(0.81)	(0.79)
Attending primary school	−0.004	−0.004	−0.004
	(0.33)	(0.30)	(0.36)
Father beyond compulsory education	0.004	0.004	0.004
	(0.45)	(0.46)	(0.45)
Mother beyond compulsory education	0.010	0.010	0.010
	(1.31)	(1.26)	(1.30)
Single parent	−0.003	−0.003	−0.003
	(0.22)	(0.17)	(0.22)
Number of siblings	−0.016	−0.016	−0.017
	(3.25)**	(3.29)**	(3.36)**
Second income quartile	0.009	0.009	0.010
	(0.77)	(0.79)	(0.85)
Third income quartile	0.045	0.045	0.047
	(3.57)**	(3.61)**	(3.68)**
Fourth income quartile	0.059	0.059	0.061
	(3.60)**	(3.61)**	(3.66)**
City size 20,000 to 39,999	0.041	0.044	0.041
	(2.06)*	(2.15)*	(2.04)*
City size 40,000 to 499,999	0.033	0.035	0.033
	(2.37)*	(2.48)*	(2.35)*
City size 500,000 and more	0.068	0.081	0.066
	(2.35)*	(2.49)*	(2.33)*
Resident in the center	−0.021	−0.023	−0.020
	(2.75)**	(2.91)**	(2.63)**
Resident in the south	−0.035	−0.044	−0.035
	(2.42)*	(2.66)**	(2.40)*
Father's age	−0.000	−0.000	−0.000
	(0.42)	(0.41)	(0.42)
Mother's age	−0.000	−0.000	−0.000
	(0.72)	(0.68)	(0.72)

Table 12.2
(continued)

	(1)	(2)	(3)
A relative full-time at home	−0.006	−0.006	−0.006
	(0.76)	(0.80)	(0.77)
Observations	2015	2015	2015
Pseudo R-squared	0.16	0.16	0.16

Note: We report marginal effects and, in parentheses, the z-statistic associated with the coefficient. Standard errors are adjusted for clustering at the provincial level. *significant at 5%, **significant at 1%.

percentage points higher than that of a child with parents in the first quartile. Private schooling is also increasing in city size and residency in northern regions. This may reflect not only the greater availability of private schools in the north but also the higher juvenile crime rate, which might induce some parents to shield their children from exposure to social problems. Contrary to some previous studies (Lankford et al. 1995; Buddin et al. 1998), we do not find that parents' education is associated with the choice of private schools.[14]

While public schools can enroll only children at least five years and six months old in September of each year, private schools are more flexible and also take younger children. One motivation for choosing private schools is therefore to anticipate the legal school age. This is confirmed by the negative coefficient of child age. The survey also includes 225 five-year-olds, 52.8 percent of whom attend first grade. As a robustness check, we estimate our model on this extended sample. The results are similar, and for brevity they are not reported.

The coefficients of the quality variables (student-teacher ratio and self-reported quality score) are statistically different from zero at the 5 percent level. In column 1, an increase of one standard deviation of the quality score lowers private enrollment by 3.7 percent, and a standard deviation increase in the number of students per teacher raises it by 0.9 percent.

In the second and third columns of table 12.2. we explore the robustness of this result by adding further indicators of school resources. While the coefficients of these variables have the expected signs (the coefficient of the proportion of students in full time enrollment in public schools is negative, the proportion in rotating shifts is positive), they are not statistically different from zero, and in column 3 the other two quality indicators are less precisely estimated.[15]

Table 12.3
Quality coefficients

	(1)	(2)	(3)	(4)
Quality score (individual opinion)	−0.007	−0.007	−0.007	−0.006
	(2.23)*	(1.97)*	(2.07)*	(1.72)
Quality of public hospitals		−0.000		
		(0.11)		
Quality of waste disposal			0.001	
			(0.39)	
Quality of local public administration				−0.003
				(0.88)
Provincial dummies	Yes	Yes	Yes	Yes
Observations	1948	1948	1948	1948
Pseudo R-squared	0.23	0.23	0.23	0.24

Note: The table reports the marginal effect of the quality score variable on the probability of private school enrollment. The number in parentheses is the z-statistic associated with the coefficient. Each regression includes the same controls as in table 12.2 (except the provincial student-teacher ratio) plus a full set of provincial dummies (excluding macro-area dummies). The number of observations falls from 2,015 to 1,948 because in table 12.2 some missing quality scores are replaced by the provincial average. Standard errors are adjusted for clustering at the province level. *significant at 5%, **significant at 1%.

12.4.2 Robustness Tests

The results for school quality in table 12.2 do not make full use of individual-level data. By averaging the quality score by province, we reduce individual heterogeneity, but we might add confounding effects (such as religion, political orientation, local labor-market conditions, crime rates) at the provincial level.

In table 12.3, we attempt to check the robustness of our results controlling for provincial fixed effects. We estimate the model in table 12.2 replacing the average quality score of public schools with the individual indicator and introducing a full set of provincial dummies. This implies dropping all objective indicators of school resources available at the province level. For brevity, in table 12.3 we report only the coefficient of quality. In the first column, the coefficient is −0.007 (down from −0.019 in table 12.2) and statistically different from zero at the 5 percent level.

The estimated effect of perceived quality on school choice, however, might result from spurious correlation because perceived quality of public schools may reflect political orientation, preferences, religion, or other factors. Furthermore, the indicator suffers from the fact that people who have chosen private schools are likely to give lower marks to public schools, an application of the principle of cognitive dissonance leading to endogeneity bias.

Even if we cannot fully address these serious measurement and endogeneity problems, we can perform some robustness checks. In columns 2 to 4 of table 12.3, we add to our model the opinion expressed by respondents on other public services (public hospitals, waste disposal, public administration). This way, we try to control explicitly for preferences for market solutions. The coefficient of the quality of public schools is still negative and statistically different from zero. This does not rule out that our estimates are biased owing to endogeneity or omitted variables. For instance, religious parents might still be more likely to choose private schools and to give a relatively low grade to public schools because they prefer a religious education.

12.4.3   Interactions with Family Background

Lower-income households might have no access to private schools regardless of quality. Thus, in table 12.4 we introduce interaction terms between the self-reported quality score, parental education (highest in the couple), and position in the income distribution (above or below the median). We also repeat the estimation distinguishing between primary and lower secondary schools.

The quality score coefficients are negative and statistically different from zero, even though they are smaller in absolute values than in tables 12.2 (where we use the provincial average) and 12.3 (with province dummies). On the other hand, the coefficient of the student-teacher ratio is no longer statistically different from zero. The coefficients of the interaction terms are positive, but they are not statistically different from zero, preventing reliable inference. The sign of the interaction coefficients suggests that parents with higher education and above-median income are less concerned of quality when choosing between public and private schools. Results by different school types (primary and lower secondary) are less reliable given the smaller sample size and the larger standard errors associated with the estimates.

12.5   Conclusions

Under the Italian constitution, privately managed schools cannot receive public funding. Accordingly, parents who choose private schools must also pay tuition out-of-pocket. We find that in Italy the choice of attending a private school is correlated with parents' income but not

Table 12.4
School quality coefficients, by school level and interaction terms

	Primary and lower secondary			Primary			Lower secondary		
	(1)	(2)	(3)	(4)	(5)	(6)	(7)	(8)	(9)
Quality score (individual opinion)	−0.004	−0.006	−0.008	−0.005	−0.008	−0.009	−0.002	−0.003	−0.005
	(1.88)	(2.59)**	(2.26)*	(1.77)	(2.82)**	(2.04)*	(0.89)	(0.93)	(2.01)*
Student-teacher ratio in the province	0.007	0.007	0.006	0.006	0.006	0.006	0.007	0.007	0.005
	(1.61)	(1.68)	(1.52)	(1.73)	(1.83)	(1.66)	(1.39)	(1.37)	(1.12)
Quality score × higher education among parents		0.003			0.004			0.001	
		(1.43)			(1.78)			(0.57)	
Quality score × third or fourth income quartile			0.007			0.006			0.007
			(1.36)			(0.99)			(2.11)*
Observations	1948	1948	1948	1172	1172	1172	776	776	776
Pseudo R-squared	0.15	0.15	0.16	0.17	0.17	0.17	0.15	0.15	0.19

Note: The table reports the marginal effect of the quality indicators on the probability of private school enrollment. The number in parentheses is the z-statistic associated with the coefficient. Each regression includes the same controls as in table 12.2 (except that the quality score is now taken at the individual level) plus the interaction terms. Standard errors are adjusted for clustering at the province level. * significant at 5%, ** significant at 1%.

with parents' education. We also find some evidence that quality considerations are correlated with parents' school choice. When quality is measured at the provincial level, both objective and subjective quality indicators are correlated with school choice. When quality is measured at the individual level and we control for provincial fixed effects, we still find a positive correlation. However, the empirical correlations that we estimate cannot necessarily be given a causal interpretation because we cannot account for residual unobserved heterogeneity and because the estimates may reflect the endogeneity of the subjective quality indicator.

Taken at face value, our results suggest that some Italian parents choose private schools to escape the lower quality of local public schools. This interpretation of our findings suggests that private schools might help to restore equality of opportunity, at least for the upper portion of the income distribution. From a policy point of view, the crucial issue then becomes how to offer similar opportunities to less wealthy children. Means-tested school vouchers, covering the full cost of tuition, could provide a solution, but in Italy they are exposed to the legal challenge that they violate the constitutional mandate.

A related implication of our analysis is that, to the extent that individual perceptions are correlated with actual behavior, it is important to improve parents' information about school characteristics and students' performance in secondary schools, college, and the labor market. Standardized national tests; information about teachers' competence, experience, and background; and information about school facilities and resources would help parents in making better informed school choices. Given the ample variability in school quality even within relatively small districts, this information should be available and comparable for all schools in every district.

Acknowledgments

We thank participants of the CESifo conference held in Munich (September 2–3, 2004) and especially our discussant, Randall Filer, and the editors, Ludger Woessmann and Paul Peterson, for detailed comments and suggestions. We also thank seminar participants at IZA, York University, and Boston College. We acknowledge financial support from the Italian Ministry for Universities and Research (MIUR) and the European Community's Human Potential Program under contract HPRN-CT-2002-00235 [AGE].

Notes

1. We do not analyze upper secondary education and the choice between private and public universities because in both cases participation is voluntary and students are self-selected. In addition, the higher-education system in Italy is mostly public, and there are only three private universities in the country. The determinants of private-school choice at the upper secondary level are described in the working-paper version of this chapter (Checchi and Jappelli 2004).

2. By comparing a sample of voucher users in New York with the eligible population, Howell (2004) finds that religious identity and practice are the most significant variables affecting the permanence in the program.

3. Teske and Schneider (2001) survey several U.S. studies and report that greater parental choice induces more satisfaction and parental involvement.

4. The OECD defines as private schools as "privately managed institutions that receive less than 50 percent of funding from public sources." Data refer to 1999 (OECD 2002, table C1.4).

5. In a 1998 survey of 20,153 Italian households, 40 percent of those who choose private schools report that they do so because they are of higher quality, and an additional 40 percent for the services they offer (Brunello and Checchi 2005). However, the survey has no information on income and public-school quality and therefore does not allow replication of the present study.

6. Sample design, interviewing procedure, response rates, and comparison between sample and population means are reported in the appendix of the working-paper version of this chapter (Checchi and Jappelli 2004).

7. The question is: "Based on your personal experience or on that of your family, can you give a mark ranging from 10 (best outcome) to 0 (worst outcome) on the working of local public schools (primary and secondary)?"

8. The student-teacher ratio is available for each of the 95 provinces in 1992 and then averaged over 20 regions.

9. The regression coefficient in figure 12.1 is -0.40 with a t-statistic of -3.25. Omitting Campania, the coefficient is -0.35 with a t-statistic of -3.19.

10. The pairwise correlations between the quality score and the proportion of students in shifts or unfit buildings are -0.84 and -0.83, respectively. The correlation with the proportion of full-day schooling is 0.35.

11. There are 1,467 households with 1,921 children in public schools and 79 households with 94 children in private schools; one household has at least one child in both schools.

12. In interpreting the results, one must bear in mind that one of the limitations of the sample is that in Italy relatively few parents choose private schools.

13. Standard errors are clustered by province. We also check for the presence of cluster effects coming from the fact that some children belong to the same households. The results are similar and are available on request. Results using a continuous income variable are similar. We prefer using income quartiles dummies to allow for a nonlinear relation between household resources and school choice.

14. We also try alternative specifications (highest education in the couple and average education of the two spouses), and the coefficients are not statistically different from zero. Only when we omit the income quartile dummies, parents' education becomes positive and highly significant.

15. Using factor analysis, we extract the first component (explaining 59 percent of the variance) from all resource indicators available. We then replace the student-teacher ratio with the first principal component. The coefficient is 0.011 (z-statistic of 2.54), while the coefficient of the subjective quality score is -0.016 (z-statistic of 2.16).

References

Altonji, J. G., T. E. Elder, and C. R. Taber. (2000). "Selection on Observed and Unobserved Variables: Assessing the Effectiveness of Catholic Schools." Working Paper No. 7831, National Bureau for Economic Research.

Bertola, G., and D. Checchi. (2002). "Sorting and Private Education in Italy." Discussion Paper No. 3198, CEPR.

Brunello, G., and D. Checchi. (2005). "School Voucher Italian Style." *Giornale degli Economisti e Annali di Economia* 357–399.

Buddin, R. J., J. J. Cordes, and S. Nataraj Kirby. (1998). "School Choice in California: Who Chooses Private Schools?" *Journal of Urban Economics* 44: 110–134.

Checchi, D., and T. Jappelli. (2004). "School Choice and Quality." Discussion Paper No. 4748, CEPR.

De Fraja, G. (2002). "The Design of Optimal Educational Policies." *Review of Economic Studies* 69: 437–466.

Evans, W. N., and R. M. Schwab. (1995). "Finishing High School and Starting College: Do Catholic Schools Make a Difference?" *Quarterly Journal of Economics* 110: 941–974.

Fernandez, R., and J. Gali. (1999). "To Each According to . . . ? Markets, Tournaments and the Matching Problem with Borrowing Constraints." *Review of Economic Studies* 66: 799–824.

Fershtman, C., K. Murphy, and Y. Weiss. (1996). "Social Status, Education, and Growth." *Journal of Political Economy* 104: 108–132.

Figlio, D. N., and J. A. Stone. (2001). "Can Public Policy Affect Private School Cream Skimming?" *Journal of Urban Economics* 49: 240–266.

Glomm, G., and B. Ravikumar. (1992). "Public versus Private Investment in Human Capital: Endogenous Growth and Income Inequality." *Journal of Political Economy* 100: 818–834.

Gradstein, M., and M. Justman. (2001). "Public Education and the Melting Pot." Discussion Paper No. 2924, CEPR.

Hanushek, E. A. (2002). "Publicly Provided Education." Working Paper No. 8799, National Bureau for Economic Research.

Howell, W. G. (2004). "Dynamic Selection Effects in a Means-Tested, Urban School Voucher Program." *Journal of Policy Analysis and Management* 22: 225–250.

Lankford, H. R., E. S. Lee, and J. H. Wyckoff. (1995). "An Analysis of Elementary and Secondary School Choice." *Journal of Urban Economics* 38: 236–251.

Long, J. E., and E. F. Toma. (1988). "The Determinants of Private School Attendance." *Review of Economics and Statistics* 70: 351–357.

Neal, D. (1997). "The Effects of Catholic Secondary Schooling on Educational Achievement." *Journal of Labor Economics* 15: 98–123.

OECD. (2002). *Education at a Glance.* Paris: OECD.

Sander, W. (2001). "The Effect of Catholic Schools on Religiosity, Education and Competition." Occasional Paper No. 32, National Center for the Study of Privatization in Education, available at ⟨http://www.tc.columbia.edu/ncspe⟩.

Stiglitz, J. (1974). "The Demand for Education in Public and Private School System." *Journal of Public Economics* 3: 349–385.

Teske, P., and M. Schneider. (2001). "What Research Can Tell Policymakers about School Choice." *Journal of Policy Analysis and Management* 20: 609–631.

Woessmann, L. (2005). "Educational Production in Europe." *Economic Policy* 20: 445–504.

Contributors

Kenn Ariga
Columbia University and Kyoto
Institute of Economic Research

Julian R. Betts
University of California at San
Diego

John H. Bishop
Cornell University

Giorgio Brunello
University of Padova, CESifo,
and IZA

Simon Burgess
University of Bristol

Daniele Checchi
University of Milan, wTw, IZA,
and CEPR

Fernando Galindo-Rueda
London School of Economics

Massimo Giannini
University of Molise

Eric Hanushek
Stanford University, NBER, and
University of Texas at Dallas

Tullio Jappelli
University of Salerno, CSEF, and
CEPR

Edwin Leuven
University of Amsterdam

Stephen Machin
University College London and
London School of Economics

Ferran Mane
University Rovira and Virgili

Brendon McConnell
University of Bristol

Thomas Nechyba
Duke University

Hessel Oosterbeek
University of Amsterdam

Paul E. Peterson
Harvard University

Carol Propper
University of Bristol

John E. Roemer
Yale University

Sofia Sandgren
Norwegian University of Science
and Technology; and Department
of Infrastructure, Royal Institute
of Technology, Stockholm,
Sweden

Jacob Vigdor
Duke University

Anna Vignoles
London School of Economics

Deborah Wilson
University of Bristol

Ludger Woessmann
University of Munich and Ifo
Institute for Economic Research

Index